Go Where You
Wanna Go

Go Where You Wanna Go

The Oral History of The Mamas & The Papas

Matthew Greenwald

Introduction by Andrew Loog Oldham

Cooper Square Press

First Cooper Square Press edition 2002

This Cooper Square Press hardcover edition of *Go Where You Wanna Go* is an original publication. It is published by arrangement with the author.

Published by Cooper Square Press
A Member of the Rowman & Littlefield Publishing Group
200 Park Avenue South, Suite 1109
New York, New York 10003-1503

Distributed by National Book Network
Book design and composition: Barbara Werden Design

Library of Congress Cataloging-in-Publication Data
Greenwald, Matthew, 1961–
    Go where you wanna go : the oral history of the Mamas and the Papas /
Matthew Greenwald ; introduction by Andrew Loog Oldham.—1st Cooper Square
Press ed.
        p. cm.
    Discography: p.
    ISBN 0-8154-1204-5 (alk. paper)
        1. Mamas and the Papas (Musical group) 2. Rock musicians—United
States—Biography. I. Greenwald, Matthew, 1961–

    ML421.M35 G6 2002
    782.42166′092′2—dc21
    [B]   2002001414

♾ The paper used in this publication meets the minimum requirements of
American National Standard for Information Sciences—Permanence of
Paper for Printed Library Materials, ANSI/NISO Z39.48–1992.
Manufactured in the United States of America.

To Diana Engle

Contents

Preface   ix

Introduction by Andrew Loog Oldham   xiii

The Voices   xix

Chapter 1   Chase the Rising Sun   1

Chapter 2   Creeque Alley   45

Chapter 3   California Dreamin'   67

Chapter 4   Go Where You Wanna Go   129

Chapter 5   Mansions   175

Chapter 6   Farewell to the First Golden Era   211

Chapter 7   Too Late   233

Chapter 8   Look through My Window   253

John Phillips Eulogy by Lou Adler   277

Tribute by John Stewart   279

Discography by Sandy Granger   285

Acknowledgments   295

Preface

There's a lot to be said of the term "family", and the Mamas & The Papas were, indeed family. The 'First Family of Rock'? Sure. 'The Royal Family of Pop'? Absolutely—they defined the term to begin with, anyway. But I would define the group as family for other reasons. Since this is an oral history on The Mamas & The Papas, I'll use some of my precious own space here to tell you why I think so, and relate my own youthful experience with this phenomenon . . .

It was spring of 1966, and I was a mere second grader in the suburbs of 'The Valley' (San Fernando, that is) in California, and my mother was taking my brother and I to school. Every day for the past week or so, the M.O.R. radio station that she listened to in the car (lots of Bacharach, Herb Alpert, Dusty Springfield, some Beatles ballads, etc.) was playing this *very* hip tune, every morning, at the same time. Each time it came on, my mother (clearly a woman who enjoyed sleeping late, when she could) would brighten up and sing along . . .'Oh!,' she'd sigh, rubbing her eyes, 'I *love* this song . . . ' "Monday, Monday . . . can't trust *that day* . . . " I didn't know who it was, but I loved it too. She attempted to explain the name of the group to me ("But whose mama and papa *are* they?!") After patient attempts to render this sense, I was instructed to consult my oldest brother, who had just got the album. That night I listened to "Straight Shooter" and "Got A Feelin" about 40 times and I believed my eyes and ears. I couldn't figure out why they were all in a bathtub together on the album cover, but Cass certainly looked like my cool cousin from back east, and Michelle looked like one of my brother's foxy teenybopper girlfriends. My dad thought that, too, when I showed him the album cover, and said that the guys were "probably beatniks"; but he smiled when he said that . . .

Yeah. This was the *shit*, all right. Anything that could unite me, my older brothers, *and* my parents had to be at least as good as The Beatles. And so it was. The Mamas & The Papas.

I first met John Phillips on July 4th, 1998, appropriately enough. I was at his Palm Springs home, interviewing him and Scott Mackenzie regarding their show the previous night at a casino in Cochilla, California billed as "The Mamas & The Papas Featuring Scott MacKenzie". I was also interviewing John regarding the possible release of his 1977 solo album featuring members of The Rolling Stones. The show was not amusing. Cochilla surely must mean 'unfit for cattle' in Navajo; and the Indian gambling vibe was a long way from the spiritual/vocal unity I once heard on "Once Was A Time I Thought". The band, while competent, was perfunctory, and the jingle singers that sang those fabulous Cass, Michelle, John, and Denny parts were an aural cartoon. "Oh, how the mighty have fallen", I thought. However, when John came out briefly and sang a new song titled "While I Hide" I knew that the pain was real and this was indeed where he was at. Did you ever want to cry, but you didn't know just why? Yeah, me too.

The interview with John and Scott was like a business meeting (which is what it was, essentially), and I was out of there with a sadness that I couldn't describe, and hit the road back to L.A. On the way back, however, I thought long and hard about that first meeting with the vibe back when I was a child, and the unity that this first family brought to my family . . . and the rest of the pop world.

In a PBS documentary on the year 1967 ("It Was Twenty Years Ago Today") George Harrison said, "Time is a very misleading thing. We can reminisce about the past, and we can think about the future . . . but we can't relive the past, and really don't know if there is going to be a tomorrow . . ."

When reading some of these recollections and accounts, please keep in mind that these are people's memories of how *they* remember things. Some who read this—particularly some of the actual participants—may strongly disagree with certain things that are said. But, there they are. The memory is a funny thing. Things like attitudes, moods, and other stimuli . . . (a lot of stimuli, if you know what I mean), will affect what people say, think and remember. This, though, is what really happened—according to those who were there—and how it happened. . . .

Then, of course, some people told me that The Beatles played at their high school prom in 1964 and performed "Sergeant Peppers" in its entirety, live.

Follow this book as a film on the printed page—or better yet, a play or a large conversation—and you'll do all right. The story of The Mamas & The Papas includes joy, sorrow, pathos, comedy, sex, drugs, and even . . . rock & roll. But these things are only secondary. At the core is love, I swear. The Mamas & The Papas. They really did put the 'fun' back in dysfunctional.

MATTHEW GREENWALD
Los Angeles, California
November 2001

Introduction

I'd met Lou Adler in the autumn of '64, theta had it be and still does. We'd met at the recording of the T.A.M.I show where his act Jan and Dean were hosting and mine were following James Brown.

321 South Beverly Drive sat down on the scrubbed 'n shrubbed Warren Beatty side of L.A's Wiltshire, and floor two housed Dunhill Records, about to get hot with "Eve Of Destruction", and formed on the heat of Adler's run of hits with Johnny Rivers. Dunhill was eared by Adler, flacked by Andy Wickham and hawked by a cigar-chomping sales suit named Jay Lasker; an agent named Landers and a tap dancer named Roberts made up the company. The latter two went on to give the world the Charles Bronson life-enhancing "Death Wish", Lasker ante'd up cut outs and returns, worked Motown and Mary MacGregor, whilst Lou gave of himself and gained the world.

That early spring in '66 day Lou Adler had said please find the time to come on down to Dunhill and be surprised, I did. I was silver bracelet clad and Lou was gold; he smoked Lucky's whilst I Salem'd my lot, though sooner and later we smoked the same brand. He wore red and I didn't know I could. Clobber was still by Sy Devore, DeVoss had yet to come on the map. We paid neat homage to Dino, Joe Di Carlo, hi-rolled button-down shirts. Our trousers were either cords, jeans or "Ocean's Eleven", and we could pass for well-meaning casual doo-wop pimps.

When I got to the second floor Dunhill abode, I greeted Lou and stopped to say hallo Andy Wickham, another English lad not getting over America. He knew he'd met the beginning of the world as he knew it as did I. Then Lou popped his head around the door, and said "Andrew, come say hallo to the Mamas & Papas . . . " We walked down the hall, into a room and saw them standing there . .

.

...John Phillips wore a darker red and wanted to know what you thought before you thought it, Cass gushed that mother lode and wondered how well you knew the Beatles, Denny cleared his majestic throat of debris and Michelle knew what she had as she kinda invited you in.

That afternoon all the leaves were modulated gold as John sat atop the oak exec desk and acoustic'd the four of them through all the hits and golden gradient moments to come and I was privileged to hear a medley of their life thus far and their career to be as their national anthems rounded the room. Later Michelle would come up with "Dedicated", Cass would call John's name with "Words Of Love", Lou would get them somewhat "Dancing in the Street" but for the most part John Boy had already written the ticket stubs, entry to the royal circle of pop, given to that golden few who manage to define the moment in the right rhythm, time and attitude of the day.

I heard 'em all that day, "Dreamin'", "Monday", "Go Where You Wanna Go"—all of the hits and the encores of that golden run. I fell in love with the choral camaraderie, the full blown bravado leads, the insolent oh-so-coherent trade-offs and your own 60's Cole Porter/Irving Berlin who got under your skin and into your heart, Papa John Phillips, who with those marvelously structured sophisticated and witty ditties captured the compass of our hearts. He would stir and scribe again with "San Francisco", "Creeque Alley" and "Twelve Thirty", but basically privileged moi had heard the lot. Not bad for an afternoon off on a busman's holiday....

... Thus far America's remaining pop chart firefight against us Brits had been the Beach Boys and Four Seasons. The Beach Boys had the sound and Brian Wilson, but alas, save Dennis, all looked like their dad Murry. And the Four Seasons looked like they would be just as happy breaking your legs as hugging your pillow.

... I left very pleased. Lou was Billy Rose and I'd just heard the Golden Horseshoe. The Mamas and Papas would unite world-pop traffic from Haight Asbury to Park Avenue. My mate had the real thing. And with a heart full of smiles all round I headed happily northeast back up to Sunset and mine.

It's January the 12th of forever, 1998 to be precise. Sonny Bono has skied his last slope, babe, and another Kennedy scion has dangered himself into dust.

My wife Esther and son Maximillian had always seen something good take me over when a Mamas & Papas song came on, they always witnessed a well-being, a good wave roll over me, regardless of whatever else was on. Something inviting and secure.

I wanted to share with them where that good place had come from. We flew up from our home in Bogota, Colombia to cold and steaming New York and California Dreamin', to give thanks and witness a voice of America get its due, as the Mamas & Papas were inducted into the Rock 'n' Roll Hall of Fame. I used to live in New York City . . . aah to feel those changes . . . and to see her again.

John and Denny, Cass and Michelle along with Uncle Lou and the pearled pen of Papa John had given America a voice and some anthems and the world some pretty good songs. The Mamas & The Papas helped America reseize the pop mantle us Brits had taken away.

And so we gathered together for the cause of this induction, a night of crips and capulets as the Waldorf Astoria beaconed fame, as the crippled and sane gathered once more for the Rock 'n' Roll Hall of Fame, Pain and a little bit of Shame. It goes with the territory so wear it well and that night we all did.

Gene Vincent crouched from up above and Santana played as one, the Eagles sounded like and on the money and Fleetwood Mac licked and played their wounds. We felt the rhythm of life and the national anthems the whole world sang, and got back to the pure joy of pop for that magical three and a half, for the Mamas & Papas had returned.

All the leaves were gold as the Mamas & Papas Spanish rose to the occasion. Allure, aura and majesty intact, they sang their swan song and inducted well. I'd never had much time for Paul Schaefer, at best, I'd thought, competent salad dressing and too much oil. That night I had cause to revise my opinion, I saw his passion for pop as he picked up the signposts and drove the Mamas & Papas well. John threw away the crutches, picked up his acoustic baton and once again the sky was grey.

Michelle thanked the academy for the nomination. Cass's spirit visited and embraced us all, and Denny sang *so* very well. I got what I came for, my three and a half minutes of golden pop. My heart swelled and I showed a joyful lump and tear of pop to my family and tablemate Lou for what he and they had all done, in raising the level of the game, entertaining and defining the world and the moment, and making that first golden era forever young.

So much had happened since that first South Beverly Drive meeting, the most important being we'd survived. When I met and embraced John on the Waldorf stairway our embrace celebrated that fact.

In 1967 whilst Cass was arrested for stealing blankets I'd nodded out en route from London to Southampton to meet them off the ship, for the previous week I'd forgotten to sleep. Lou Adler woke me for breakfast and the blankets were pretty neat.

Until Monterey the 1967 "Summer Of Love" for me had been the summer from hell. The English establishment and its law enforcing bullies had had enough of this youth movement, the swingin' '60s were already over and they wished to nip the coming revolution in the bud thus they aimed for it's frontrunners, heroes and spokesmen and Beatles and Stones were being busted left, right and planted.

The Paris and Europe of '68 was just around the corner, dancin' in the street was off until disco, and fighting in the streets was on.

I fled the London coup to avoid getting busted and ended up having a vital summer of love. Arriving in Los Angeles I unpacked in Stone Canyon and headed for the festival office on Sunset Strip. John and Lou put me to work on things international, which was a breeze, it had to be Hendrix and the Who.

Sir Paul McCartney, from a distance and Lord Derek Taylor, from a warm and present, seconded the Who and Jimi emotion. A few phone calls to the wonderful Chris Stamp and Kit Lambert and Chas Chandler, and the U.K's contribution was on. I sat back, tabbed up and had a wonderful summer, went back to England in the fall and took one.

In London in the early '70s I was continuing this rough patch and at the local green grocers at the top of the King's Road ran into John, who was not very well either, though we both carried this meeting off with wasted aplomb. I was buying beef stew, Rose's lime juice and a bunch of roses swathed in camel hair and tweed, whilst John was decked as wolfman, very furred and wan, buying both the evening and rolling papers, before heading next door for wine and Cadbury's snack, then home to Cheyne Row and Keith. We hallo'd, sorta spoke, ground our teeth in prescribed and scripted harmony, thought of getting together (... or was it thought of getting it together? ...), both shrugged and moved along.

Later in the '70s in New York I stopped off at his narrow East Side of Manhattan townhouse, where there was blood on the ceiling, snot on the floor and a drug filled freezer. It was a far cry from the Bel Air Nelson Eddy and Jeanette MacDonald dreamy and altered existence and a long way from the Hall of Fame. In the mid '80s we met again on a day we were both blond and on. John was working the telephones of an east side bar called Yellowfingers, and I was marking time till my dealer deigned to arrived home. I had a gram in reserve and a Bloody Mary so we congratulated each other for still being there.

So we all climbed our different stairs, fell over, got up and moved on up again, until we all met under the chandeliers of the master ballroom of the Waldorf Astoria, hugged, marveled at the night and of going full circle. Their greatest contribution to my life? ... being part of my musical recall and helping me remain a fan.

The story you are about to read is told by the people like us who were there. It contains our truth, as it was and is in our now. ...

ANDREW LOOG OLDHAM
Bogota, Columbia
May 2000

The Voices

(in order of appearance)

Andrew Loog Oldham Original manager and producer of The Rolling Stones, and close friend of The Mamas & The Papas and Lou Adler, then and now.

Cass Elliot, John Phillips, Michelle Phillips, and Denny Doherty The Mamas & The Papas.

Scott Mackenzie Vocalist and former member of The Smoothies and The Journeymen (both with John Phillips, pre-Mamas & Papas), and singer of "San Francisco."

John Stewart Legendary singer/songwriter, member of The Kingston Trio and early songwriting partner of John Phillips.

Clark Burroughs Founder, vocalist and architect of The Hi-Lo's, a formidable jazz/pop group from the 1950s. One of John Phillips' greatest musical influences.

Henry Diltz Co-founding member of The Modern Folk Quartet, one of the most respected pop/folk/rock vocal groups of the 1960s. Renowned rock photographer.

Dick Weissman Founding member of The Journeymen, and considered one of the greatest folk banjo virtuosos of all time. Presently professor of music at the University of Colorado, Boulder.

Frank Werber Original manager of The Journeymen and The Kingston Trio.

Roger McGuinn Founding member of The Byrds.

Jim Mason Former early '60s folkie and later a member of mid '60s folk/rock band Webster's New Word, who toured briefly with The Mamas & The Papas.

Russell Gilliam Sister of Michelle Phillips, and friend of the group.

Cyrus Faryar Founding member of The Modern Folk Quartet.

Eric Hord ("The Doctor") Legendary guitarist/banjo player who backed up virtually all of the individual The Mamas & The Papas members in all of their early folk group incarnations. Later to lead The Mamas & Papas road band in 1966–67.

David Crosby Founding member of The Byrds and Crosby, Stills & Nash. Close friend of the group, especially Cass Elliot.

Peter Pilafian Musician, friend, and eventually road manager/ 'aide-de-camp' for The Mamas & The Papas.

Jerry Yester Record producer, musician, co-founding member of The Modern Folk Quartet as well as a member of a later incarnation of The Lovin' Spoonful, and friend of the group.

Nurit Wilde Photographer and close friend of the group members in Canada, New York and California.

Mark Volman Co-founder of The Turtles. Friend of the group, particularly Cass Elliot.

Stephen Sanders ("The Bomber") Boyhood and lifetime friend of Cass Elliot, filmmaker/photographer and eventually early road manager of The Mamas & The Papas.

James Hendricks Songwriter/musician. Co-founder of both The Big Three and The Mugwumps (with Cass Elliot and Denny Doherty), friend of the group.

Kim Fowley Notorious Los Angeles music gadfly, manager, record producer, and songwriter.

Bones Howe Legendary Los Angeles recording engineer and producer. Engineered all of the early Mamas & Papas recordings.

Steve Barri Dunhill Records in-house songwriter, musician and record producer.

Joe Osborne Los Angeles-based session bass guitarist. Performed on most of The Mamas & The Papas recordings.

Hal Blaine Los Angeles-based session drummer. Performed on most of The Mamas & The Papas recordings. The most recorded pop musician of all time.

P. F. Sloan Legendary Los Angeles-based singer/songwriter, as well as in-house Dunhill Records session musician and record producer. Performed on many of The Mamas & The Papas early recordings.

Lou Adler Legendary Los Angeles record and film producer and song publisher. Co-owner of Dunhill Records, he produced all of The Mamas & The Papas early records from 1965–68.

Bud Shank Los Angeles-based jazz flute player, as well as one of the architects of Los Angeles "Cool Jazz". Performed the flute solo on "California Dreamin'."

Larry Knechtel Los Angeles-based session keyboardist and bassist. Performed on most of The Mamas & The Papas records.

Guy Webster Los Angeles-based photographer and music publisher. Shot all of The Mamas & The Papas album covers, 1966–67.

Donovan: Legendary Irish folk and rock singer/songwriter.

Graham Nash Co-founder of The Hollies and Crosby, Stills, Nash & Young. Close friend of Cass Elliot.

Rodney Bingenheimer Los Angeles disc jockey and entertainment gadfly.

Ann Marshall Close friend of all of the individual Mamas & Papas, and member of the extended family.

Jill Gibson Singer and painter, she replaced Michelle Phillips in the group briefly in 1966.

Ray Manzarek Keyboardist and co-founding member of The Doors; performed on a 1966 Mamas & Papas studio recording before his band got signed.

Gus Duffy Co-founder of Webster's New Word, who briefly toured with The Mamas & The Papas.

Al Kooper Musician, singer/songwriter, film/television composer, record producer, founding member of The Blues Project and Blood, Sweat & Tears. Assistant stage manager at Monterey Pop.

Marilyn Wilson Ex-wife of Beach Boys architect, Brian Wilson.

Chapter One

Chase the Rising Sun

PART ONE

Alexandria, Virginia...John, Cass, Scott MacKenzie...The Smoothies...Hi-Lo's/jazz influences...Dick Weissman...Dancing in the Streets of Greenwich Village...The Big Three...Agents can't be trusted...Strange Young Girls at The Hungry i... If you're goin' to San Francisco...

Cass Elliot: John and I were from the same hometown. I had never met John, although I had heard about him. John is a few years older than myself, and he was a few years ahead of me in school. John had been singing around in our area for several years in various groups. He had a group called The Smoothies, I remember, when we were in high school.

John Phillips: I can't write a note on paper, it's just that I know a lot about music. I spent most of my life on street corners, singing.

Scott Mackenzie: Cass was from the same town we were, and we never met her in Alexandria, Virginia. She lived like a quarter of a mile from me, and I never met her until New York.

John Phillips: Her father had a deli there. I remember her as a little, chubby girl, with the stained apron on, behind the counter. We were sort of infamous in that area, and when she got to New York, she knew who we were, but we didn't know who she was.

Scott Mackenzie: Ramsey Alley in Alexandria, Virginia. I think I was about fifteen and John was twenty-five. He was having one of his famous two-week-long parties or something, I don't know. I don't know how I ended up there. But he was sitting in the corner of a room with a guitar and I said, "Hi. How you doing?" He says, "Can you sing?" I said, "Yeah." He says, "Sit down and sing this part. And that's what he's been doing ever since, telling me what part to sing.

John Phillips: It's sort of a passion of mine. If people can sing, I think, "Well, let's sing something. You sing this part and I'll sing this part."

John Stewart: Back in the '50s when he had The Smoothies with Scott, he was writing things that sounded like The Lettermen. And then later when folk music came along, he *got it* and started writing those songs, and was able to pull it off. Just amazing . . .

Scott MacKenzie: He's only three years older than I am, and he had been singing since he was a kid and wanting to have vocal groups all over the place. He knew from the time he was about ten years old. We were in several vocal groups together in Alexandria. You know, the local kids on the corner, the doo-wop. Although, we were more jazz—tried to be more jazz.

Clark Burroughs: A lot of people thought of us (The Hi-Lo's) as a 'group's group.' We didn't have a lot of commercial success. The things that we did that probably influenced John, was that we were doing four-part harmony. Nobody was really doing that, everyone was doing three-part, and our four-part went back to the big-band jazz days. The doo-wop singer would occasionally stick one extra note in, a fourth part. We would just grab the whole chord and just run all over the place. It wasn't any big deal for us to do four or five parts, because we had come from a whole other different place. But we did have kind of a special, sibling blend. We were kind of the last gasp of the big band thing.

Jazz and folk music are kind of so far apart, and yet in a certain sense so close together. With folk and country music, it's the people that are what's important, and it's the heart—folks getting together and singing songs that they like. With jazz, its digging the way the music goes, and it doesn't matter much what the lyric is, so long as the music has the heart.

John Phillips: Hi-Lo's, Four Freshmen, The Modernaires. Paula Kelly and The Modernaires. The first time I heard those kinds of chords sung. And I always liked the sound of men and women singing together, like in church or at work or whatever. I always thought that kind of very moving. That's what we ended up with The Mamas & The Papas, as a matter of fact, to get that choral blend like that. I really admired The Hi-Lo's harmony and The Four Freshmen's harmony and Modernaires, people like that. So we started off that way. And that's what eventually led to The Mamas & The Papas' sound. We were drawn to jazz, because we were sort of beatniks, really, rather than hippies, or whatever, flower children. So we wanted to sing modern harmonies, like Lambert, Hendrix, and Ross. Dave Lambert did a lot of our arrangements for us, as a matter of fact. I don't know if you remember Dave, the father of bebop, he's called. At that time we were The Smoothies. And we had always played guitars and banjos and things, and Scott and I, the survivors of The Smoothies, Bill Cleary and Michael Ren, threw the whole thing up in the air and said "forget it." We put an ad in the local newspaper, *The Village Voice*, for banjo/guitar players. A fellow, Dick Weissman showed up, answering the ad. And he turned out to be about the world's virtuoso banjo player, and still is.

Scott MacKenzie: Pete Seeger used to send—I believe I'm right on this—he used to send tapes to Dick for his opinion and everything and they would get together and talk and play banjo together. More than one airport, they'd sit on the luggage carousel or whatever and take out their banjos and play together.

Dick Weissman: The first time I met John was in, I think, 1960. He was in The Smoothies. The Smoothies had a contract with Decca. John had a girlfriend in the Village, and he wandered down to The Folklore Center, which along with McCabe's in L.A.

was the first acoustic music store in the United States. It was run by this guy Izzy Young. He told him that he needed a couple of people who understood guitar and banjo to play on this record they were making. Frankly, John didn't know much about all this. He had heard The Kingston Trio, and I think John's reaction—and some people think this may be arrogant, but I think it's pretty accurate— was, "Hey, I can do that . . . " So, Izzy was a good friend of mine, and in some ways a bit of a mentor for me, and he told John, "You need to contact this guy named Weissman."

I was living uptown at the time, and John called me up. I was at Columbia graduate school, where I was studying sociology and playing in sessions and stuff, mostly banjo. So, we met and we liked each other and he said, "I want you to play on this thing, but we need another guy too." So, I brought in my friend, Eric Weisberg. The session that we played on was contracted by this bass player named Sandy Block, and I knew him from sessions. There were other players, like Don Arnoon, who was a big session electric guitar player, sort of like a Tommy Tedesco. Anyway, Sandy later told me that he thought that this was the first big folk session in New York, meaning that it integrated people like Eric and myself, kinda with some of these more standard studio guys . . . I think we did four tunes at two sessions. I don't think this stuff ever came out on Decca, for whatever reason. But John and I started to become friends and we started hanging out together quite a bit. It was really kind of funny, because I would take him to parties in the Village, which even though I lived uptown, most of the people I knew were in the Village.

Cass Elliot: And in that group was Scott MacKenzie, so Scott and John had worked together for some time. Then Scott and John put a group together called The Journeymen, and they worked around for a while.

Dick Weissman: We started to rehearse at my place, which was on 106th Street, between Amsterdam and Columbus in lower Harlem. John moved in to the place. It was a five room flat, and I think the three of us were paying $110.00 a month. We rehearsed for six weeks, about eight hours a day. It was probably the most intense rehearsal that I've ever done. We went through *Billboard* magazine, and we targeted about six record companies. We were only doing a couple of John's songs at that point, the ones that are on the first Journeymen album: "Soft Blows The Summer Wind" and "Ride, Ride, Ride". John called these record companies up, and our rap was, "We don't want to make a demo; we're all experienced musicians, we've done a lot of studio stuff—we want to sing for you live." The only one who would listen was MGM. The other ones said that they'd listen to a tape, but they didn't do live auditions anymore. This is 1961 now.

We went in to MGM and sang for them, and they really liked us, and the guy said, "We're interested in doing a deal." The chief A&R guy was a guy named Danny Davis, who was later Danny Davis and The Nashville Brass. Trumpet player. Good musician, actually, and a pretty nice guy. So we thought we had a record deal, but now we needed a booking agent, so we went through Billboard, and there was this agency called I.T.A.—International Talent. They had booked The Kingston Trio, The Brothers Four, and later they booked Peter, Paul & Mary. John called them up, and we went down and sang for them. What happened next was like the scene from "Viva Zapata," where Zapata is being arrested by these Mexican 'gendarmes,' and he's in the middle of nowhere, but suddenly dozens and dozens of people appear from the hills. That's what I.T.A. was like. We started auditioning for two or three people, and suddenly people were coming out of the offices, and suddenly there were 15–20 people there! They loved it, because we had this interesting balance. John had all of this charisma—they didn't know about the writing thing yet—John had the personality, Scott had the voice, and I could play. If you think about it, all of these bands like The Kingston Trio, The Brothers Four, nobody could really *sing*, and nobody could really *play*, relatively speaking. We went with them, and unfortunately for us, Rene Cardenas was there, and he became our manager, along with Frank Werber. Frank has an interesting prospective on John; I think he was always a little afraid of John! He thought that John was a loose cannon. And it's true, from Frank's point of view. They signed us.

Frank Werber: Some years back, I had taken in a partner to help me keep on top of all this shit. His name was Rene Cardenes. He handled the publishing, and also found talent. One of the groups that he found was John Phillips and The Journeymen. We funded them and got them jobs. We got them the deal with Capitol. We sort of put that together, and Rene sort of took that and ran with it. We had a run with them for a while, about two years. I got involved because Rene had limited experience in dealing with artists.

Dick Weissman: We were sort of at a stalemate with MGM, because they said, "We don't hear any hits in your stuff, and we want hits . . . " They brought a lot of Broadway songwriters in front of us, and we didn't like any of their stuff, and we didn't feel that they were even close to knowing where we were at. Finally we had a showdown. Rene went in and said, "We want a $5,000 promotional guarantee and a two album deal . . . " Back in those days, you wanted to do a two album deal, because it didn't take a long time to make an album. This other guy, Chip Vienneau, who had come into the picture, looked at me straight in the face and said, "You'll never get a deal like that in the record business." Ten minutes later we were at Capitol, auditioning live for Andy Wiswell, who was East Coast A&R and later produced the first two Journeyman albums. He got on the phone with Voyle Gilmore, who was on the West Coast, and he told him what we wanted, two albums, etc. and you could hear on the other end of the line, "Okay, that's no problem . . . " So, that's how we got our deal.

We were pretty together at the time, because we had done all of this intense rehearsal. Scott, by the way, was living in the Albert Hotel in the Village. He wasn't living uptown with John & I. We went in and recorded out first album for Capitol at their studios on 46th Street. Meanwhile, Cardenas and Werber got us a gig at The Hungry i, in San Francisco. Before this, we had done a television show in Canada called "This World In Music," or something like that. That was a big gig, and we were pretty excited because it was a big CBC production. Probably the best TV stuff we ever did. We also did gigs in New York—I had some contacts and we did gigs at

Folk City and The Second Fret in Philadelphia. And we finished the album.

I remember one thing, this funny memory . . . John was kind of a rough kid, and John wanted to have a fight with this guy, and he kind of insulted him. He might have been a little bit drunk. But anyway, I had to sit down with John and explain to him that this is not the way we do things here in The Village! "Maybe you'd do that in Virginia Beach, but not up here. We don't do the fighting thing in the Village. If you wanna go uptown, you can get in as many fights as you want to."

Henry Diltz: John Phillips was a big hero of mine, when he had a group called The Journeymen. They also had a great banjo player named Dick Weissman. *Great* banjo player. I saw The Journeymen at The Troubadour, when I had just come over here from Hawaii with The Modern Folk Quartet. They were just so great. John had also been a songwriting buddy of John Stewart, who was a good friend of mine, so I heard a lot about John Phillips from Stewart.

Jim Mason: I met John in 1961, and I knew of The Journeymen, because I booked them, I think in '62 at a college spring break social event. I was Student Council Social Guide or something at Kellogg Community College in Battle Creek, Michigan.

What attracted me to The Journeymen was that after I first heard their recordings, I thought that they had an amazing vocal blend. I thought they were very sophisticated as singers and just in terms of vocal ideas, for being a 'folk group'. I later learned that they had a jazz background, and they got into being a folk group because it was very trendy in the early '60s, and it was an easier way for them to make a living as opposed to being a jazz group. They were incredible live. They were a dress-alike, matching shirts and blazers, skinny ties group . . . very professional. The thing I remember from this show is that I'd never seen anybody take their vocal performance so seriously. They were warming up backstage, and John had all of them doing vocal exercises; one thing in particular that's pretty famous called "Seiber Syllables"—it's a series of vocal exercises where you enunciate different vowel and consonant sounds. It had the effect of clearing your head, and it's something that really good, operetta singers do. I thought these guys were really slick and very professional; this is a folk group doing that! I was privy to be backstage during the warm-up. I just thought these guys were so cool . . .

My little group got to hang with them, and we got to play a few tunes with them after the show and had a few drinks and things. It was fun. John was a fun guy to hang out with. He was 'Mr. Charm', like the social director, and obviously the leader. He was very outgoing, very pleasant, and very charming.

Dick Weissman: Then we went out to California, and we did the gigs at The Hungry i. We started in January, and then it moved into February. John moved Suzie, his wife, and his kids, Jeff and Laura—or MacKenzie, as she's known—out there. They were living in Mill Valley. We were making about $1,500 a week, which for us, was a lot of money. After commissions, we would each take home about $300, which was not bad for 1961. And it was there that John met Michelle.

Michelle Phillips: I used to sing in church. My grandfather was a minister, so I used to sing there. But I never had any ambition to be a singer, I never wanted to get up on-stage. I didn't have that burning desire to pursue a career of any kind, actually. I was modeling in New York when John suggested that I join the group, and I laughed in his face. He said, "No, no, really . . . you're gonna sing because it costs too much to keep you on the road." For me, it was a lot of work to learn really how to sing in a group, and I really had to learn how to do it practically overnight. First we had the group with Marshall Brickman on banjo, but only for a very short period time. But everything that I was doing was new to me. I had never been on television before, and we were doing a television show. I had never been on stage before and it was freaking me out. And having to really learn how to sing, how to blend, how to remember my parts. Just everything! I had to learn *everything*.

Russell Gilliam: She certainly hadn't sung much, and I remember it was very traumatic for her. At that point, Marshall Brickman was in The New Journeymen. Apparently, some people were making fun of Michelle's singing abilities, and John arranged for her to take some singing lessons from a very famous voice teacher in New York, and he really taught her how to project and how to sing on key.

Dick Weissman: John had met Michelle at the Hungry i. I think that she decided that he was 'the one,' and he was kind of enamored of her. This left him in a very difficult position, because he had moved his family out there. You know, you didn't ask people what they were doing in those days. I was too busy figuring out what I was gonna do. Scott was the same way; we weren't worrying too much about what John was doing. We didn't get the feeling that John needed too much help, anyway.

John Stewart: As soon as John came out to San Francisco with The Journeymen, he was playing the Hungry i, and the next thing I knew, he was with Michelle. I would go over to his house when Mackenzie and his older son, Jeffery were there. He'd come in about noon, after being out all night with Michelle . . . The kids were sitting there having peanut butter sandwiches, and Suzie his wife was there . . . I was in a very distant marriage at the time, so I fully understood the appeal of Michelle, yeah! She was 16 or 17 years old, and just *loved* John. They were inseparable.

Michelle Phillips: I have to tell you that when I first met John Phillips, I met someone who was so decent, and such a fine human being. He exuded that. He was a very, very good man. He cared about his family, and he cared about his music very, very deeply.

Dick Weissman: I was probably a little bit moralistic and a little appalled. It wasn't that I was especially close to Suzie, but I realized that he had two kids, and I thought, "What the fuck is he doing?" But I would talk to Michelle and I was friendly with her. To be honest with you, she seemed to me like a teenage Hollywood starlet, and that was not my particular world. I didn't have any particular impression of her, and John didn't seem like the kind of guy who had any trouble finding girlfriends. But I couldn't quite figure out what he saw in her. Part of it, I'm sure was her persistence. Michelle's a pretty ambitious person, and she's pretty good at getting what she wants, and probably in that sense, was way mature beyond her years. I think she was 17 or 18 at the time. Rusty, her sister, was around then, too. She was hanging around with Scott at the time, and I liked Rusty quite a bit.

Russell Gilliam: Because of the way that we were brought up, the age difference between John and Michelle wasn't an issue. You have to remember that my father was dating girls who were *a lot* younger than he was, and he was already on his fourth marriage by then. By the time she was living with John, I was dating and living with Scott MacKenzie.

Michelle and Russell Gilliam, Mexico, late 1950s.
Courtesy of Michelle Phillips.

Cyrus Faryar: She had grown up in Mexico, and had had a childhood upbringing that was not conventional. Both Michelle and her sister, Russell, were both cut from a different cloth. Rather bohemian.

Russell Gilliam: I had so much fun with John. We would stay up all night long singing and laughing. At one point, John wanted to actually put me in a group with Scott. It was going to be Scott, John, Michelle and me, I believe, and we were going to be dressed in this very pure . . . like, the girls were going to dress like these Puritan wives, and it was going to be rock & roll and roll and country!

Eric Hord: I met Michelle first when I was playing at The Ash Grove in L.A. I was playing with Judy Henske at the time, and I think that Sonny and Brownie were also on the bill. She was hanging out with Carmine Paz, who was this Cuban girl. They always showed up when Bud and Travis played. The Ash Grove was a real artists' club, and on any given night, you would see Bud and Travis, Henske, Lightnin' Hopkins, all of 'em, hangin' out. This would be '58, '59. After that, I made it to New York with this group called The Highland Three, and then we played in Minneapolis at a club called The Padded Cell, and that's where I met John, when he was playing with The Journeymen. Later on back at the hotel, John and I started talking, and saw some kind of potential in me, and he told me that if I was ever free to give him a call, because he was using guitar players all of the time. Basically, the one thing he wanted from me was that when we would get together, I'd sit down and explain guitar chords to him, and what went to this, and what went to that—the relationships between the chords. So that's the first time I met him . . .

David Crosby: I met Cass when she was in the Big Three, and they were on tour with us on a terrible tour back in nineteen hundred and frozen to death . . . 1963, I think, and she was a pal. We stayed friends for a very long time, because she was without a doubt one of the funniest and nicest people I've ever met in my life. It just was one of my best friendships, ever. I knew Denny earlier, when he was in a group called The Halifax Three, who were playing in the folk circuit, and I had run into them there. I liked him too, I thought he was a wonderful guy. A bit of a drunk, but a very funny drunk. I only knew Michelle from a distance, and thought she was a tremendously attractive girl. You know, she was everybody's idea of what it was to be good-looking. All of us wanted her desperately.

Russell Gilliam: John wanted Michelle to move with him to New York. I remember I had to buy her a coat. John wanted her to come to New York with a coat, so I bought her one and got her on the plane. After that, I went to college and went back to live with my father. I didn't hear much from them for a while . . .

PART TWO

Halifax Denny . . . good fortune at the pawn shop . . . Damon Runyon & The Colonels . . . The Halifax Three . . . John & Michie in California . . . The Big Three . . . Denny & Zally sing for their supper to puking teens . . . gettin' kinda itchy . . . Wavy Gravy stops the party . . . Whatcha Gonna Do . . .

Denny Doherty: I was working in a hockshop, and we used to take in a lot of instruments. One night on a dare, I went up and sang at a local rink. This guy stopped into the hockshop the next day, and said that he heard me sing, and would I be interested in fronting a band in Spryfield, Nova Scotia, playing weddings and dances and shit? And I said, 'Sure, why not?!' That was The Hepsters . . . before there was 'hip', there was 'hep'—and you had to be a *'hepcat,' daddy* . . . Oh, man . . . this is 1956 . . . Little Richard had just come out, and everyone was shocked, stunned . . . we loved him.

In this hockshop there were all of these sort-of Damon Runyon characters. It was the underworld, man. We all drove these big cars and were wearing diamonds and watches. Of course, all of this stuff had all been taken in hock. So, from that, and being able to sing, and being asked to sing and hanging out at the jazz clubs where The Hepsters—those finger poppin' daddies'—were hangin' out. There was a pretty good jazz scene up there, because there were a lot of military bases.

There was a guy, Pat Le Croix, who was in a group called The Colonials. He went to Westlake School of Music in Los Angeles. He had come back from L.A., then bummed around Europe, playing jazz little coffeehouses there, and wound up back in Halifax. I met him in the jazz club, and the other guy was playing folk music, because you could make a living playing that at the time. So that was The Colonials. We were trying to make a living as an act. It was more show biz oriented than anything related to folk. Folk music just happened to be what was going on at the time. If it hadn't been folk music, I probably would have wound up playing bass in a rock & roll band. That didn't happen. What happened was folk music got real popular with The Kingston Trio, The Brothers Four and The Travelers and The Weavers and everything. It had all changed. But, there was nowhere to work. We had played all of the fraternities, the local coffeehouses, and we had a 15-minute television series on local TV but that was like, end of '59, early 1960. So, we had exhausted these avenues, so it was, "What do we do next?"

One of the guys in the group, he and his wife had been to Montreal . . . as a bullwhip act. He's telling us that we've *got* to go to Montreal. We're saying, "What the fuck are you talking about? *Montreal?*" He said that there are about 300-plus nightclubs that are open until four in the morning featuring every kind of entertainment; dancing bears, fire-eaters . . . everything you saw on the Sullivan show? That was performing in Montreal in the late '50s and early '60s. Wide open town, and that's where we headed with our folk group; because if it was popular at the time, we could get into some clubs. And we did.

We left town in an MG. One of the guys had an MG, a two-seater. He cut the back off this car and stuck a Studebaker back end on there! A '47 Studebaker back on an MG . . . I think he was

trying to make it look like a Jaguar. All he made it into was this
weird-fucking-bug thing. You had to get into a pre-natal position
to sit in the back. We arrived in Montreal, but on the way, the push
rod broke, and we had to sell one of the guitars in order to get one.
So, when we got to Montreal we had about thirty five cents, and
we were looking for gigs . . . We eventually got a gig at this coffee-
house, where the owner put us up upstairs, gave us food and
lodging and ten bucks apiece a week, which wasn't bad. Then we
could also get work at other clubs, so were running up and down
St. Catherine Street. We were doing all of these folk songs like "All
My Trials, Lord" and "Call The Wind Mariah." I turned 21 in Montreal, and then we went to Toronto, so Montreal was our way out
of Halifax. We played Toronto and eventually went down to New
York. We had a pretty good sound. We all sang, and we all knew
harmony.

Peter Pilafian: I had just arrived on the West Coast. I was
playing upright bass and some fiddle; I was mainly a violin player.
Mostly folk stuff. I was a roommate of Chris Hillman's, and in the
early days of The Byrds, these were the guys I was hanging out
with. I just came out to California to see what was happening—a
little bit of surfing, a little bit of drugs, everything. One of the girls
that was hanging out was Russell Gilliam, and her and I kinda hit it
off and started spending a lot of time together, and eventually
started living together. There seemed to be a changing of apart-
ments every few months, and people writing songs in the bedroom, taking drugs in the living room, that kind of thing.

It was because of Russell that I got involved with them. We
went up to San Francisco a few times, and we went to New York
once, and John and Michelle had a little apartment in Greenwich
Village. John and I immediately got along very, very well. We were
all friends during this period, and Michelle was taking singing
lessons from a lady in San Francisco. So it was during this period of
transition that John decided to bring Michelle into the group and
form the more 'decorative' Journeymen, The New Journeymen.

I remember that John was very sincere. Very warm, open and sincere. He loved his music, and he loved the songs. It was so comfortable and inspiring to sit with him in a room. He always had his guitar, and was always singing songs, and there was such a warmth in that. There was also a real sincerity in that. He didn't seem phony or contrived; his music came from a really deep place, and there was a lot of clarity in his music because of that. He knew so many songs, and had such a phenomenal memory and a grasp for things. Consequently, he was able to work the nuances, which as a musician it was very delightful and impressive to be around that kind of talent. That's what led, of course, to his ability to construct those four-part harmonies. He had such a grasp of the basic music that he could embellish and expand it.

Michelle had a kind of personality that she still retains, a general sort of good-heartedness, a cheerfulness and a positive attitude. Like a shining light; a happiness about people, about life. That never seemed artificial. She just looked at the good side of things. I certainly didn't identify this at the time, necessarily—I was just a drug-talking hippie kid! But I definitely responded to both of them, and always had a good time with them. We got along really well. Also the openness at that time to bring people into the circle. I never felt that I needed to go through a baptism or challenge to prove myself.

Music was more prevalent than conversation, in a way. Like right now—we're sitting here talking—but in these cases, John would have a guitar, and we'd be sitting and fiddling with tunes. And if there were people around, like, say, Michelle, he'd say, "Here, sing this part." It was a good, loose environment, and consequently led to a lot of creativity, and things were thrown into becoming songs.

Barry McGuire: The first time I met Cass was at Fordham University. She was in The Big Three at the time with Tim Rose and Jim Hendricks. Sometimes you meet people that you have an instant affinity with, and it was certainly that way with Cass, it was awesome. We just looked at each other and went, "boing!" and we were friends. And through her I met Denny Doherty down in The

Village, and Zal Yanovsky and John Sebastian—they were all kinds hangin' together. It was always a lot of fun, and a lot of laughs. It was just a fun, exciting time with music just floating in every direction. Then I met John and Michelle on the road one time when they had The New Journeymen when I was in The New Christy Mistrels. John knew a friend of mine, Art Podell.

Jerry Yester: I met Cass around the time of The Big Three; she was friends with my wife, Judy Henske. When Judy was playing somewhere in the Village, Cass would usually drop by the dressing room and say hello.

Cyrus Faryar: That first Big Three album had a fantastic cover, which was done in the style that was to become known as 'Pop-Art'; it had a great photo and the design was very cubistic. I think on that album, Cass sang "Wild Women Get The Blues"—one of her all-time greats.

Henry Diltz: I met Cass a little later in New York when she was a member of The Mugwumps, so this must have been around '64. Zal Yanovsky and Jim Hendricks were in the band, and John Sebastian would sit in and play blues harp with them. I remember that they were practicing at the Albert Hotel. My roommate was Eric Jacobson, who produced some Mugwumps stuff, and later produced The Spoonful. So I saw them around The Village at clubs about this time.

Cyrus Faryar: We were in the Village, and the MFQ were in transit to becoming a folk-rock band, and we were all sort-of hanging out. Cass had a friend named Muffy, and they were hanging out a lot together, and I remember that they had gone to Coney Island and she had got her hair caught in a ferris wheel or something, and they came back with all of these heavy stories.

This was around the time when people were taking acid and you had to talk them out of jumping off buildings because they thought they could fly. But mostly it was about the music, and at the time there was a lot of talent floating around . . . and the beauty of that moment was that everyone was accessible to everyone then. It was tribal, kind of. Very friendly. No one was locked really hard into any one group or identity. People shared their talent. If someone had a particular kind of voice that you wanted to use, if they were in town, they'd happily come over.

Denny Doherty: While our band was in New York, we changed our name to The Halifax Three, and we went on tour. Folk music was dying, Kennedy was assassinated, and that's where I met Cass; on that tour. John, Michelle, Scott, and Dick Weissman were The Journeymen, and Cass was The Big Three. Everybody in the world was workin' on something. David Crosby was singin' in Les Baxter's fuckin' 'Balladeers.' John Denver was in The Chad Mitchell Trio, and Jim McGuinn was playing banjo for Chad Mitchell.

I met Cass first, through Zal Yanovsky. He was her guitar player, and he was from Toronto. In our group, we only had one guitar player, and he wasn't that great. I couldn't really play guitar; I had played bass back in Halifax, and in The Halifax Three, I took a nail and drove it into a Martin D-18, made an extra peg and tuned it like a banjo, and played banjo chords on that. It looked like I was playing guitar. We also had a washtub bass player. So musically, we were rather light.

During the time that The Halifax Three were working in New York on Bleeker Street, Cass and The Big Three were hitting the big time. They were gigging at The Bitter End and clubs uptown like The Blue Angel. They were on their way, and they were doing pretty good. John and The Journeymen were also doing pretty good. They were playing a lot of college dates, and they were more cerebral and less commercial than The Halifax Three. John could write stuff that sounded more like obscure folk songs. Him and Dick Weissman would get together and write something that sounded like some old English ballad. You could get away with it, if you were 'hipper than thou.' The folkies couldn't really question it, it was like, "Oh, what a beautiful song," and they'd say, "Oh, it's a thing that needed to be translated . . . an old Gregorian thing that I did at university!" Dick Weissman is, to this day, a professor of music at the University of Colorado at Boulder. They did it in such a way that they were more authentic and they weren't getting labeled like The Kingston Trio for being 'commercial', which is what we were labeled with. We didn't give a fuck, anyway. If being 'commercial' meant getting paid, that's us! "Show me the money!"

When that ended, Zal and I hung out played as a duo in Washington, D.C. The Halifax Three had played there earlier, at clubs in Georgetown like The Shadows and The Cellar Door. Zal and I were befriended by this guy named Jack Boyle who owned a bar called Max Fife & Drum, and we played surf music. Zal played guitar, I played bass, and we also had a drummer. Jack liked us, so he went out and bought us the instruments. We were living above the bar . . . oh, my . . . Zallman and I living upstairs above a beer bar, in a university full of college co-eds . . . it was bizarro to the max. After we would do a 45 minute surf band set, we'd go out and wait on tables to these puking college kids, and then when the bar would close, we'd take 'a selected few' upstairs and boogie 'till dawn . . . See, I was into rock & roll before folk music, so when folk was dying, what do ya do? "Time to play rock & roll again . . . " [hums melody to "Walk Don't Run"] on and on and on. These college kids didn't care, as long as we turned it up to ten . . .

Across the street was The Cellar Door, and they had folk acts, as well as comedians. Hugh Romney—now known as Wavy Gravy—was there. Wavy Gravy actually got us kicked out of Washington! The kid that we got to play surf music was this rich kid that owned a set of drums. He used to hang out at the bar, because Zal and I were rather worldly. We were friends with the sculptor who lived upstairs, who was into Ravi Shankar. Anyway, this kid who had the drums was Ted Hamm. Hamms Beer? Yeah. Huge Romney came into town with some grass, and we went, "Oh shit, man! We haven't smoked any grass in months . . . " It was really good shit, too. Anyway, we turned Ted on, and he's never smoked grass before in his life. He freaked out and went home and laid in his bed screaming, "Oh no, Denny did it! They gave me poison!!" Then his father, Mr. Hamm, came down to Max's and said, "I don't know what you did . . . I don't want to know—but Theodore is *beside* himself, and we've had to have him sedated . . . *just make sure you're outta town by sundown . . .* " Thank you, Hugh Romney!

Nurit Wilde: I knew Cass in The Big Three and Denny in The Halifax Three. I was a student in Toronto, and working in the clubs. I don't exactly remember how I met Cass, but she had already met Denny, and was already in love with him. I think I met her through Zal Yanovsky; this is before the Mugwumps. A little later on, I worked at The Bitter End, and I saw The Mugwumps perform there. They were good; they had Cass and Denny, and John Sebastian was a sideman, and Zal was playing guitar. He was always cutting up, so he was a good foil for Cass. James Hendricks was usually stiff as a board. But they also played at The Village Corner in Toronto, which was on Avenue Road.

PART THREE

Denny & Cass in The Mugwumps . . . John & Michelle in The Journeymen . . . Sebastian & Zal form the Spoonful . . . I used to live in New York City/California Dreamin' . . . Life in the Village Meets The Beatles . . . and back to California . . .

Mark Volman: John wasn't the kind of guy who was going to be able to go up on stage and sing his songs as a singer-songwriter. He had to put himself in the context of a group. When he had his group going in New York in that college folk scene, The Journeymen, it was a perfect situation. There were all these groups like The Kingston Trio, Bud and Travis, The Brother Four, all that scene—that's where he came out of. That was a good time in music, but it lived and breathed in kind-of an East Coast, collegiate thing. Left Coast was starting to take on a harder, electric guitar-driven edge, and that was spawned by the surf music.

Jerry Yester: I met Denny through Zally, just pre-Mugwumps in Washington, in '64. Cass was *always* a great singer, even back then. I never noticed a difference in her voice from those days to The Mamas & The Papas.

Cyrus Faryar: A lot was going on—Tim Hardin had just come into town as an unknown, and he obviously had a very unique talent. John Hammond Jr., Felix Pappilardi, who was very talented and was a bright light. The Lovin' Spoonful were gathering their resources together, and started playing at this place called The Night Owl, and also right around this time, Jim McGuinn—before he was Roger McGuinn—was starting up The Byrds.

Michelle Phillips: We had known John Sebastian in New York, and Cass had been in a group with Zal and Denny, The Mugwumps. So we were kind of hanging with them in New York, before we even came out. I remember John playing "Do You Believe In Magic" for me in our apartment. He said, "Do you like this song?" I said, "That's a *hit* song!" "Do you really think so?" I said, "Absolutely!!" Then later on, we heard it in the Virgin Islands.

The Mugwumps, 1964.
Courtesy of Michelle Phillips.

Denny Doherty: When Zal and I left Washington and got back to New York, we stayed at the Albert Hotel, which was our home base. The owner, Miss Feldman . . . god bless her, she's dead . . . but she would give us credit, because she knew that we had no where else to stay. A lot of people stayed at The Earl, we stayed at the Albert, and that's where Cass and Jim (Hendricks) were holed up. They were lookin' to so something, because The Big Three had broken up. At this point, The Beatles were starting to happen. "I Want To Hold Your Hand," "Please Please Me," all of those were on the radio. I remember hearing that last chord of "I Want To Hold Your Hand," and we said, "How the fuck did they do that!? We gotta get into *that* shit!" So, we put together a folk group called Cass Elliot and The Big Three, which was Zal, me, Jim, and Cass out in front. We were doing sort of Springfield's-type stuff . . . we were going electric, but we weren't going to get a drummer. We went to Manny's and got out instruments and our amplifiers, and then we went up the street with Jim, who was a clotheshorse, and we got the suits and ties and shirts and everything. Cass got her chiffon gown.

We went back to Washington, D.C., where Roy Silver, who was Cass's manager at the time, became friends with Bob Cavallo, who owned the club, The Shadows. They got into management, because he had the club, and we were the house act, and we went back to Washington D.C. as The Mugwumps. We took a drummer with us, and Sebastian, playing harp. We had already played The Bitter End and around New York as 'Cass Elliot and The Big Three'. This was *before* The Beatles, before 'A Hard Day's Night' came out, we had gone electric. And it wasn't because of The Beatles, it was because of The Springfield's and Dusty Springfield; we were lookin' more like that. They were a studio group, and they used bass, drums and guitar. "Silver Threads and Golden Needles". We used to do that on stage, as a matter of fact. It was in our repertoire; Cass sang it. But, we weren't going to make in Washington, D.C., especially the way *we* looked. But we couldn't get any work, and the album that we started to make was too contrived. It wasn't *our* stuff. It was The Mugwumps, but we weren't playing and singing and writing our own material. We were looking around for material.

We also couldn't always connect with younger audiences. Cass and Jim would consciously take time out, because kids couldn't get in at The Shadows, which was a gin mill, not a nightclub. We would do Saturday morning, teenage juice bar and sandwiches shows for the kid. They'd jam the place with teenagers who were all into the British Invasion, and were into The Beatles. We had long hair and looked freaky and played rock & roll. They ate it up, and from those sessions, Cass and Jim would go back and write songs. They wrote "Everybody's Been Talkin" and a bunch of others. We were just starting to write our own stuff when the club closed up to do 'disco' or something. When we got back to New York we sort of finished the recording we'd already started, but that only lasted a few months, if that. The Mugwumps were dead. Mainly because we were all just laying around the hotel with no money. Management didn't have any cash to give us. Miss Feldman was getting a little antsy about payment. We had paid her *some* money, but . . . god, there was Cass and myself, Jim, and Jim's girlfriend, Vanessa. We had this one huge three-bedroom suite with a big living room, and like, nine people were living there. [Bob] Gibson would come by and stay for a day or two. Sebastian would come by . . . everybody would just hang out. We'd pull the mattresses off the bed so that we could all sleep. But we had to pay for it . . .

The year before, when we came down from Toronto to New York in '62–63, we got that Southern bus tour. Cass got us that. John and The Journeymen were also on the show, and we were with the same agency, I.T.A., who also had The Brothers Four and The Cumberland Three and a whole lot of other people. I'd seen John at the agency before; it was just a nod and a 'hello'. But on this bus tour through the South, we got to talkin'—ya know, you're on a bus for a month, so . . .

Dick Weissman: Back when we were on the Hootenanny Tour with The Halifax Three, I remember Denny and Pat LeCroix taking John aside all of the time and saying, 'Let's sing something . . . ' and they would, and then they'd say, 'Doesn't that sound *good?*' It was sorta like they wanted to be with John rather than the leader of their group. That may have been the first time that John and Denny sang together, so there was some connection.

Dick Weissman: John and Michelle decided to get married. I think we were playing in D.C. and The Shadows. Scott and I bought them a very nice little wedding present, a Lady Martin guitar. So, they're getting married, and we get them this guitar, and we go to this justice of the peace. Scott and I were looking at each other while the justice is reciting the vows—because there was this noise. The Justice of the Peace never turned off the FM musak that was playing! Here we are, musicians, and this was like the most ironic thing that could happen. It was hysterically funny. The next

Soon to be married, John Phillips and Michelle
Gilliam, Alexandria, Virginia, 1962.
Courtesy of Michelle Phillips.

day, we left the motel, and John, I think, left the guitar next to the car we were driving, and drives away. We get about ten minutes away, and someone says, "Where's the guitar?" Of course, it was gone when we got back; but that's a vintage John story. He's probably lost more tapes than anyone in the universe.

I.T.A. called us, because our record had come out, and we had a turntable hit—meaning it was played a lot, but didn't sell much—with this song, "River Come Down." These guys were older guys and they actually listened to M.O.R. radio, and every day when they'd drive into work, this one station in New York would play "River Come Down." It was drivin' them crazy, because they liked us, and they didn't want to let us go; they had to because of some union technically with Werber that they hadn't gotten us enough work. We ended up going back to New York, and I.T.A. said, "Contracts can be gotten out of, potentially. We'll get you a lawyer, and you'll work it all out . . . " David Braun was the lawyer. Very well known lawyer. We're sitting in the lawyer's office, and they're doing projections of our earnings. Now mind you, we don't have enough money between us to get a can of sardines. But they're saying, "Well, they're going to make $100,000 this year, probably $150,000 next year . . . " and the three of us are looking at each other like, "What in the hell are they talking about?!" Meanwhile John was in debt to Werber and Cardiens, because they had advanced him money to pay the rent and things like that. We also owed them commissions, because they deferred commissions on the Hungry i, because we had no work . . .

Frank Werber: John Phillips was, I have to say, a major pain in the ass. Every turn of the card, we had to take care of him. He always needed something done, he always needed some money, and he was always draggin' his heels about what management and producers wanted. He was, in general, a pain in the ass, and we let him go. After a while, it proved to be taking up way too much time for any returns, and it also was encroaching on our energies, which we used on other projects. I don't remember how, but we released him.

Dick Weissman: Also, we did five weeks in a club in San Jose, and that was a pretty neat gig, because it was a very informal club, and it really tightened us up, because we had to a lot of stuff. Definitely 'trial by fire'. And every week more and more people would show up. We started out making almost nothing, and by the end we were making a reasonable amount of money.

But after that, we agreed to get out of the management contract, and we hooked up with a manager named Stan Greeson. We did our second album, "Live At The Padded Cell," which was probably our worst album. Right after that, Michelle moved with John back to New York. Just how John and Suzie got divorced, I don't know. Michelle was fascinated by New York; she'd never seen snow before, growing up in California and Mexico. Also during this period, John didn't show up for a couple of shows, one in Cleveland and the other in Vermont. He missed the plane or slept through it. Scott and I did the shows as a duo, which was kind of fun, as well as a challenge.

There was one rehearsal we had at John's. He and Michelle were living in the Upper East Side, around 70th Street. We went to a rehearsal, and we never rehearsed with the intensity that we did for the first album. John was really, really stoned, and he left the room and was gone for about 15 minutes. I looked at Scott and said, 'Let's just get out of here.' He never mentioned it, and I doubt that he was ever aware the we'd left.

John Phillips: Well, after the Kingston Trio sort of came in and boosted, not traditional folk music, but commercial folk music, the whole folk music thing died right after that and just became persona non grata in the music field. We had resisted going in the pop field for years and years because you couldn't do anything intelligent in it. It was all, [sings] "Venus, goddess of love—" that kind of stuff, and bobby socks with blue jeans. We just didn't want to sing that. The only thing that we could sing was jazz. So we did that. And then when The Beatles came along and sort of opened this whole new door of songwriting, where you could express personal feelings—when I first tried to sell "Monday, Monday" or "California Dreamin'" and things like that to publishers in the Brill

Building, Scott and I together, and we had a guitar, I think. They would say, "Who wants to hear a song about a state? Where's the girl interest in this? Who wants to hear a song about a day of the week? Come on, get out of here." And this happened in the whole building. It was nine floors. And we persisted and it just sort of came around.

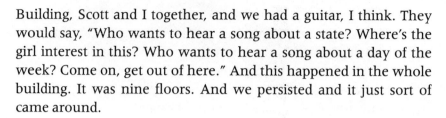

Dick Weissman: John would always like to work late at night, like about 10 or 11 at night. And basically, he liked to have company, so say, if you were there, he'd say, 'Hey, help me write this song . . . ' By helping him, that might consist of staying awake with him, getting him a beer or whatever, and throwing in one word. If you did that, he'd give you 20 percent of the song! Now, I wasn't there when John and Michelle "wrote" "California Dreamin'," but it's my guess that this is what happened there. I have some pieces of songs that John gave me for keeping him company. He likes different influences, also, and different people bring out different influences. He's a smart guy. Also, if you're there, and he doesn't finish the song, he feels bad about it.

Roger McGuinn: I used to live at the Earle Hotel in the Village, in room 707, and John and Michelle lived downstairs. They had a big suite, and I used to visit them all the time. I'd go down and jam with them quite frequently; literally hundreds of times. I wouldn't say we were close friends, but we were acquaintances, and we liked playing together. I knew them in California, too, prior to the Village. I met Michelle and Rusty in San Francisco, and I met John around the time when he was in The Journeymen with Dick Weissman and Scott McKenzie. I was in The Chad Mitchell Trio at the time, so we were all part of the commercial folk music scene of the period. But I lived in the Village for about a year, and spent a lot of time at the Phillips's apartment. In fact, I kinda turned them on to mixing folk and rock. They were purists about folk music at that point. I was getting into The Beatles, and I'd been working with Bobby Darin, who had influenced me to go into rock. So, I kinda started mixing it up with traditional folk songs and rock. I was playing down at some of the coffeehouses in The Village, and I remember showing John and Michelle some of the things I was doing, and they thought it was pretty weird. It was pre-Beatles; it was just some compositions that I'd came up with that had a rock beat with folk music changes. I don't think Michelle was singing with them at that point, but she was sittin' around lookin' pretty!

It was hard for John to break out of folk music, because I think he was real good at it, conservative, and successful, too. Remember, The Journeymen were a pretty big group. John was a pretty traditional singer, and I think he was doin' what we were all doing, which was adaptations of traditional folk songs and claiming arrangement credit for them. We all did that, and he was into that. I don't remember him writing any original material at that point. I was also hangin' around with The Doc—Eric Hord—around this time.

I met Cass when he was in The Big Three, and I also knew Jim Hendricks. I remember seeing them at The Bitter End; I used to hang out there a lot. But Cass's voice was a standout, even then. No question about it. Great lady and a great singer.

John Phillips: It's my recollection that we were at the Earle Hotel in New York and Michelle was asleep. I was playing the guitar. We'd been out for a walk that day and she'd just come from California and all she had was California clothing. And it snowed overnight and in the morning she didn't know what the white stuff coming out of the sky was, because it never snowed in Southern L.A., you know, Southern California. So we went for a walk and the song is mostly a narrative of what happened that day, stopped into a church to get her warm, and so on and so on. And so as I was thinking about it later that night, I was playing and singing and I thought "California Dreamin'" was what we were doing, actually, that day. So I tried to wake Michelle up to write the lyrics down that I was doing. And she said, "Leave me alone. I want to sleep. I want to sleep." "Wake up. Write this down. You'll never regret it. I promise you, Michelle." "Okay." Then she wrote it down and went back to sleep. And she's told me—up to this day—she's never regretted getting up and writing it down. Since she gets half of the writing of the song for it.

Michelle and I were in New York, and it was four below zero, we were broke, and in the Earl Hotel, and the heat goes off at ten o'clock at night, ya know? We hadn't gotten out of bed until eight o'clock at night that night. So we were up all night long. Michelle went to sleep about five o'clock in the morning, and I started writing, freezing to death. She would talk all night about L.A., how she wanted to go back to Los Angeles, her home town, and get out of New York.

Michelle Phillips: The first time I ever heard John mention that he was the sole writer of "California Dreamin'" was when I went on "The Conan O'Brien Show," and Conan said to me that he had had John on the show a week before and said, "I just have to ask you about this: John claims that you didn't write any of the song "California Dreamin'," and that he only woke you up in the middle of the night so that you could "write it down."

Now, at this point, John was either just about to go in for his liver transplant, or he had just come out of it. I was so surprised, and I was stunned that John would have said something like that, and yet I knew that he had, because Conan O'Brien wouldn't have put himself in that position even though I hadn't seen the show; I knew that John must have said it.

At the time, I said, "You know, Conan, John has been very ill, and I am not going to attack him, and I think that [in] the 35 years that the song has been in publication, I think it's been pretty well established that we were co-writers on the song. But I don't want to say anything inflammatory or derogatory. I think that John is going through a lot of—besides physical stress—he's going through a lot of emotional stress. I feel badly that he said this, because he knows that we wrote the song together."

I have *always* maintained that he wrote most of it. There wasn't a song that we wrote together that he wrote most of. "Creeque Alley," "Free Advice," all of 'em. There's never been any question as to who wrote most of the songs. But for him to say that he woke me up in the middle of the night to have me "write down some lyrics" so that he could give me 50 percent of the publishing is the most absurd piece of *fiction* that I've ever heard!

What led to the writing of the song was that it was a *very* cold, bleak New York City day, and I wanted so desperately to go home to California. And it didn't seem like that was gonna happen soon, because all of the agents offices, the music offices—G.A.C.—were all out of New York City. I remember that at one point—see, John had gone to a military Catholic school from the time he was seven years old. At one point during a day—and I don't know if it was *the* day we wrote the song—but I was raised in Mexico City, and used to go to Catholic churches all of the time. And I wanted to take him into I think St. Patrick's Cathedral. I wanted to go in, I wanted to light some candles and he did *not* want to go in. He had an *aversion* to anything that had to do with organized religion. In fact, I remember us *not* going into the church. But for me—I am at best an agnostic and possibly an atheist—but I love the lighting of the candles and I loved going in and praying in a church. It was like my spiritual expression, and John did not like this at all; he hated it when I went into church. He had such a bad experience with the church; yet myself growing up in Mexico City—which is very much based in the concept of the 'Mother Church'—and the fact that all of my friends were Catholic, if I wanted to hang with them at all, I went to church with them; to mass with them on Sunday morning and that was that.

We were either at the Earle or the Albert Hotel in New York City in 1963, he woke me up in the middle of the night, he had started the song with the line, "All the leaves are brown, and the sky is grey/I went for a walk on a winter's day." This was very much parallel to what had happened like, maybe the day before. And it was indeed bleak and *windy* and cold. When he woke me up in the middle of the night, he played me those first eight bars, and I knew exactly where he was drawing from, and I said, "That's beautiful, John," and he said, "Well, help me write it," and I said, "I will help you write it, tomorrow," and he said, "No. Wake up now and help me write it now." And he was also totally strung out on Bennies, so there was no *way* I was gonna get any sleep anyway!

I woke up, and because of that walk to the church, I started to write the second verse: "I stopped into a church I saw along the way/ I got down on my knees and I pretend to pray." John did not like this lyric at all. As a matter of fact, he felt that it was too secular, too religious. Everything he hated about the song was the second verse. We finished the song, and the line about "The preacher loves the cold"; that was all my verse. Now, John may have tweaked it here and there, but that was my idea, which he *hated!*

There was never any question; no one ever asked me what I wrote in that song, because we didn't write that way. You know, "She gets this much, because she wrote these lines, etc." But when he said what he said on Conan O'Brien, I was really hurt, and I thought, "I really feel sorry for John, because I think this is all going to his brain; that the illness is going to his brain. But I'm not going to attack him or kick him when he's down." But you know what? Every time I see "Behind the Music," *he's* the writer, and he "woke me up in the middle of the night to be the 'secretary'." I think that the more I let this go, the more this is going to be the "story" that everyone's going to believe. And he doesn't say it about the other songs, just "California Dreamin'," because that makes the most money.

You know, it's really unfortunate that he got together with this woman to conspire to make everyone in the group *meaningless* except John Phillips. I think that he used Farnez [Phillip's third wife and widow] as a foil, because he wanted it to be all Farnez's fault, so that the entire family could say, "That damn Farnez; she doesn't let him see his children." Well, the truth is that John Phillips never had anyone in his life that prevented him from doing what he wanted to do. It's such bullshit. John didn't see his children because he didn't want to see his children. Because he didn't want to have to fess up to the neglect that he had inflicted on all of them. I don't blame Farnez completely; but I believe that the little "mix" that they created, this "concoction" was perfect for both of them, because she was so desperately jealous of me that she wanted to tear any relationship with me down.

Dick Weissman: We had all moved out to the West Coast,

which was a big deal for all of us. Then, Werber got into a big fight with I.T.A., and he wanted to get The Kingston Trio out, but he pulled us out first on some union technicality. We went from making $1500 a week to almost starving. Scott and I were living in a $9.00 a week Chinese hotel. I think I was budgeting like, $3.00 a day for food! Meanwhile, Werber entertained the notion of John being in the Kingston Trio . . . See, we didn't know that Dave Guard was going to leave The Kingston Trio, but Werber did, and it's our theory that he signed us as an 'insurance policy.' He figured that in some way, he could keep something going, and we were certainly sufficiently talented enough. There were different ways of dealing with it. At one point, he thought John would take Guard's place, and that I would be the instrumentalist, and spin Scott off into a solo career. He appreciated us on some level, he didn't think that we were 'nobodies,' but he did have an investment to protect. Which is, of course, what he had to do. We didn't understand any of this very well, at all. I think we went to some rehearsals. It would be interesting to know exactly why it didn't work out, other than that Werber didn't trust John.

John Stewart: I don't know anything about John joining The Trio, but if that's what you heard . . . I think it's pretty ridiculous, only because of the fact that John and Frank Werber didn't get along at all. But John would have made a great replacement for Dave Guard, but they needed someone who could play banjo. And John was too independent, anyway.

John and I had talked about me leaving The Kingston Trio, and becoming a new group with Scott and us. In fact, I told Frank and the rest of the guys that I was leaving, and that this was our last gig, and they said, "Yeah . . . right. . . . " Then John called and said, "I don't think we'd better do this . . . " I went back and said it was really the money, and I did get some more money out of it, so it turned out okay. I'm glad that it happened before I made the final walk, than after . . . But it's interesting to think about it now, if I had joined the group with John and Scott, and having John be the leader. I would have slipped into the role of being one of the band members. We loved each other. Scott wasn't too big on my singing, and neither was I. But we worked well together, and I was good on stage, and the camaraderie was there.

"Chilly Winds" was a song for The Kingston Trio that he and I wrote, and he had the first verse, which was "heading out on a westbound train . . . " and he pretty much had the structure, and said, "Let's write this together." So, we went out on a rowboat in San Francisco Bay, and we wrote some more of it, and then we went out to Charlotte Larson's house, who was the Kingston Trio's secretary. We sat up all night, and we must have written 40–50 verses, and then we pruned it down to a few verses . . . Another time, this waitress at The Trident was humming this old folk song, "Mary, Mary, where are you wandering?" That was all she knew, but I thought it was wonderful, so John and I went up to Nick Reynolds's house; he was married to his first wife. John came up with this chorus that went, "Oh, Miss Mary . . . " and the two of us just sat down and wrote all of the verses. We recorded both of those songs on the second Kingston Trip album that I was on, called "College Concert," and that was a very big album. We were best friends, and we were together almost 24 hours a day, every day.

Dick Weissman: But during this period when we were basically starving—which we were, that Phillips and Stewart were doing some writing together. Scott was living with some woman, and I was doing some copyright research for the Trio, like finding old verses of things like 'Old Joe Clark,' so that they could get the copyrights for them. Like, they were recording songs, and they would say, 'Well, make sure these are verses that you didn't write or that Phillips didn't write . . . ' They flew me down to UCLA, and I went through the library there, and that kept me alive for three or four weeks. And John was makin' some money, because he was writing with Stewart. They were writing, "Oh Miss Mary," "Chilly Winds," things like that. I don't know exactly what happened, but John probably got an advance from Werber's publishing company. It was never clear to me. But it was obviously to their benefit to keep John around . . .

Towards the end, we were playing a lot of schools. The problem was that because our records didn't sell that well, we were usually playing secondary schools. Like, instead of playing the University of Wisconsin, we'd play the University of Wisconsin at Milwaukee, things like that.

Ultimately we did a third album in L.A. with Voyle Gilmore. We recorded at The Tower, and used some other musicians. After that, we played at The Troubadour with Hoyt Axton. By the time we played there, things were already falling apart, and this was the time when John and Scott did not talk to each other. They had been the closest of friends and now they were the worst of enemies. They talked through me, like I was a medium. It got to the point where we'd be standing in the dressing room, and John would say to me, 'Tell Scott that his right sock doesn't match his left sock...' Things like that, when they were standing five feet away from each other. By this point, I was engaged and was already thinking about getting out of the group. Scott wanted to be a solo. And that's how we broke up. The worst thing about this was that we had this deal with Schlitz Beer, recording all of these commercials for them. The first year we had a guarantee of $25,000, and we went way over that. They wanted to pick up the option for the second year, but when they found out that we were breaking up, they didn't want to do it.

Eric Hord: Around this time, I got a call from John asking me if I'd come and play some concerts with him, Michelle and Denny as The New Journeymen, back east. We played in Washington and a few other cities. We were playing things like "500 Miles," which was a very popular song at the time, and things like Tom Paxton's "The Last Thing On My Mind" ... Phil Ochs things ... it was a trio thing, like Peter, Paul & Mary.

We had done a gig in upstate New York somewhere, and they had given me a medical bag, and at the gig John broke a string, and I fixed it on stage. I had to go into the bag to get the new string, and that's when John said, 'That's why we call him The Doctor, 'cause he takes care of us...' and that's where I got the nickname, 'The Doctor.'

Michelle Phillips: We had money, as a matter of fact. Life was good. When he was in The Journeymen, they were making quite a bit of money, and John was not out of work for long periods. We went to Sausalito to rehearse with Marshall Brickman, and we rehearsed for probably a couple of months. It wasn't a long time, really. We lived in Sausalito in a new house, and I remember them taking me to Sacks Fifth Avenue to buy my stage dress. It was very exciting, even though I was very unprepared. I remember the two of them saying, "You're ready, you're going to be fine . . . this is not brain surgery, it's just singing. You'll be great." This was also a very good period of our marriage. Very nice.

Dick Weissman: Scott went on and did a couple of singles for Capitol and Epic; none of them did anything. I went back to doing studio work, was a contracted songwriter. One thing that John did for me was this: I had always written songs, but I had always pretty much written them in the form of folk songs. In a way, I introduced him into folk music, and he introduced me into commercial music. The John formed The New Journeymen with Michelle and Marshall Brickman. They made some demos, and John played them for me, and frankly, they sounded terrible. But that was before Denny was in the group.

Eric Hord: John was very serious about his music. He knew that he could make money off of his writing and that he could make money from publishing, and he still knows it to this day. He was always a total businessman. If you listen to people like Dylan or someone, they're singing songs that sound like traditional folk songs, and the songs that John was writing songs that sound like traditional folk music songs. He was a great interpreter, and because of his background in jazz, he was very influenced by writing things for Scott, because Scott has a great voice, and a real commercial, selling voice. John knew that once he was in the studio he was halfway home. Because if he had a record in production, he could get money in advance. One of the things I remember was that we'd write a couple of songs in a blithered drug state, and then go up to the Brill Building and sell 'em for $50 apiece. There was always some publisher up there that would buy stuff like that, so that's how we existed for a good six months. Get a bunch of songs, play 'em on stage, and if people accepted 'em, we'd go and get some money for 'em. So John was basically the kind of person who was going in the right direction as far a commercial music is concerned.

Michelle was basically the kind of girl who would go along with anything. She was doing modeling, and she was very, very beautiful in a strange, weird way. She was hangin' around with John and getting into all of that, and when The Journeymen broke up, John looked around and got Michelle in the group. She just had to stand there and sing, she didn't necessarily have to have a great voice. He still had a great tenor, Denny, and he still had choral backgrounds, and someone who could play guitar behind that, meaning me.

Denny was a true-born singer who had aspirations to go from Toronto and come to New York and be a part of the city thing. The excitement of the city at the time we're talking about was just amazing, and there was a real buzz. The city was just *charged* every single night. There were six or seven coffeehouses where you could go on any night and hear all of the prominent singers who were making the set. Also, the city at the time was just at the *peak* of social reform, while a war was going on. There were always the greater things—there was always civil rights, or the war. That was the background to all of this.

We all hung out at this bar called The Dugout, which was the main watering hole. On any given night you would see John, Michelle, Denny, Cass, Dylan, Phil Ochs, Freddie Neil, everybody. It was literally right next door to The Bitter End. There was also The Cafe Wha?, The Kettle of Fish—which was *real* traditional, and that's where people *seriously* talked folk music, *seriously* talked war, *seriously* talked civil rights. All of the editors and writers from the local papers like *The Village Voice* were always there.

The drug scene was speed and marijuana. Methedrine. Some of the singers were junkies, like Freddie Neil and Bob Gibson, and a lot of those guys would also go to the black clubs like The Five Spot or The Blue Angel and see the jazz players. The thing was, was that a lot of the jazz players found great comfort in the folk music, because the music being played let itself so readily to jazz thing. Now, when I met John, he was amazed at my modern compings and guitar styles. See, he was interested in me for one thing, and that was that I played choral-style guitar, as opposed to straight lead. And I also played banjo, too, from the Bluegrass school. But the fact that I was a West Coast, choral guitar player, which went real well with the vocal thing. That was the interest that Cass had with me, too. She was a singer of pop and commercial jazz music. So, falling into this group of people was real easy. With Michelle, I could fill out Michelle real easy, and the same way with Denny.

It was all a mish-mash at the time. All these groups; The Mugwumps, The New Journeymen, The Big Three—they were all vying for spots in the folk thing until The Beatles came along. Then everything changed from folk music to 'folk-rock.'

Denny Doherty: When we got back to New York from this bus tour, when Kennedy got assassinated—Cass was also on tour at the same time up in the Northeast, with David Crosby and his brother, Ethan—both tours folded. We all wound up back in New York. Tour's canceled, whole thing's over, finished. I then get a call from John saying that he's got some gigs left over from The Journeymen, and would I be interested in going on the road for six concerts for two weeks at The Shorham Hotel with Bill Cosby? I said, "Oh yeah . . . ," 'cause we needed the money and I wanted to work with John and Michelle. I sent the money home so that we could pay the Albert Hotel. So then everyone leaves the hotel and I'm ensconced with John and Michelle in The New Journeymen.

Cass Elliot: Denny and I had been singing right up to that point in a group called The Mugwumps, which was really a tragedy. Not musically, but in a time warp, it was just too much before its time, really, I think. Or at least I like to think about it that way. We heard that John needed a tenor for his group, and our group was breaking up. So we got Denny all cleaned up and sent him over to

John's house for a job, 'cause Scott was leaving. And Denny got the job and started singing with them, and the three of them traveled around for a while.

Denny Doherty: John had a working relationship with the chemist on the corner, actually. The pharmacist. We had a prescription for Esktrol, diet pills. Black Beauties. I dunno, fifty or a hundred of each. I came over on a Monday, had dinner, and sang with them for a day or two. Meanwhile, I find out that we have to open at the Shorham Hotel in Washington, D.C., that weekend! "Ha-ha, let's learn the repertoire!" We gotta do three sets, 12–15 songs per set . . . you're talkin' 40 songs and lyrics. And the shit that they were doin,' I'd never heard before. So, we took our diet pills and rehearsed for three days and then got on the train for D.C. Next thing I know, I'm on stage at the Shorham Hotel singing with The Journeymen . . . Marshall Brickman was still playing banjo, but he was weaning himself out of the group. He was world class, one of the best three-finger Earl Scruggs-style banjo pickers around.

At this point, John's hangin' on like death and he's not gonna let go of folk music, and he's trying to book The New Journeymen any which way he can. But that dried up, so 'what to do, what to do . . . ?'

PART FOUR

The Mamas & The Papas are born on Seventh & Avenue LS"D"…an evening in the birdcage with the magic circle . . .

Russell Gilliam: John and Michelle were living on Seventh and Avenue D, I believe. Peter and I got an apartment on Fourth Street and Avenue B, so we were just a few blocks away.

Peter had been given this LSD by a friend, not the same stuff we later took with John and Michelle. I didn't know what it was, he didn't know what it was. But everywhere we went, it was wrapped in this aluminum foil, and we would store it in a refrigerator

Michelle Phillips, Greenwich Village, 1964.
Courtesy of Michelle Phillips.

wherever we were staying. We knew nobody who had ever taken it. When we moved into our apartment in New York and we got settled in, Peter said, "Hey, let's take that acid." And I said, "Okay." Back in those days, everything was "Okay, let's go for it!"

We had bought this old dresser, because we wanted to furnish our place, and it needed to be painted. We mixed the acid up in some coffee—he drank half, and I drank half—and then we went down to the hardware store and bought about four cans of different colored paint. By the time we got back, I became convinced that whatever this stuff was, it had become impotent, and it wasn't doing anything to me . . . So I put out the newspaper and the dresser and paint and brushes . . . let me tell *you* . . . that I spent the entire eight hours painting this dresser, having the *most* wonderful time! I not only painted the dresser, but all of the cabinets, in the Jackson Pollock 'splattering' style . . . it was *so beautiful,* so incredibly beautiful, that when I woke up the next morning, I could not believe that I'd painted it. It wasn't messy, it was just *gorgeous.*

At one point John and Michelle came over to watch us. I remember also that it was at that moment that I lost my prudeness about nudity. It was hot, and I was just wearing a full slip and a bra, and I remember looking at John when he came in—he had never seen me almost nude before, except in a bathing suit, which is appropriate—and I started to cover myself up, and I looked at John, and there was nothing. I thought to myself, "What are ya doing?! You're covered..." And I kept painting! After that moment, I was not prudish at all: In fact I later did nude modeling at UCLA. So that was kind of a typically '60s moment, if you will.

John Phillips: Cass had met Denny, and Denny said, "I know this girl that sings wonderfully. We should have her over and sing with her." It happened to be that LSD was actually legal at the time. It wasn't a banned drug or anything. We searched all over the Village and found some contemporary artist who had some and he gave it to us. We were about to take it that night, when the knock on the door came and Cass came in. So we all had it together the same night, for the first time, and I think that formed a bond between the four of us that we just never stopped singing. We just went on and on and on and on, until the trip wore off, which was about four years later.

Peter Pilafian: At the time, John and Michelle had an apartment on the lower East Side, and I had an apartment a couple of blocks away, so we would get together a lot. We went over and walked in, and as I recall, things were already under way. Experimenting with drugs at the time was just sort of matter of fact; "Hey, I've got this new drug, you wanna try it?" "Sure..."

Michelle Phillips: It started with Stewart Reed coming over to bring us some pot. He pulled out these little sugar cubes and said, "Do you want to try this? It's LSD-25." We'd all heard about it, and I think that Denny and Cass had taken it once before. John and Denny and I each took a sugar cube, and I remember waiting and waiting and waiting . . . and at that point, Denny had told us that his friend Cass was going to coming over. We had never met, but we had heard a lot about her. I never envisioned what she would look like, and I don't think that Denny mentioned that she was a great big girl or anything like that. He just said, "You're going to love her, she's so funny and so talented and such a great singer, and I used to work with her in another band . . . "

Dick Weissman: Stan Greeson told me that he had told John about Cass. He told him, 'Hey, there's this girl in the village named Cass and she's a killer; you ought to hear her . . . ' I think that later he got some money out of John or something, because I think that Stan thought he was gonna manage The Mamas & The Papas. I don't know if John would remember this . . .

Michelle Phillips: I went down to the corner drugstore to get some things and came back. I remember saying to the guys, "I don't know about you guys, but this drug does nothing for me . . . '"At that point, there was a knock on the door, and as I opened the door and saw Cass, the acid hit me *over the head*. I saw her standing there in a pleated skirt, a pink Angora sweater with great big eyelashes on and her hair in a flip. And all of a sudden I thought, "This is really *quite* a drug!" It was an image that I will have securely fixed in my brain for the rest of my life. I said, "Hi, I'm Michelle. We just took some LSD-25, do ya wanna join us?" And she said, "Sure . . . "

Then, I think that she was the one who brought the Beatle album with her, and we *rocked* to the Beatles. I don't know where we were up until then. I'd heard of them, and I may have heard a single, but I'd never heard an album. In our folkie circle, it was almost a sacrilege to listen to rock and roll. So we put the album on. My sister was there, Peter Pilafian was there, and this was the first time Cass, Denny, John, and I had spent any time together.

Rusty Gilliam: I was out one day, and when I got home there was a note from Peter saying that he was at John and Michelle's, and that I should come over. I walked in, and as I came inside,

John handed me the acid and said, "Eat up," and of course I did. At the beginning, it was just Denny, John, Michelle, Peter, and me, and then Cass arrived. Everything Michelle says about that moment is absolutely true. It was mind-boggling. She had on a white pleated skirt, false eyelashes. These were the kind of eyelashes that when you put them on, you were supposed to trim them to an appropriate length, which she didn't, and when she blinked, she looked like a cow, or those dolls that you get when you're little, and the eyes open and close. And we're on acid. *Oh my god!* It was a *sight!* And everything she was wearing were things that you weren't supposed to be wearing if you were heavy—white pleated skirt, mohair sweater. You know, until she became famous, she suffered so much, and was poked fun at.

Peter Pilafian: For a long time I remember that there was this peculiar fascination with the discovery of the shadow of the birdcage, which when it was placed under a hard lightbulb or a candle, would make the room seem like it was the inside of a birdcage . . . and we were all coming in and out of the birdcage. Probably John was the 'birdcage master', I suppose, like a puppeteer, and we would all get freaked out! Kinda symbolic actually, because as benevolent as John was, he was definitely a benevolent dictator. He was the ringleader. As far as I'm concerned, his talent made that perfectly appropriate. He had the intellect and the talent to justify it.

Michelle Phillips: Then we started playing the 'bird in the cage game,' which I remember being a very, *very* scary game, under the circumstances. What we did was put a candle inside this big birdcage, and put it in the middle of the floor, so that the light from the cage was illuminated all over the ceilings and walls. We would pretend that we were the little birds in the cage, and that John was the cat coming to get us. It was *really* scary! It went on for a long, long time, and we were *squealing* laughing. Then John and Denny disappeared into the kitchen for a long time, and when they came back, they had deviled ham in their ears and noses! And Cass and I were having our talk; it was the first time we had a talk . . . She was telling me that she'd been raped in Florida, and that it was a really big guy with a knife, and when she had woken up, he was straddling her with the knife to her throat, and told her what he was going to do, and that she'd better be quiet. I said, "My god, what did you do?" and she said, "I let him ball me." But then she said that he collapsed on her . . . *dead*. I said, "*Dead* ?" and she said, "Yeah, I was too much for him!" So, the whole story was probably just made up! To this day, I do not know whether she was raped in Florida. I kinda doubt it. I think that it was a way for Cass to 'get' me, I don't know. I don't know if she was ever raped in Florida, but I know that the guy did not *die* on top of her . . . but it would be something that she would love; to think of herself as a 'femme fatal.' "I was much too much for him . . . *died right on top of me!!*"

Peter Pilafian: Cass and Denny were there, and I remember there was some music, and the birdcage, and later on, Russell and I decided it was a good time to leave. It had been a great night, and it was almost dawn. We went to the Staten Island Ferry dock, and I remember being very calm and peaceful. It was a real revelation, and I remember it being a very positive thing, and feeling a great inspiration and the transformation of the environment into something magical. At that time, of course, that drug was not illegal, so there was no need for paranoia.

Michelle Phillips: The whole experience changed all of us, and brought us all very close together. I knew that Cass was my new best friend. I would have done anything at that point to have her join the group. I had never heard her sing, and it wouldn't have made any difference at all. I wanted her to hook up with us on a personal level. I was so *desperate* for a girlfriend. I had been very, very close to my friend Tamar, and been very close with my girlfriends from high school. But from the time I left Los Angeles, I hadn't had a friend, a *buddy*. I was *married*, and John and I did not hang out with women, we just hung out with men, and especially not people my age. John was nine years older than I was. And here was a fun-loving, intelligent woman. She captivated me. I was as close to in love with Cass as I could be to any woman in my life at that point.

She also represented something to me: freedom. Everything she did was because she wanted to do it. She was completely independent, and I admired her and was in awe of her. And later on, Cass would be the one to tell me not to let John run my life. And John hated her for that. She'd be the one to say, "Don't let him do this. You're a person, too!" She was *completely* emancipated. And as emancipated as I may have seemed to people of my own age, I was not emancipated at all. I was completely dependent on John. I was Mrs. John Phillips, which is exactly what I pretended to be and wanted to be.

John Stewart: After that initial 'meeting of The Beatles' by John, when Denny played them for him, his writing changed, and he started writing things like "California Dreamin'." After I heard that, I said, "John . . . you can do anything and make it your own thing. Man!"

Chapter Two

Creeque Alley

PART ONE *Early 1965*

End of The New Journeymen's road . . . Go Where You Wanna Go
. . . LSD and the Virgin Islands trip . . . Camp Torture . . . come
along, everybody come along . . .

Denny Doherty: It was the end of The 'New' Journeymen; we
had done all of the gigs there were to do. The folk scene had dried
up; there were no more bookings that were going to lead anywhere. It was time to do something new, but John was holding on
like dreaded death to folk music.

Eric Hord: I got the call from John and Michelle to come back
East and do some concerts with The New Journeymen, and after
we did a few shows, we had taken acid and decided that it was time
to split. I had to get Davine, who was my girlfriend, out there, and
she was on her way. This was during the first contact with acid and
the group, and the idea was that if we were going to take acid, we
were all going to take it together.

They were in a real quandary about where to go, because folk
music was dead as soon as The Beatles came along. That was a real
big thing. See, Dennis turned John on to The Beatles, and he told
him, "If you can write like *that*, then we're in business." John *was*
hanging on like death to folk music. Like death. Anyway, John got
the idea that we had to re-group somehow, and that's how The
Virgin Islands trip got started.

Michelle Phillips: The story that John tells is that while we were on acid we decided to go away, and that I was blindfolded and threw a dart at a map of the world and that it landed on the Caribbean. . . .

Denny Doherty: We were going to the Islands and get it together somehow, and we ended up in St. Thomas, because Michelle took some acid and pointed at a map blindfolded and put her finger on St. Thomas.

Michelle Phillips: That sounds more like it. I do remember that we did have a map of the world on the wall, that's for sure. I remember going up to the G.A.C offices—our agent—and saying that were going to go to The Caribbean, and someone said, "Go to St. Thomas." So that's how we ended up in the Virgin Islands.

Denny Doherty: Before we left New York, we went to Third Avenue to a surplus store and bought tents and cots and Coleman stoves, all that shit, put it into a container of a Pan Am flight, and shipped it all down there. It was then all loaded on to a ferry from St. Thomas to St. John. All of the natives didn't know *what* the fuck was goin' on . . . "Jah mon, you da orchestra, mon?! Where you *play*, mon?" We had trombones . . . Pilafian brought a bow (bass) fiddle. It was nuts!

Peter Pilafian: Russell and I went back to L.A., and sometime during this period John called and said, "Could you guys join us in the Virgin Islands? We wanna head down there . . . " There was no reason not to, so he told us to be at J.F.K. by a certain date. I don't remember it being a big decision, really. I think we said, "Sure, why not?" We had a drive-a-way car, which in those days a good way to get across country, and I put my big stand-up bass in the passenger seat, and we went. We drove for four days, and arrived at J.F.K. with three or four hours to spare, and get in the plane with John and Michelle, Denny, McKenzie, Billy Throkmorton, who was John's cousin, and off we went. John bought a ticket for my bass. John was doing it all, he was a very magnanimous guy. He just took care of everything.

We didn't know what to expect. It was the age of exploration and discovery. We were young and it was the 1960s, and it was wide open. The future was a marvelous thing.

Denny Doherty: We had about nine grand in cash, and John had The Journeymen's American Express Card, which had a limit of another $5,000 on it. We went to St. John first. We were looking at National Parks, and St. John had one. The *Rockefellers* owned the fuckin' island. We went and camped out for $30.00 a month, each. It was Russell and myself, and John and Michelle, The Doctor and his girlfriend. Five tents. And Mackenzie—she had her own tent. We were living on a campsite on Cinnamon Bay. There was a swamp, a campsite, and the beach, so we were between the swamp and the beach . . . and the mosquitoes were just brutal. But, there was nothing to do; it was a national park out in the middle of The Caribbean. After about a week or two it got real old *real* quick, and John took to his tent. It was time to do something. We had motorcycles, our instruments, camping gear, all this shit.

John Phillips: We went to the Virgin Islands the summer of '65, to rehearse and just put everything together. Cass and Denny and Michelle and I and The Doctor (Eric Hord), who played guitar, and Peter Pilafian, who played violin. All these strange people. We took dogs with us and motorcycles and children. Mackenzie, my daughter, went with us. She had her own tent on the beach. We were the last campers to arrive and we got the worst camping site. We called it Camp Torture. There was a mosquito bog right behind it. We had this on St. John.

Russell Gilliam: We all lived communally, right in the beach. The mosquitoes were *horrendous*. Poor Eric Hord's girlfriend, Davine. She was so allergic to these mosquitoes. It was terrible. She was actually hospitalized at one point earlier, for the same reason in Hawaii.

Peter Pilafian: We camped out at a state park campground or something there, and maybe rented space or tents for a few bucks a day. I think the idea was just for us to take a break and kind of unplug. I never quizzed John on his motivations, but I think that he kind of knew that beyond The Journeymen he wanted to disconnect and get some free air and fresh inspiration, and god bless him, he just loved hangin' out with his friends

Denny Doherty: We had a tray of sugar cubes, "for the dog's medicine"—that was the acid supply. We kept it in the refrigerator at the commissary, and we'd go over every day to get the dog's medicine . . . . "Don't want the dog to get mange!!" The dog ended up getting pregnant, is what happened . . .

Michelle Phillips: It was just heaven. We were living on a very deserted island at the time; I don't know what it's like now. But there was nothing on St. John at all but the Rockefeller Hotel. Other than that there was nobody there. We went to St. John in January of 1965, and we were there for three months, I think, and then April through June we were in St. Thomas. I think we left at the end of June. We did nothing but dropping acid, snorkeling, and smoking a lot of pot, and drinking. We would actually slice the top off a coconut and pour rum into it! This is how we were living . . .

Peter Pilafian: Exactly, exactly. It was fabulous that way. John was making it seem easy. I didn't know what the economics or the cash flow was. But I don't think it was a big deal. You get down there, and its a couple of bucks a day for a tent or whatever, buy food at the grocery store and cook it on the beach. I think the whole thing was low-impact anyway, and that gave it the feeling of freedom and low-pressure.

Eric Hord: I remember this one night, Dennis and I and Peter went to this native bar about ten miles away from where were. It was all black, *100 percent black.* We were the only white people there, that's for sure, and it was like Friday night in the jungle. We were all on acid, and we were drinking rum and everything in sight, just getting shit-faced. We got back from the bar later that night, and Dennis said, "Come on, let's go for a ride . . . " So we took one of the little scooters, and about halfway up the hill in this big tree with vines all over the place. We were hallucinating our brains out, and I thought they were anacondas.

John Phillips: It started off very carefree and very happy. It really got rougher as time went on. After we camped out for two months, I got us some rooms over on the big island on St. Thomas, because we were living on St. John. I went back to the camp to pick the people up, there were ten people there. All of them were sitting there with vacant stares and slack jaws, wide-eyed and just staring at the wall of the tent. They'd just lost all interest in everything. No one bathed, no one shaved, everyone just sort of sat around. It was really just sort of a vegetation.

Denny Doherty: We stayed on St. John's for about a month or so—maybe more—I don't know, and then John took a ferry over to St. Thomas, and met Duffy, and we wound up at Duffy's in Creeque Alley. John said, "I found this guy who's got a hotel and a nightclub, blah-blah-blah . . ." We said, "Great, where is it? Just get us the fuck outta here . . . "

Michelle Phillips: We would wake up in our bathing suits, go to sleep in our bathing suits, we had two little Yamaha '80s that we got around the island with. My sister was cooking for us; we had a little outdoor grill. What was there not to love! Every full moon we would take a catamaran out and take acid and hold on to the nets and go in and out of this *warm* water. It was the most sensual living that I have ever experienced in my life.

PART TWO

St. Thomas . . . Cass can't make it; we knew she would eventually . . .
Greasin' on American Express Card . . . Cass' fixation on Denny . . .
Duffy's good vibrations . . . Mitchie & Denny 'tapping toes' on
Caneel Bay . . . and we all fall down . . . "Yes It Is, it's true . . . "

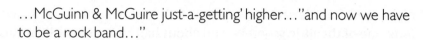

...McGuinn & McGuire just-a-getting' higher..."and now we have to be a rock band..."

Stephen Sanders: I first met Cass in Washington, D.C., when I was working at The Shadows Nightclub. Owned in part by Bob Cavallo and I think that Kenny Fritz was also around by then, were producing concerts in Virginia Beach . . . Stevie Wonder and things like that. Anyhow, Cass was singing in the upstairs lounge and then later as an opening act. Her pianist was Martin Seigal. I was sound and light man and once had a wonderful tape of her singing blues and standards. But either I lent it to her and never got it back or it was stolen. Too bad.

So she also needed money and worked days doing payroll, books, etc. and I would come by and work with her and we would hang out. Sometime have a drink and a Desbutal—pharmaceutical amphetamine—to start the day. Not often.

Cass Elliot: I was down in Washington, D.C., working as a single, and working as a secretary in the club I was singing during the daytime. It ultimately folded and went bankrupt, which had nothing to do with my presence I'm sure, but I just happened to be there. Denny, John and Michelle passed through on their way to the Virgin Islands, and I hadn't really known John and Michelle that well, but Denny had been talking about them a lot. In folk music, when you traveled around, everybody sort of came together. When you'd go into a strange town you'd find out who was playing, and weather you know than or not, you struck up a friendship, because there wasn't anybody else there that you could talk to, you didn't know the people who were in the town you were working in.

Steve Sanders: Then the club closed. Costs of acts went too high and people were not coming so often. So when the club closed she asked me if I would buy her an air ticket to the Virgin Islands. By now she had met John Phillips, Denny and somehow they all decided to get together down there. John and Michelle—who had their wedding reception in The Shadows—were already there and I think Denny as well. So I gave Cass a round trip ticket figuring it might fail and she would need a way back and also loaned her something like 200 or 300 dollars. That was the end of it for me.

John Phillips: Cass followed us around for months, maybe six or seven months trying to join the group. We kept saying "No, no . . ." She'd get jobs as a waitress at clubs wherever we were working, just to be around. She knew she was going to get in the group, and we knew she was going to get in the group also, it was just a good game to play for awhile. She just had to keep following us around, and she followed us down to the Virgin Islands where we were camping out. You can imagine Cass camping out!

Eric Hord: We headed down to Camp Torture, camped out for a few weeks, whatever, and made it over to Duffy's. Then Cass shows up, with John's cousin Billy Throkmorton. It was a situation where the one thing she wanted in life that she wanted the most, she couldn't have; that was Denny. She had a great voice, and she knew she could make it on her own, but she came down to be in close proximity to Denny.

Denny Doherty: We came back to New York, but not before Cass came down to join us—she was following my ass around.

Cass Elliot: I traveled down to the Virgin Islands to see them. And John had written a new kind of music that he couldn't iden-tify, he had no frame of reference for it. We didn't either. He had written "California Dreamin'," "Monday, Monday" and a few others. He knew they weren't folk songs . . . he didn't know what they were. He got his first electric guitar down there and he started flailing away, and it turned out that it was sort of, rock and roll.

Eric Hord: There was a great anticipation in the air that the music was changing, and if the music in changing, you gotta have a new sound.

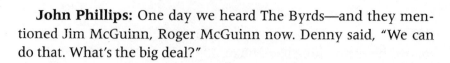

John Phillips: One day we heard The Byrds—and they mentioned Jim McGuinn, Roger McGuinn now. Denny said, "We can do that. What's the big deal?"

Scott Mackenzie: Denny was a great influence. That's not surprising that he said, "we can do that", because he was one of the few white guys who could really sing rock and roll. He could sing it in the '50s.

John Phillips: He was just a natural.

Michelle Phillips: We also heard The Byrds "Mr. Tambourine Man" which Dylan had written, but they had a hit with it. We couldn't believe it. We were sitting down saying, "Wait a minute, The Byrds have a hit, The Spoonful have a hit . . . we'd better get to California! We can have hits. We can have hits, too!"

Peter Pilafian: It seemed like it was gravitating more from the vacation mode to a "Let's form a band" thing. I guess the St. John's thing served its purpose. Cass had brought down this vile of clear Sandoz acid, which was just wonderful stuff. That whole situation was just so extraordinary. I remember going snorkeling in Caneel Bay on acid with Michelle and maybe Denny. It was fabulous. We were young and free and there were no constraints. It was a world of discovery, both internal and external. At night there would be these giant land crabs rattling around the trees near our campsite. We had a rental jeep that we would cruise around in. For some of us, it was our first taste of that sort of tropical life.

Russell Gilliam: The whole trip to the Virgin Islands was an incredible turning point in all of our lives.

Michelle Phillips: My affair with Denny started on the beach in Caneel Bay. I can't exactly say how or when it happened, but even before Cass came down and the acid arrived, Denny and I were lying around together a lot in the hammock, etc. To see Denny and I lying around together in each other's arms would not have been a suprising sight. Palling around together, it was hot, we were drinking a lot of rum . . . Denny and I were spending a lot of time together; we were snorkeling together, hanging out. It was a very sensual experience, being on the island of St. John, lying on the sand. It was very beautiful. And there was no feeling that you were ever going to leave. This was our life now, and we were singing together. And I remember that we were always in each others arms, or we always had our feet entwined and we were playing footsies . . . it felt really *good*. And sometimes he'd brush a strand of hair out of my face . . . .

Then Cass came down with the liquid acid. Denny and I were pretty much practically sitting on top of each other all of the time. It wasn't until we came back to Charlotte Amalie, that we took acid one night, and we all ended up at the docks. Denny jumped in the water, and I jumped in after him, and we were swimming around the little fishing boats. Then I saw Cass and John wave good-bye to us; "Bye you guys, we're leavin' . . . " And they very naively and very innocently walked away. Denny and I got up on a boat and woke up the fisherman; we were just carousing. They all knew us. Denny and I swam back to shore, and then, and as we were walking together down Creeque Alley back to Duffy's, we were holding hands. And all of the sudden Denny took my arm . . . and *threw* me against the wall, and came towards me and said, "I'm going to kiss you now." I can't remember anything so sensual in my life as Denny coming at me and kissing me *straight* on the mouth. I thought, "*Wow* . . . " He didn't say another word, and we just walked back to Duffy's.

I remember later that morning lying in bed with John and telling him that I felt that it was time for us to live apart from Cass and Denny. He asked me why, and I said, "To be honest with you, I find myself being attracted to Denny." He said, "I wouldn't worry about it, Mitch. He has no interest in you . . . " I thought, "*Okay*, you can't say that I didn't warn you." Because I *wanted* to continue this flirtation with Denny; it was something that was drawing me like a *magnet*. I didn't want to stop, but I was doing my wifely part by saying, "This is what's going on. I'm attracted to him." I didn't want to get anybody in trouble, I didn't want to say that Denny and I kissed. But it *infuriated* me when John said that. It hurt my pride, and I think I've said before, that it was like red to a bull. I thought, "All *right*, we'll see . . ." And we did not consummate the relationship until we got back to Los Angeles.

Denny Doherty: We had started tapping toes on St. John. John was hangin' out in his tent grumbling, "Arggh, it's all fucked up, we're doomed, we're all doomed!" So, Michelle and I would go down to the beach and play footsies, and go into the water and get better acquainted. John didn't want to come out and play. It was paradise, it was 'Blue Lagoon' time. Acid, the tropics, the incredible fucking sunrises and sunsets. More beauty, more beauty, more beauty and . . . take 'The Love Drug.' "But don't touch! Yeah, right . . . we can handle that, sure. We're being tested, I know it." Didn't know it at the time; wouldn't have cared. The libidos were very strong at the time. But that was just furtive, that was just a stolen kiss on the beach. We both looked at each other and went, "Ah . . . no. This is not gonna work, this is counter-productive." But a lot of eye contact and a lot of longing looks saying, "Oh, if it were only otherwise . . . " [sings "Glad To Be Unhappy"] 'Unrequited love, and I've got it pretty bad . . . but for someone you adore, it's a pleasure to be sad . . . '

Eric Hord: As far as I can remember, I don't recall noticing anything happening between Denny and Michelle, but you have to remember that everyone was concentrating on their own little thing. I had my whole thing with Davine, because we found out that she was pregnant, and she went to live with my cousin in Puerto Rico, because by then we didn't have any money. So, I was just hangin' around, watching everything go down. It was around this time that Cass and I went to this open-air bar and dropped acid. See, Cass came into it, and she came down there, but she didn't know what to do, because John still concentrating on a trio—and to have Denny play bass and Peter Pilafian to play drums. But Cass didn't have anything to do. John, I think, introduced her to Duffy and asked him if he had a job for her, and he put her to work waiting tables at the bar. So, she was tending the drinks while we were rehearsing. Also, we were rehearsing all the time when we were doing the stage, and Duffy would listen because he wanted some assurances that this was not going to be a fluke. When he heard us, he gave us the go ahead to perform. And that's how the band got started.

John Phillips: Went across the main island, St. Thomas, and we got a job there, working at a club, Duffy's. Duffy was a great help to We were trying to sing country pop, folk-pop at that time, and we weren't quite sure how to do it or what to do.

Peter Pilafian: John being somewhat older than I was, he was probably on a more determined course. I was still discovering life, rather than in the mode of 'let's create stuff.' I just kind of followed his lead, and at a certain point what was in the air was to form another group. We moved back to St. Thomas, and we were listening to The Beatles, and John said, "We need a drummer; you play drums." I told him that I had played in college for a couple of weeks in a little jazz trio, and he said, "Okay, fine . . . you're the drummer!" We went out and bought a practice pad and some sticks, and every day I would work on my drum licks, and John, Cass, Michelle, and Denny were going over Beatles tunes, and doing respectable covers of those things.

Denny Doherty: [sings] "If you wear red tonight . . . ." That one. ("Yes It Is" by The Beatles). We did "Ticket To Ride," too. We weren't doing stuff like "California Dreamin'," in fact, I hadn't heard it yet. See, John had finally acquiesced and said, "Okay, what's this Beatle shit?" And I said, "Well, we gotta have a back-beat—we've gotta have a drummer. We need electric instruments and we've gotta be a *rock and roll band* . . . 'if it's gotta a back beat you can't lose it'—yeahhh!'" John's going, "What does that *mean*??" We're on this island, and we had to go looking for drums, electric guitars, amplifiers, and we needed a drummer. Peter Pilafian!? He'd never played the fuckin' drums before in his life. He fell asleep at the drums on opening night, as a matter of fact. On stage, in the middle of the set he fell asleep and hit the back wall!

Well, we'd worked so hard getting the place into shape, that he wasn't getting much sleep. So Peter Pilafian was our drummer. We had Eric Hord—The Doctor—on guitar, and he scoured the island for drums. He found a couple of old Silvertone guitars for he and John. I played a bass.

Eric Hord: "Twist & Shout," "Yes It Is"—and Michelle wore her red dress. "Ticket To Ride," early Beatles. I was left to do the instrumental, which was "Walk, Don't Run," which Denny knew how to play. We were trying to get ourselves together a la The Lovin' Spoonful, The Byrds, etc. and John saw it, but Denny had put him in the right direction. Peter Pilafian was getting more into like management stuff and rock climbing. But he still played, and he's a brilliant violin player. We were working on "Spanish Harlem" during this period, too.

Denny Doherty: So, we were renovating Duffy's, and we rehearsed in the loft, just above Duffy's. Still, Cass was not rehearsing with us; it was John, Michelle, and I doing the vocals. Peter was playing drums, The Doctor was playing lead, John was playing rhythm, and I was playing electric bass. We were doing three-part harmony on "Mr. Tambourine Man," but a lot slower. As a matter of fact, Duffy used to get 45s from the mainland, he had friends in New York who used to send the latest 45s down and he'd put 'em on his jukebox—the best jukebox on the island. We're rehearsing "Mr. Tambourine Man," [sings a spry polka] 'Hey, mister tambourine man, play a song for me . . . ' like a polka or something! And I tell John, "No John, we gotta slow it down and give it a backbeat . . . " Finally, we get The Byrds 45 down there, and we put it on and turned it up to ten . . . and John says, "Oh, like that?" Well, as you can clearly tell, it had already been *done*. So John goes, "Oh, ahhh . . . that's it . . . " A light went on. So we started doing Beatles stuff. We dropped "Mr. Tambourine Man" after hearing The Byrds version, because there was no point.

We rehearsed for weeks and weeks, and decorated the place with burlap tables and candles, but we were off the island before we knew it. Flash, bam, get off the island. Cass saw the writing on the walls, and she took off. We had to sell everything to get off the island, and ended up on San Juan. The material we were playing on stage was leftover New Journeymen stuff that we tried to rock up, and Beatle songs. We also got into doing "Searchin," which we had done in The Mugwumps.

Michelle Phillips: It was terrible. It wasn't that we were terrible, we sounded good, but we were singing folk in a club. It was just John and Denny and I, with The Doctor on guitar and Peter Pilafian playing drums. It was such a transitional period. We were trying to sing a little more contemporary, but we weren't quite there yet. Next door was a very good group . . . a rock band, and that place was always full, and we were like, "Oh, shit!" We couldn't drag those people out for anything!

Eric Hord: There was another band that came down from New York City, and they played the club opposite ours, and that got to be a competition thing. Yeah, that band next door was really a very slick Top-40 cover band. We were just this 'other' band next door. Almost like a 'homegrown'-type of act. It went over to the audience real good actually, it was exceptional. The other group across the way was for a strictly commercial, Top-40 audience, and they did all covers. We were sort of like a group that had two Jimmy Buffets, and two Linda Ronstadt-type chicks, and people dug it. St. Thomas at the time just exploded, and it was a time when there was a lot of sailor action, and Duffy's bar was always crowded, and these sailors were throwing a lot of money around and having a good time. In the meantime, we were still maintaining our acid intake. Nobody ever stopped taking it. We were always making runs to the refrigerator . . .

Peter Pilafian: It was a breezy kind of feel. The only serious activity was when the navy boys would come into port, and at night they would try to fill things up and get some action. Other than that it was kind of laid back. It was an upstairs joint, and it was open to the breeze as it would blow through. It was an out of the mainstream situation where you could do no wrong, because nobody cared anyway. Playing loud rock and roll was a whole new idea, because all we knew about was folk music, and now we had these Beatle things with drums, and we would get up there and play and people would get up and be dancing. It was quite amazing. I remember one night this navy guy came in, and he had been playing for years, and he sat in, and it was wonderful because he kind of upgraded the whole thing.

Michelle Phillips: Then Cass was singing the fourth part from the floor, she was waiting tables. She wouldn't get on-stage with me. She said that she wouldn't let an audience make that comparison between us. The "obvious distinction" between Cass and Michelle. It wasn't until Lou offered us the contract when we got back to Los Angeles that she actually agreed to be part of the group. I've realized that there's a lot of speculation as to whether she wanted in the group, or John didn't want her in the group, or what it was.

Eric Hord: John was always the head guy that wanted to do the business. Denny was this guy that said, "Do whatever you want to do, I just want to sing." Michelle says, "Do whatever you want to do, I just want to be myself." Cass says, "Can I be in the group?" And John said, "No," until later. She was never on stage singing with us during that period—maybe one or two times.

Russell Gilliam: When we were in the Virgin Islands, Cass and I were the only two who worked. The others were rehearsing on the beach and singing at the club in the evening. See, the Virgin Islands was a port, and all of the sailors and marines would stop there, looking for action, and when we were waiting tables, these sailors were *so cruel* to her. "Hey fatty, get the hell over here!" That was mild. Cass and I became very, very close, because everybody else was busy, and were working together, because Cass wasn't in the group at the time.

Russell Gilliam: There are two things that I disagree with, that they usually talk about. One is this story about Cass being hit over the head with a pipe. That was stupid. The entire time Cass was in the Virgin Islands, Cass wanted to be in the group. John refused to let her into the group for one reason, and *one* reason only. She was too *fat*. Once they got famous, he couldn't say that. They made up this story about that she couldn't hit a certain note, and that it changed when she was hit with the pipe . . . where they get this, I'll never know.

Michelle Phillips: I remember when she was hit in the head with a pipe, but if you listen to Cass singing on her own before she joined the group, she's singing *way* up there, she sings very, very high.

Peter Pilafian: My reflection was that Cass was on-stage. I remember that Cass was kind of an oddity in the equation; that she kind of put herself in the equation. She came down bearing gifts, namely a bottle of acid. She decided that she wanted to be part of this. She was a friend if Denny's, of course. Cass was a more domi-nant personality, and Denny would have been happy to be dragged around anyway, back in the old Mugwumps days or whatever. It seems to me that Cass wasn't necessarily John's type, but she came in, and she was good-hearted, and a great singer and all of that, and sort of said, "I'm here!" The whole feeling at Duffy's was that we were experimenting with a whole new form, "Hey wow, rock & roll—let's give it a try, let's see how it feels." We found out that it worked, and that people loved it, and that we could do it. It felt good, and the songs were good, and it was well received.

We did lot of things that we could get off The Beatles' first record that we could get, and some stuff of John's, I'm sure—there had to have been. The Beatles stuff was so wonderful, and such a revelation. As musicians, we were sucking it up. From my end, and a sideman, it was simple enough so that I wasn't overly challenged. Duffy wasn't paying us, although he gave us room and board, I think. But there wasn't enough cash to support the operation. And then John's credit cards went bad. Suddenly money is running out.

I was not really concerned about how we were going to survive—totally oblivious!

Michelle Phillips: That's where I thought we were going to live for the rest of our lives. When John told me that we had to leave, and we didn't have any money, and they cut up the American Express card—which was pretty tragic—it was terrible. When Cass was told she went over and put her fist right through a window. She was very dramatic.

Russell Gilliam: Later on, we were living at the hotel. We had no money, they tore up the American Express card. When we snuck out, it was the slinkiest, *sneakiest* sneaking out I've ever seen! We left owing money to *everybody*. We had tabs, we had rent we had to pay, they had a tab to the seamstress. So, we left at six o'clock in the morning. We went to the airport—and it was a tiny airport. We were instructed to separate, and talk in small groups, so that we weren't seen as a large group. I think Michelle had on a warning of some kind.

Michelle Phillips: I had been arrested in Charlotte Amalie, by Sergeant Hershey, ostensibly for not stopping when he supposedly tried to stop earlier in the day. I had, in fact, not been out of the house all day. He said that he had tried to stop me, and that I had driven off. I got into a mild altercation with him, a verbal, and people were stopping, and staring at us, right in the middle of town. I told him that I had not been out of the house all day, and he said, (stern, condescending voice), "Don't tell me, I know . . . " Then this little crowd gathered, and he turned to me and said, "You're under arrest." And I said, "For what!?", and he said, "Disturbing the peace . . . ", as he waved his hand towards the crowd. So, they took me to the old prison, and locked me up. When we were really ran out of money, I was awaiting a hearing on my arrest by Sergeant Hershey. We also owed money all over the island.

Eric Hord: At one point, the governor of the island asked us all to leave. Things were rocky, and the people of the island were growing very suspicious of us, going, "Who are these people, and what are they doing?" It was basically an ultimatum to leave the island.

Denny Doherty: Long story short, the governor of the island came down and kicked us off because his nephew came down and wanted to play with us—see, we were the only action from the mainland for a long time. The nephew partook of some of our 'controlled substance' . . . no, it wasn't illegal at the time. Anyway, we were partying hearty, redecorating Duffy's, and I guess this kid couldn't handle it, so he went home screaming that those people at Duffy's stole his brain or something . . . "My hair is burning . . . flames are coming out of my toenails!!" "Have a drink, kid, it'll calm ya down . . ." He said, "I don't drink." "You will *now*, kid . . . "

Cass had just escaped. Her and Billy had round-trip tickets, and they just left. It was all falling down around us. The American Express card had been cut, and we had spent a lot of our own money getting uniforms made. John made sure that we all had matching suits, and Michelle had to have a matching dress. We went around the island and found this seamstress and found this bulk silk, which cost a fortune, and had these Harry Belafonte-type Calypso shirts made with the big sleeves. That's where the last of the money went. An investment in the future, so that we could hit the big time! We were broke, that was it! Duffy was goin, "Ya know guys, I've done all I can do . . . and I'm almost outta business myself . . . " We had two motorcycles—John and Michelle had these little Hondas, all of our instruments, and all of our tenting gear that we dragged off of St John's. The cots and the stove . . . anything that we could sell, we sold to the people that used to hang out at Duffy's on the waterfront. We got everybody plane fare on Carib Air, to San Juan. That's as far as we got, that's all the money we had. The governor told us, "If you're here tomorrow morning, I'm putting you all in the fort," which was the jail. At least for disturbing the peace, and then he would look into whatever nefarious things we had been involved in. Okay, "We're *gone* . . . let's get to the airport. . . . " It was like Bosnia coming out of Croatia; it was awful.

Michelle Phillips: We were pretty much sneaking off the island, 'under the veil of darkness . . . ' and Sergeant Hershey was actually *at* airport. So we were really keeping a very low profile, very quiet. So, we got to the airport, we had my dog with us, we had Maude, and they wouldn't let Maude fly with us, so they put her in a crate, and they took our bad check. I could hear Maude yapping away through the whole flight, which was only about twenty-five minutes. When we got to Pan Am, they would not take the check, for us to get back to New York. And they were adamant about it. I think it was me, John, Denny, The Doctor, his girlfriend. We were quite the little village. We didn't have more than about $25. I really didn't know what we're going to do.

Denny Doherty: Everybody's just fucked up, hadn't washed for days, mosquito bit, the dog is pregnant, Davine is pregnant . . . it was just awful. Displaced persons with their luggage piled up in the Pan Am lounge. Not a fuckin' place to go, and no way to get there, anyway. John is up at the counter trying to give the guy a personal check for *eight people . . .* the Pan Am guy is *laughing* at him . . . We were one step away from calling home: "Hi ma, you're never gonna believe this. . . ."

What we did though, was pool our recourses, which turned into about fifty dollars. John and I put on our Journeymen suits, Michelle put on her red clinging dress, and off we went to the Carib Hilton, to the casino.

Michelle Phillips: When John said that we were going to go to the casino, I thought he was joking, because then we would have *nothing*. But John said, "It doesn't matter; we have nothing now, so we're going to go to the casino and see what happens." I don't think that Cass was with us.

Denny Doherty: We go over to the craps table with our $48 or whatever, and start playing craps. I didn't know; I had never been in a casino before in my life. John gave Michelle the dice and said, "Throw . . . "

Michelle Phillips: I had done precious little gambling before. I started to throw, and we won, and we won . . . and we won . . . I threw seventeen straight passes.

Denny Doherty: Now, if you know the game of craps, if you win when you throw the dice, you get 'em again. Now, the odds of getting them seven or eight times is *ridiculous*. She got the dice *eighteen times* . . .

Michelle Phillips: There were people at the table that won *a lot* of money. We won enough money to fly us all back to New York; and I think that we all flew first class.

Denny Doherty: The place went *bananas* . . . people are screaming, "Go Blondie!!" During this time, everybody in the casino crowded around the table. You've got to realize in the time it takes to throw the dice, scoop up the money, do the bet thing, this takes 15–20 seconds. She did this *eighteen times*, so you're talkin' 15–20 minutes. The place was freakin' out, they closed the other tables, pit bosses were coming over to see what was goin' on. There were some high rollers at the table, like that one guy won $50,000—he had never won like that before, and he took all the focus. John, meanwhile, scooped up the money we won, around six grand, went up to the Pan Am guy, paid him cash, got on the plane, and came back to New York. It was magic.

Russell Gilliam: The other story that I disagree with, was the story about the casino. It was much better than that . . .

We got to the airport in San Juan, and there were a *slew* of us. There was Peter, me, John, Michelle, Denny, The Doctor, and Davine. John goes in and tries to get them to accept a personal check for our airfare back to New York. John's going through all of these people, until he gets to, like, the president of the airline counter. And this is taking a while, and we're all standing around wondering what's going on, and he finally conned them into accepting a personal check. And then John comes back, and we're going through all of the luggage—I remember this *vividly*—all of the luggage being tore apart on the floor, while John's looking for a personal check. And he can't find one! He doesn't have one! And he has to go back in, and talks the guy to accepting a counter check He *did it!* And, of course, it bounced! But that's how we got back . . . Now, I do remember that they—John and Michelle—did go to the casino in San Juan, and that supposedly Michelle threw 17 straight passes, but that was certainly before the airport, and before we went into this check business.

Michelle Phillips: Then I got to take Maude with me in first class; they gave me a little thing to carry her in, and after we got in the air, I put her in my lap. She was bleeding profusely through her vagina. I kind of can trace the break-up of my marriage back to this occasion. We took her to the hospital when we landed in New York, and they wanted to keep her overnight. They called the next morning and said, "Can we speak to Mr. Phillips?"—and I knew she was dead. She had torn seven fetuses apart from her uterus. We had no idea that she was pregnant. I grieved so much for this dog; and I don't think that John really ever understood how much it meant to me. It's not his fault; it's just the different way people respond to a tragedy like this. To me it was a monumental loss . . .

When we got back to New York, we came back to our apartment, which is where Scott McKenzie and his girlfriend were living, and they were just breaking up as we got there. It was the strangest thing: when we had left, Scott desperately needed a place to stay, and when we came back, he was literally packing and walking out the door. We were only there maybe a week, and then we left everything we owned there and got the drive-a-way and came out to California.

Peter Pilafian: We got back to New York. I was completely goin' with the flow, obviously. I didn't dream of even trying pry into how things were happening. So it seemed that this chapter was over. We flew back to New York. Russell was pregnant with our child, and along with John and Michelle, it was obviously a time re-group. It wasn't so much that the vacation was over, it was just that it was time for the next unknown thing.

Chapter Three

California Dreamin'

PART ONE

Finally . . . California via Drive-A-Way. Fowley's Crescendo and Werber's cold shoulder . . . Hoyt Axton's chili . . . snipers on the freeway during the Watts Riots . . . McGuire's free advice . . . Uncle Lou joins the family . . . Cass 'joins' the group, and California Dreamin' is becoming a reality . . .

Barry McGuire: When I came up through L.A. 1961–62, L.A. was just a sleepy little town. The hit singers were The Everly Brothers, people like that. When I came back in 1965, everything had changed. Folk/rock was coming in, all of these psychedelic little clubs were opening up; the first one was The Trip. It was just a much faster pace. Drugs had come into town. Before that, somebody may have had a little marijuana, maybe a little speed, but I didn't know anything about that. But in '65, drugs were really moving in. Lots was going on; a lot of people, and just a non-stop party.

Peter Pilafian: We felt that we were being constantly transformed, that our lives were being transformed. Everything we did was new and exciting and into the unknown. It was wonderful. When we took the drugs, it was the same thing, too. Drugs were exploratory. We'd take them and find out things that we never knew.

When we got to New York, I called some of my friends and

associates, and one of the people that I called was Conrad Rooks, who was making a film called "Chappuqua." I had worked with him earlier as an audio and soundtrack man. He was a pretty free-form and wild guy. He had inherited some of the Avon Cosmetics fortune. He was pretty well known in the New York underground as a druggie, but a stylish one. We talked, and he asked me what I was doing, and offered me a job that consisted of packing and transporting all of the audio and post-production equipment for the film company to France on a Swedish freighter. So I said sure, and we ironed out the details and I crossed over the Atlantic and helped set up the studio over there and worked with the French film editors. I produced the soundtrack sessions with Ravi Shankar, and got to become friendly with him back then. I was in Paris for three months, and meanwhile John, Michelle, and Denny got the famous drive-a-way car and made it out to L.A.

Denny Doherty: I'm back in New York, in Peter and Rusty's apartment on East Seventh Street. Cass was gone. We were going to get a U-Drive, and then The Doctor got arrested for hash possession with these girls, Muffy and Rachel. They were just swinging along Bleeker Street, and the cops nailed them for possession. But we were gone by then. Michelle, John, and I, and Billy Throkmorton got the U-Drive—a '63 or '64 Cadillac—out of the paper. They gave us about $700 traveling money, and about a week or so to do it. We had a week to do it, so we drove straight through, because John still had a friend at the corner drugstore; we just needed some Peruvian marching powder. Actually, we got some methamphetamine, and we drove straight through to California, stopping off in Las Vegas to see if we could duplicate the feat we had done in San Juan, but, no. Outside the casino in Vegas the police looked at us changing in the limo, and said, '"Where do you think *you're* going?" So, it was on to California . . . .

Barry McGuire: I'd left the Christy Minstrels—I'd sung "Green, Green" a thousand times and I didn't want to sing it again. This is January of 1965. I went back to L.A. to meet some producers, and I was broke. Nobody had the time of day for me. I was walking down street one time to go see "Dr. Strangelove" and I walked by the music store, and I heard "Green, Green" comin' out of the store, ya know, on Hollywood Boulevard. And I heard my voice, and I thought, "I got four dollars in my pocket!" I couldn't believe it, my voice is comin' out on Hollywood Boulevard, and I'm broke. And right at that moment, a car pulls up, and the radio is playing "Chim Chim Cherie" also by the Minstrels! So I got my voice comin' at me in stereo, standing on the sidewalk there, and I'm broke, and I can't get anyone to sign me!

A few weeks later, Roger McGuinn was staying out at Hoyt Axton's place in Topanga Canyon. He had this bunch of songs that he really liked, and he sang 'em for me one night. Then one day about a month or so after that, I ran into him again, and he said he'd just finished recording this song called "Mr. Tambourine Man." We were driving in the car, and he sang the whole song to me driving down Melrose Avenue. He told me that this band that he had—The Byrds—were opening in a week down at Ciro's on The Strip, and he told me to come down, and so I did. Everybody was there: Jack Nicholson, Lou Adler, Phil Sloan, Bobby Dylan. It was a big party. While I was there, The Byrds were playing, and this big tall guy had his arms flopping at his sides, and he was jumping up and down, looking at the ceiling. And I thought, "Well, I can do that!" so I started bouncing around the floor, and I thought, "This is fun!" This is the first time in my life where I'd really gotten into dancing, and The Byrds are playing the great, new 'folk/rock'; it *was great.*

Then Lou Adler comes over, and he says, "Aren't you Barry McGuire?" "Yeah" "Well, what are you doing these days?" "Well, I'm dancing right now!" He asked me if I was singing, and I told him I really wasn't, and he asked me if I wanted to, and I said, "I'd love to . . . " and he said, "C'mere to my table . . . " So I go over to the table, and there's P. F. Sloan and Bobby Dylan and a couple of guys from Dunhill Records. So I met everybody, and Lou said that he had some songs that he wanted me to hear, and would I come down to the office?

So we eventually hooked up, and Phil Sloan played me a bunch of songs, and I really liked 'em and we decided to record some of

Lou Adler, Western Studios.
Photo by Bones Howe.

'em. So we worked on the songs, and a couple of weeks later, we went into the studio. It was like, a three hour-session. We did two songs, and then the third one wasn't turning out. We only had about a half hour left in the session, so I said," Let's do this tune . . ." and I pulled "Eve Of Destruction" out of my pocket, and it just had Phil's words scrawled on a piece of paper, all wrinkled up. Phil worked the chords out with the musicians, who were Hal Blaine on drums, and Larry Knechtel on bass. Phil was playing guitar and harmonica. In those days, we did everything live. We did a take, and then went into the booth to listen. I missed the last note, so I went back out and 'punched in' that note. I wanted to go in and re-do the whole vocal track, but we were out of time . . . Lou said we'd come back next week.

Back then, they had acetates—little demonstration discs that had about 20 plays on them before they ran out of fidelity. Lou took this to his office, and one day this record promoter named Ernie Farrell came by to see him and to see what was happening. At one point, Lou had to leave the office, and before Ernie left, he grabbed these acetates off of the desk and threw 'em in his brief-case and left. Ernie was also a photographer, and he was shooting photos of a birthday party a couple of days later for the head of pro-gramming of KFWB Radio, which was the big Top-40 L.A. station at the time. He went out to his car to get some flashbulbs and saw his briefcase in the trunk, and said, "I'm gonna take these in and play 'em for the kids, see what they think." So they played a couple of songs and the kids thought they were okay, and then he played 'em "Eve Of Destruction", and the whole party stopped. "Play that one again!" He played it again. The third time, the KFWB programmer heard it and it blew him away . . .

He called Lou Adler, and told him, "If you get this pressed and shipped, it'll go on the radio Monday morning as a "Pick To Hit." This is like, a couple of days after the session. I had split for Mexico for the weekend, so I wasn't around. Lou went back in the studio, added some background vocals, mixed it down. By Monday morning, man . . . I got a call at 7 A.M. Monday morning, and this guy says, "Turn the radio on to KFWB . . . " And there I was.

Jim Hendricks: I came out there in early '65, and I came out there because a friend of mine told me of some opportunities for songwriting and folk clubs. And I was ready to get out of New York anyway. This was in about February '65. We got a little apartment about two blocks down from The Whiskey. I don't remember exactly how Cass got a hold of me—it may have been through Barry McGuire—we all knew each other real well. But she got a hold of me, and told me that she was coming to California and could she stay with us? So I said, "Sure!"

Cass made it out here and stayed with my girlfriend Vanessa and I. She had told me what had happened in The Virgin Islands, and I think that she felt the rest of the group might come out, but I can't remember her being definite that they were coming at that point. I can't remember, but I think that she was there for about a month, or maybe two. At that point she was doing nothing, she just came to cool out. Then Denny called me, and said something about coming out, and I said, "Come on, come out!" Well, we were up there in this little apartment, a one bedroom, and we took the beds apart, put bedsprings and mattresses on the floor, we were sleepin' all over the place. It was kinda rough.

Denny Doherty: When Cass came out to California, before we came out there, Jim put her up in his apartment, where he was living with his girlfriend Vanessa. But while she was living with Jim, they tried to take anything that they could sell and flog it in Hollywood, and one of those things was "Everybody's Been Talking," which is now owned by Kim Fowley. But it didn't do much good, because when we got to the apartment, there was an eviction notice on the door and it was only a matter of time before everything would be turned off and everybody would be thrown in the street . . .

We came over the San Bernardino foothills . . . we had two more days; the idea was to get to L.A. and use the rental car and make some contacts. We're coming into L.A., and it's the weekend of the Watts Riots. 1965. We didn't know. Michelle's driving, and she says, "Okay, we're in San Berdoo . . . " I think we were on the Harbor Freeway, and the radio reports were that there were *snipers* on the Harbor Freeway! There were plumes of smoke and flames and fuckin' army trucks on the street. We get off, and this soldier sittin' on top of a tank says, "Get back on the freeway." Welcome to L.A.!

So then we ended up at first staying up at Michelle's friend Markia's place in L.A., sleeping on her floor. I don't remember singing for anyone, but we were rehearsing, and that's where John and I wrote "Got A Feelin'." We hadn't been doing "California Dreamin'" because John had written it, and put it away. We hadn't been doing it in the act, although we had rehearsed it. But I don't know if we had really done it until we hooked up again with Cass . . . I'm not sure. I was singing the lead, and John and Michelle were doing the backing vocals, but I don't know how doing that with just the three of us would have been conducive to working out a whole arrangement. But at that time we'd just arrived in L.A. to see what the fuck was gonna happen . . .

We went around to the clubs, and we saw Hoyt Axton when we first got into town at his house. He had a big pot of chili on his stove. That was great; cornbread and chili, thank you, Hoyt! That got us through that night. Nothing happened there though, although he may have turned us on to Nick Venet. I'm not sure which came first—this was like, a 48-hour period. We came back from San Francisco, and we rented a car. We had Scott MacKenzie's credit card—Phil Blomdheim—and we rented a car, made it back to L.A., checked into The Landmark Hotel. Woke up the next morning and the car was gone. Stolen. It had all of our shit in it, and wound up in Mexico, stripped. That's when we started looking around for a place to live and we hooked up with Cass.

Jim Hendricks: I knew that they had a great sound. Basically, John and Michelle weren't great singers, so anything involving Cass and Denny I knew was great. John did have a great ability for vocal arrangements, things like that. From my previous experience working with Cass and Denny, when we were in The Mugwumps, we would get together and start harmonizing, and we just did all the arrangements as 'head' arrangements, there wasn't anyone taking it apart, and handing out parts, which is what John was doing. But I knew it was a great sound . . . I thought that they needed to do a little woodsheding, but that's all it was. Just a little woodsheding, a little rehearsing.

John Phillips: So we got to California. Everyone we had known in the Village, before we left for the islands, was in California. I mean, Crosby was here, McGuinn was here. McGuire was here. I don't know, thousands of people who were singing in the Village when we left, were now making records in California.

Kim Fowley: I was working for Gene Norman at GNP Crescendo; I was allegedly a talent scout and a West Coast A&R guy. Later I produced The Seeds for GNP Crescendo. I was sitting in the office one day and Cass Elliot called and said, "My friends from The Virgin Islands have arrived, so why don't you come down and hear the stuff?" I had ran into her around town earlier; everybody knew everyone else in those days in L.A.. So I walked down to this place off San Vencente south of Sunset, and there they were,

Denny and Michelle and John. They played three songs: "California Dreamin'," "Monday, Monday" and "Straight Shooter." I called up my boss, Gene Norman, after I asked them how much they wanted—they didn't want much. So, Gene says, "What are you doing? . . . where are you? . . . are you working??!" I told him that I found a great group with good songs. "Yeah? What's the concept?" "Harmony." "What do they want?" "$250 a month, and the guys will do the janitor work at the studio, and the girls will do the accounting work." He said, "*Nobody's* worth $250 a month, not even *you!*" He said "No" and hung up the phone. I told them that Norman wasn't interested, but I was sure that my friend Nick Venent would be. So I called up Nick and told him about the group and said, "I'm the publisher, you're the producer." So, he went to see them sing these three songs, and said "If they're any good I'll put 'em on Mira Records," 'cause he had just done "Hey Joe" by The Leaves.

Jim Hendricks: Nick Venet came to our house one night. I remember it seemed like everyone was singin' together. Cass, Denny, John, and Michelle had obviously done some rehearsing down in the Virgin Islands. They were the ones who were singing, and Nick was there while we were all kind of harmonizing on these songs. He offered them a deal, he offered John a deal at that point. As a matter of fact, I don't know what it was, but some money changed hands right there, it was cash. This is just my recollection, but it seems that Nick said, "I want to sign you" and John said, "Man, we need some money . . ." because everybody was *extremely* broke. We were barely eating. They had nothing, because the American Express card had been cut off, and they had no cash. So, Nick gave 'em some cash.

Kim Fowley: Remember, it was a trio that sang for me. When they rang Nick's doorbell, he looked out and saw all of them, and said, "What a great image the four of you have!" They said that they were a trio, and pointed to Cass and said "She's a friend of ours, and she just drove us over here. She's not part of the band." Nick asked if she sang, and they said, "Yeah, I know all the parts . . . " So the four of them sang for Nick, and he said, "I won't record you unless she joins the group. The four of you are remarkable; I don't know what the three of you are like, and I don't care to know." He asked them if they needed some money to eat on and gave them $150.00. Nick then said, "Here's the deal: tomorrow you'll go to this address at 3:00 and sing for Randy Wood, and if all goes well, you'll get a contract with Mira Records. Kim publishes, I produce, and we'll put out a single, and hopefully it'll be a hit. . . ."

The next day, at around 11 A.M. they were getting nervous, and apparently they needed some 'refreshment' to calm them down or rev them up, so that they could go to Mira Records at three. So they called up Barry McGuire and got him to come over and bring some 'refreshment,' so that they could stabilize themselves to audition for Mira with the Beach Boys producer, who has a hit at the moment with The Leaves. Well, Barry was trained pretty well by Lou Adler, because he said, "I have a label that I have a hit on right now. Sing your stuff for me right now, and if it's any good, you can talk to Lou Adler and get another opinion." Barry called up Lou and says, "Hey, I'm sitting with a group from New York, and they have a great look and fantastic sound and great songs. There's another label that's interested in them, but can I rush them over to see you." Lou said, "If they're that good, bring 'em down." Remember, Barry had the number one record in the world at the time, "Eve Of Destruction."

Denny Doherty: Nah . . . no, no. Venet couldn't get anybody at Capitol interested, so he was trying to raise it himself. We sang, "California Dreamin'," "Monday, Monday," "Go Where You Wanna Go"; stuff from the first album, that's what Venet heard. But I don't remember Kim Fowley. But he had a relationship with Jim and Cass. So, in his memory, there was more to it than that; but this was before John, Michelle and I got into town. You know Fowley? He'd say, "You gotta hype, you gotta puke, you gotta grease, you gotta happen . . . " Whatever *that* means. That's *very* Irish. "Ya gotta come and do stuff. *Stuff.* You gotta come and stuff'll *happen* . . . it's the law of nature." Well, that's his recollection. He 'found' us, too. A lot of people 'found' us. Oh yes. But John and Michelle didn't 'find' us until three days later, when we went to San Francisco, because we had to drop the car off. John and Michelle and I went to sing for Frank Werber, who said, "Get the fuck outta here."

Frank Werber: I had established myself with The Kingston Trio, and The We Five happened as well with "You Were on My Mind," which had made it to #2 on the charts. Everything was going pretty well. We had moved to a complex at Columbus Towers, in San Francisco, and we had offices and were building a studio in the basement.

The day John came back to see me, I remember it being a day of tension, as most of them were at that time. Production, getting things ready for shows and what have you. And John Stewart came up to me and said, "Listen, John Phillips is here . . . " He had this tape, a cassette. And without thinkin' about it, I'm real busy, and Stewart comes in again, and goes, "Phillips is gonna leave, he's getting tired of waiting . . . " They go into another room in the same floor. I've reviewed this moment many times since, by the way . . .

I took the cassette, and I marched in, and I say, "Hey John, how ya doin'? Stewart tells me that you wanna blah, blah, blah . . . and I have to tell you, that I have not had a chance to listen to this tape. I believe that you are a most talented individual, and that's why we took you on in the first place. But I also believe that you are also a drag to work with. A pain in the ass. So I'll tell you what; before whatever you have on here sways me, I'm gonna give it back to you and say that we're not interested." And that was it. I don't mind tellin' that story. Ya gotta lose a few, ya know? But I'll tell ya, if I'd have played it, I would've been in. For sure. It was *gold*. That group was just, creatively, great. Knowing what I know about John and his complete control of his music, I'm not too sure what Adler had to do with it. Nothing against Lou; he did his thing well.

John Stewart: John, Michelle, and Denny came into Frank's office in the Columbus Tower, on Columbus and Kearny. They played me this song, "California Dreamin'", and I called Don Graham, who was Frank's record promoter, and he was promoting The We Five, which was my brothers' group. Don came in, and we went up to Frank's office, and Frank said, "Get John Phillips out of this building!" Don said, "Frank, this is gonna be huge . . ." and Frank said, "Get 'em outta here." John had come with Michelle and Denny, to ask me to produce them . . . and I couldn't do it because Frank was the whole thing.

Denny Doherty: Werber wouldn't talk to John about anything. John Stewart and his brother Michael wanted to get something going. There was a studio in the basement, and The Kingston Trio were in the building. Perfect, perfect! But I guess Werber and John had been at loggerheads to begin with. We were like a pinball bouncing around. We turned in the car, and then came back to L.A., where I guess that Hoyt Axton/Fowley/Venet network happened. Finally we get back down to L.A., where we hook back up with Cass. She calls McGuire, who comes over and says, "Come on down to the studio and sing for Lou Adler . . . " We went down and sang for Lou and got the deal while Venet was out beating the bushes for money. First one to the starving artists, wins.

Lou Adler: Barry had told me that he had some friends that were in San Francisco that were going to be coming through L.A. . . . they didn't have a recording contract, and would I take a listen to them? I said, "When they come into town, have them come by . . . ," because we were in the recording studio quite a bit, and I'd listen to them. During a break—we were at Western Recorders on Sunset—I was recording Barry in Studio Three. We went over to Studio A, the large one in the back, and it was John playing guitar, and Denny, Cass and Michelle. The title of the album, *If You Can Believe Your Eyes and Ears* comes from the way they looked, and when they started singing. They sang "California Dreamin'," "Monday. Monday." and "Go Where You Wanna Go"—I think either three or four songs. It's amazing in retrospect; I felt like, and I've said it before, like what George Martin must have felt like when he first heard The Beatles. Maybe even more so, because vocally, everything was *there*, and each one was outstanding, and they were incredible looking. I couldn't believe my eyes and ears, is what happened to me.

James Hendricks: The next thing I knew, they were going off with Barry to go see Lou Adler. Barry had come over. He was just starting to go up with "Eve of Destruction," and he had a new motorcycle, new clothes. I can remember him pulling up in front of this little apartment with this brand-new motorcycle, and all this sort of stuff. I was there. I remember Cass coming back and being very excited about getting signed at Dunhill.

Barry McGuire: Cass was staying with James and Vanessa. The rest of the group came into town, and they didn't have a label, a producer, nothin'. And they were broke. Kind of like I was at the beginning of the year. So they thought, "Well, McGuire's got a big hit, let's talk to him . . . " So Cass called me and told me what was going on, and I went over there. Cass was ironing, and they were rolling joints and we were all singin'. Cass was singin' too, at the ironing board. It just blew me away, it sounded *so* good. So I said, "I'm working with this guy Lou Adler, and he's a great guy, and he's treated me with dignity and respect, and he's just easy to work with. I can take you to him, see what happens . . . "

So I talked with Lou and told him what was happening, and he said, "Okay, bring 'em down to the studio and I'll listen to 'em . . . "

Lou heard 'em, and he loved 'em, and his jaw fell open. I think he fell in love with Michelle, too! He asked me, "Hey, who's the blonde?" And I said, "Well, she's *his* wife; that's John's wife . . . " So then the next thing I knew, is that they signed on the label, and Lou said, "Why don't we have 'em sing background vocals on your album so that they can make a few bucks?" So, they're on about seven or eight songs on my *This Precious Time* album.

I was gonna release "California Dreamin'" as my second single. After we cut it, John came up to me in the hall and asked me, "Is it okay if we put this out as our single?" And I said, "John, it's your song; of course it's okay! And if you have a hit with it, then *you* can buy the grass next year!" So we laughed about it, and then we went back in. But I didn't know that they were going to use my backing track. They just took my voice off and put Denny's on, and got Bud Shank to play the flute solo. They took off my *wonderful*, moaning harmonica off! I was moaning; I was howling at the moon! And, on the left channel at the very beginning of the track, you can hear a bit of my vocal. But I think that's cool! I thought that was very cool when my son discovered that one day . . .

Kim Fowley: They went down and sang for Lou, and he loved it, and he asked them who are the people that they'd been talking to. "Who's involved?" "Kim Fowley." "Oh!" "Nick Venet." "Oh!" Lou told them, "I'm the label, and I'm going to give you three grand *right now*. I'm gonna walk you to the bank, and you're gonna sign an agreement before we get there, and we're gonna do an album. You don't have to talk with Nick Venet or Kim Fowley or Mira Records—you're on Dunhill Records now, you're with Lou Adler, and I'm gonna give you three grand right now."

Meanwhile, it's after 3:00, and Nick calls me at GNP Crescendo, where I'm waiting to find out what happened. "Where are they? Maybe someone else grabbed them . . . " Well, we all know what happened. P.S., a couple of months later, I was at a party, and John was there, and he had a record there called "Daydream" by The Lovin' Spoonful that he was playing for everyone, and I said, "John, you owe Nick $150," and he said, "Right!" "Well, you ought to do something about it . . . " John sent Nick a check for $150, and Nick never cashed it. He framed it.

Michelle Phillips: I don't have any memory of this whatsoever. When we went to Hendricks' apartment, we didn't know that Cass or Barry was there. We called over there because he was the only person we knew that we could crash with. Barry said, "Why don't you go sing for my producer, Lou Adler?" And that's when we pleaded with Cass and said, "Why don't you come and sing with us, if only for the audition? *Please* sing with us" She hemmed and hawed because she didn't know if she really wanted to do this. But when we sang for Lou and he heard us . . . the minute those contracts were on the floor the next day, she was like, "Gimmie the pen!!" It was a *job* . . . money, *now*. We're gonna make an album, "Great! Where do I *sign?!*" This was *right now*. We didn't have *any* money. And then she was in the group, and there were no more questions about it. When we left, someone said, "Lou Adler . . . what did ya think of that guy?" Cass and I looked at each other and said "Don't trust him . . . " He just asked us to sing one thing after the next, and wouldn't move. "What else do ya have?" He was *very* cool. Mr. Cool, oh yeah.

Barry McGuire and The Mamas & The Papas, Western Studios,
Los Angeles, summer 1965.
Photo by Chuck Boyd. Courtesy of the Michael Ochs Archives.

Denny Doherty: We went down to McGuire's session to sing backups, and Lou heard "California," and said to Barry, "This is your next single. Who wrote that?, where's that?, who the fuck is the blonde?!?" McGuire has said this to me subsequently: "Whose song is that, and who's fuckin' the blonde?!" In the first ten minutes!!! Hello, Uncle Lou! So anyway, we did the track. The

Wrecking Crew was there—Blaine, Knechtel, all of 'em. So they were at the session, and they learned the song and laid it down right there. We did all the background vocals and then Barry did the lead. Lou went, "No, something's not right. . . ." and then I put the lead on it, and that was our first record.

It only took a little while. That initial meeting was enough for Lou to say, "Okay, we'll give you some session work to keep you alive." We did the backing vocals, and then he heard the song . . . it wasn't like 'bam' that first night. But it was through that evening of introductions—Cass calling McGuire, McGuire telling us to come and meet Lou that it happened. Lou said, "Here's the money, don't worry about it . . ." It just so happens that his partners are Jay Lasker, Bobby Roberts, and, at the time, Pierre Cosset. Apparently Cosset said, "If you hire these people, I'm out. You're not hiring *those* people." Lou hired us, and Pierre quit Dunhill. He walked; he's a man of his word.

Cyrus Faryar: We (the MFQ) headed out to California, and The Mamas & The Papas showed up, and they had gotten a house on Flores street, and it was just like a work-a-day event. They were looking to get a deal. I guess they were evolving into The Mamas & The Papas at that point.

Barry McGuire: I do remember a little later, some guy—I don't remember whom—being pissed off that they signed to Dunhill, and that this, "Cost me a hundred million dollars!" Yeah, that's right, *everybody* discovered them, after the fact. Just like The Beatles. And it's *my* fault, because *they* didn't have the hit with it!

When I went up to that apartment, she was *singing* with 'em, but Denny told me that Cass wasn't part of the group. I don't know if John was very excited about having her in the group, ya know? When they went down to sing for Lou, they were thinking, "Well, we'd better take Cass with us, because Barry thinks she's part of the group, and Barry knows Lou . . ." and talked her into coming down for the audition. But they wouldn't have made it without Cass. And they wouldn't have made it without Michelle, or Denny. Or John. You have the great songwriting and arranging of John,

AMERICAN FEDERATION OF MUSICIANS N°. 243803

Local Union No. **47** OF THE UNITED STATES AND CANADA

THIS CONTRACT for the personal services of musicians, made this **4** day of **November** 19 **65** **7** musicians
between the undersigned "employer" (hereinafter called the "employer") and _____ (including the leader)
(hereinafter called "employee").

WITNESSETH, That the employer hires the employees as musicians severally on the terms and conditions below, and as further specified on reverse side. The leader represents that the employees already designated have agreed to be bound by said terms and conditions. Each employee yet to be chosen shall be so bound by said terms and conditions upon agreeing to accept his employment. Each employee may enforce this agreement. The employees severally agree to render collectively to the employer services as musicians in the orchestra under the leadership of

HAL BLAINE as follows:

Name and Address of Place of Engagement **Western Recorders, 6000 Sunset Blvd, Los Angeles, Calif.**

Date(s) and Hours of Employment **November 4, 1965   1 P.M. to 4 P.M. (same men with overtime)**

Type of Engagement: **Recording for phonograph records only.** Plus pension contributions as specified on reverse side hereof.
WAGE AGREED UPON $ _____ **UNION SCALE**
(Terms and amount)
This wage includes expenses agreed to be reimbursed by the employer in accordance with the attached schedule, or a schedule to be furnished the employer on or before the date of engagement. **WITHIN 14 DAYS**

To be paid _____
(Specify when payments are to be made)
Upon request by the American Federation of Musicians of the United States and Canada (herein called the "Federation") or the local in whose jurisdiction the employees shall perform hereunder, the employer either shall make advance payment hereunder or shall post an appropriate bond.

Employer's name and **Dunhill Records**   Leader's name **Hal Blaine**   Local No. **47**
authorized signature _____   Leader's signature _____
Street address **321 So. Beverly Dr.**   Street address _____
Beverly Hills, Calif.   **CR-45201**   **Hollywood 28, Calif.**
City   State   Phone   City   State

(1) Label Name **Dunhill Records**   Session No. _____

Master No.	No. of Minutes	TITLES OF TUNES	Master No.	No. of Minutes	TITLES OF TUNES
	2:12	"TOM THUMB"		2:14	"I'D HAVE TO BE OUT OF
	2:21	"THIS PRECIOUS TIME"			MY MIND"
	2:16	"CALIFORNIA DREAMIN'"			

(2) Employee's Name (As on Social Security Card) Last First Initial	(3) Home Address (Give Street, City and State)	(4) Local Union No.	(5) Social Security Number	(6) Scale Wages	(7) Pension Contribution
Blaine, Hal ½ O.T. (Leader)	Hollywood 28, Calif.	47		162.68	13.01
Howe, Dayton B. ½ O.T. 1-hr O.T. 2-Dbls.	Los Angeles 27, Calif.	47		81.34	6.51
Knechtel, Lawrence W.	Sherman Oaks, Calif.	47		127.10	10.17
Lipkin, Stephen B. 3-Dbls.	Los Angeles 46, Calif.	47		61.00	4.88
Osborn, Joe ½ O.T.	No. Hollywood, Calif.	116		109.81	8.78
Phillips, John E.A.	Hollywood 46, Calif.	161		61.00	4.88
Sloan, Phillip	Los Angeles 48, Calif.	47		61.00	4.88

NO ARRANGER OR COPYIST THIS SESSION****************************

(8) Total Pension Contributions (Sum of Column (7)) $ **53.11**
Make check payable in this amount to "AFM & EPW Fund."

FOR FUND USE ONLY:
Date pay't rec'd _____ Amt. paid _____ Date posted _____ By _____
Form B-4 Rev. 4-59

Courtesy of Elliot Kendall.

you have the great look of Michelle—every guy in America wanted to fall into bed with her. You had the voice of Denny Doherty—who could sing the birds out of the trees, and you had the charisma and voice of Cass Elliot. She had this incredible, *rich* timbre in her voice. So you had two real incredible singers, a great looker who had a good voice, and the incredible songwriter, who was a good singer and arranger. If one of 'em had been missing, I don't think they would have made it. Just like The Beatles. They wouldn't have made it with any of 'em missing; it was a *great* balance, and that's what it takes.

John Stewart: I later talked to John, and he said that they'd been to see Lou Adler, and that they played him the songs in the studio, and that the 12-string sounded like an orchestra in there. Lou asked 'em what they wanted, and John said, "I want a steady stream of money from your office to my house . . . " They lived in this little place up in the Hollywood Hills, Jim & Vanessa's place. Real nomads.

I came down to L.A. a bit later, when "California Dreamin'" was a hit, and they had this party at the house . . . probably on Flores Street. There were just people *everywhere*. Barry McGuire came through the room dancing through the house nude, and nobody said anything. I came back the next morning, and John said that there were people waiting in line to buy "Monday, Monday". And I thought, "Okay . . . here we go. This is it . . . " The next time I saw him, he was livin' in a Bel Air mansion!

PART TWO

This Precious Time . . . The Mamas & The Papas become that magic circle, or vice-versa . . . and sign with Dunhill . . . McGuire and Roberts 'negotiate' . . . Bones, Sloan and early sessions . . . Duck a l'Orange at The Landmark and Michelle and Denny on the wall to wall . . . Lasker's bottom line: "Remember, Lou, they're just animals."

Bones Howe: I started with Lou, doing all the Johnny Rivers stuff, "Memphis," everything. Lou did those for Imperial Records as an independent producer, then he started this label called Dunhill Records, and they signed Shelley Fabares, and this guy Barry McGuire. This would be late '64, goin' into '65, right in the middle of the folk/rock period. So we made "Eve of Destruction," which was written by Flip (P. F. Sloan) and Steve (Barri), two of the staff writers for Lou's publishing company, Trousdale Music, and it became a *huge* hit.

Steve Barri: Myself along with Phil Sloan were songwriters for Lou when he was running the publishing over at Screen-Gems. When he left to start the publishing company (Trousdale) along with Dunhill Records, we went with him. We were like staff songwriters at the company, and we had already started to have some decent success, a couple of local hits and whatever. Then we did "Eve of Destruction," that song, for Barry McGuire. What Lou was doing for us—we were just a couple of scuffling guys in our teens—was to kind of give us an education in terms of producing records, and learning how to be producers along with being songwriters, and doing our own demos and stuff. It was a learning process. I always tried to be around the studio with Lou when he was producing records, because, like Lou, I didn't have much knowledge of music, other than the song sense that we had. I realized that he was a guy that couldn't read or write music, but he was producing all of these hit records. I always found it fascinating, the way he could relate to musicians and cut great tracks and everything. Basically we were songwriters, and when "Eve Of Destruction" took off—which is a whole story in itself, because it was put on the radio before it was even finished and mixed—and it exploded, and we had to finish up an album really quickly. Lou was having us work with McGuire, in terms of writing the songs for him and sort of co-producing the record with Lou.

Bones Howe: We went to make the album, and one night in the studio, McGuire shows up with these four scruffy kids with a guitar. McGuire said that he was going to cut this song, "California

Dreamin'," and he wanted them to sing on the record. He also said to Lou, "Hey, you've got to hear them sing, they're really good."

So we cut the track to "California Dreamin'," which is the same track that The Mamas & The Papas used on their record, except for Barry's vocal and the harmonica solo. For The Mamas version, I got Bud Shank out of Studio Two in the back to play the alto flute solo. But anyway, before that, we were tracking for Barry's record with Hal Blaine, Jo Osborne, and Larry Knechtel.

Steve Barri: The first time I ever remember meeting The Mamas & The Papas—and I don't know what may have gone on behind the scenes—but Barry McGuire brought them into the studio one day over at Western Studio #3, where we worked all the time, and he said, "These are some friends of mine, and I'd like them to sing background on the record." We had only worked with studio background singers up until that point, and we said, "Sure, great, let's hear 'em." So they just sang a couple of songs for us that kinda blew everybody away. As it turns out they had been to see Nick Venet at Capitol records, the same day.

Bones Howe: I was just blown away. Lou turned to me and said, "Whadda you think of 'em?" and I said, "If you don't take 'em, I gonna. . . . ." At that time I was producing The Turtles, and starting to get active as a producer. Lou made a deal with them. He asked them how much Nick had given then to get through the day, you know, which I think turned out to be about $50.00. So, Lou gave them the $50.00 to give back to Venet, and told them to come into the office the next day to make a deal, and get an advance, etc. They came into the office the next day, because Lou came in to me and said, "We signed 'em, and we're going to make a record."

Joe Osborne: It was at a McGuire session. They were just there, and came in to sing. I thought that they were really, really good.

Steve Barri: I don't even remember them even being on-mic.

They were just singing live out there in the studio, I just remember them and John on guitar, and them singing and they just blew everybody away. You didn't really have to be a rocket scientist to figure it out. These guys were really, really good.

Bones Howe: We were just laying down tracks for McGuire's record. The Mamas & The Papas were out in the studio singing with Barry. We usually cut the track and the sent the musicians home, and then laid down the vocals. There weren't any written arrangements, except maybe a chord sheet, they were all worked out right then as 'head' arrangements. At one point, the band was taking a 'ten' or whatever, and Lou said, "Let's go back and hear this group sing . . . "

So, Lou and I want back to Studio Two, which is the studio in the back of Western. Studio Two was kind of a big barn of a rectangle in the back. We went back with the four of them, and I remember they sang "California Dreamin'," and "Somebody Groovy." I think they sang "Go Where You Wanna Go." They sang four songs, as I remember. This was before "Monday, Monday" had been written, I think, before John started really digging in and writing, before he knew he was going to make a record.

P. F. Sloan: Barry brought them in, and he said, "These are some friends of mine from New York that I want you to listen to. They've been turned down by a lot of other people, and would you give a listen?" They broke into a rendition of "Go Where You Wanna Go", which was fairly complete as a song. "California Dreamin'" is nothing like it turned out to be, chord and structure-wise. It was basically incomplete. I listened to the harmonies, and I just hadn't heard joy and exuberance like that. It was comparable to The Beatles, in my mind. They were bigger than Peter, Paul & Mary—there was obviously that connection—but they went beyond that, *way* beyond that. I told Lou that I would produce the group. I told Lou, "If you won't, then I will." That was the initial meeting. I told McGuire that I had no problem working with them, and anything he wanted to do was fine with me. Steve Barri liked them, he thought they were really good.

Steve Barri: For whatever we knew in those days about what was great and what wasn't, whatever, you knew this was something special. Of course, those songs we so great also, but at that point we were only thinking in terms of that they'd be great to do background vocals, and especially because McGuire's a friend of theirs, this would fine . . .

P. F. Sloan: The fact that Barry McGuire was not acceptable as a recording artist was because "Eve of Destruction" had brought death threats to Dunhill as a company. They didn't want Barry McGuire as a recording artist anymore. The country basically said, "We will not play Barry McGuire's music." So Dunhill did not want anything to do with Barry's friends, or anything like that. They were trying to distance themselves from McGuire, as best they could. The word was out.

Barry McGuire: "Eve of Destruction" was a scary song, because it made it on its own; it had no 'payola,' no disc jockey manipulation. Phil told me later on that there was a letter that went out from The Gavin Report or something, saying, "No matter what McGuire puts out next, don't play it . . . " After that, I put some great stuff out: "This Precious Time," and some other cuts with The Mamas & The Papas on it, and they wouldn't play it.

I'm glad it happened, because if I'd have had another hit, I'd be dead now! I would be, I know that. If I had had a string of hits, I'd be just as dead as Cass or Hendrix or Elvis, any of 'em. I'd have been *outta here.* It was just enough to make a little niche for me.

Michelle Phillips: I remember at first not really trusting Lou. I remember the first day we met him he seemed *awfully* cool. He revealed nothing. There we were, singing all of our material, and being funny and witty, and he was being very . . . careful. Well of course, that's how Lou is! We grew to love Lou in about ten minutes. The next day we realized that he really loved us. The next day when we went to see him, we didn't know that we were going to

Cass, Denny, and Lou Adler, Western Studios, 1966.
Photo by Don Paulsen. Courtesy of Michael Ochs Archives.

sign contracts. He just said, "Hey look, why don't you kids come back tomorrow at about three?" I thought we were going to have to come back and sing some more, which I was dreading, and that maybe he was going to bring some other people in from Dunhill. But, there was a whole room full of contracts, they were all out on the floor. I'll never forget that. And Lou just wanted to get those signatures, because he just didn't believe what had walked in the door.

Cass Elliot: Even when we went into Dunhill records to write up our contract, John asked for things that had never been heard of in the recording business, except for The Beatles, who got pretty much what they asked for, there had been no other groups, certainly in this country, and no single artists who got the kind of creative freedom that we had gotten, and John knew what to ask for, he knew what we were worth. I'm not talking about financially, 'cause money is no criteria. It is a criteria in one way, because the record company believed in us, they gave us money to live, and when somebody puts their money where their mouth is, you know they have faith in you. But that's not the point, the point is they trusted it artistically, they didn't tell us what to sing, they didn't tell us how to sing.

Lou Adler: They asked for a couple of things, as I recall. First thing was, as far as "California Dreamin'," I wanted to try that with Barry. I said we could record that, and then we could try and record the group. John said, "Well, we've got another deal goin', and somebody is looking at us . . . " I don't know if that was ever true or not. I'm not sure if he said Warner Bros. or Nick Venet. Later on, I learned that Nick Venet had been talking to them. John said, "We're looking for some things, because we've got other deals . . . " And I thought, "These guys are worth quite a bit more than I'm going to be able to afford in a new company." It was so small. I was amazed at what they asked for. John later became a good negotiator, but at that time particular time . . .

I think I got 'em a house on Flores, and an old car, and maybe $1,500. I think it was on a Friday, so it might have not been the next day. By Monday we had the contracts all written up.

Michelle Phillips: I was very hopeful that Cass would join the group. I knew the difference between the way it sounded with her and without her, and I didn't want to carry the girl part all by myself. It was a great relief to me when Lou put the contracts out on the floor and Cass was *right* there! That pen was out and she was signin'!) She was on, and I was very, very glad that she was on board with us. It was such a big difference in the way it sounded. It wasn't until Lou offered us the contract when we got back to Los Angeles that she actually agreed to be part of the group. I've realized that there's a lot of speculation as to whether she wanted in the group, or John didn't want her in the group or what it was.

Barry McGuire: I didn't have that much relationship with Dunhill. I went in and met Lou Adler, Jay Lasker, Bobby Roberts, and another guy I hardly ever saw . . . maybe Andy Wickham. I didn't really hang out at Dunhill hardly at all. They were the suits, and I was into flowered pants and smoking dope and wearing ribbons in my hair. I knew that I was like, the 'token hippie' on the label. Denny told me one time that Jay said, "Remember Lou, they're just animals." So Jay was ridin' it like a toboggan down a mountain. I never really went to the office much; I think I went there one time to pick up a check. In fact, I went to see Bobby Roberts, because he was going to be my business manager. I was whacked; I was living in Topanga Canyon, and I rode my Siata roadster in there, and I went into the office just *stoned . . . out there.* And I'm sitting there lookin' at him, and he looks like a cartoon person sitting at his desk. He's going through all of these body language wiggles and twitches, and to me, every movement was *so* magnified. I thought, "Why's he so uncomfortable? Why doesn't he mellow out?" He says, "Well, listen, my normal manager's fee is 40 percent" I'm so stoned that I'm sitting there trying to figure out what 40 percent *means*! "If I get $100.00, he gets . . . what?" I'm not saying *a word*, and my brain is working so slowly, and my face is crunched up, concentrating, or *trying* to concentrate. So he got uptight and said, "Well listen, I know you're a new artist, so I'll do it for 30 percent . . . " Then I had to concentrate again on 30%, which was even *more* difficult! "If I get $70.00, he'll get . . . what?" Then he says, "Okay, 20 percent!" Again, I'm thinking, "Okay, if he gets $20.00, *what do I get*?!" Finally he says, "10 percent! And I don't work for anybody for 10 percent!!" And I said, "Okay, that's cool . . . " and he said, "You're a *great* negotiator, Barry . . . you are *tough.*" I would have gone for 40 percent; I didn't know!

Michelle Phillips: It was Cass's birthday—September 19th, 1965, at The Landmark Hotel. Cass made Duck a l'Orange, which was the only thing I think she knew how to make, but she made it *very* well. We had a long table, and Cass and John were each at one end of the table, and Denny and I were sitting across from each other with our feet on top of each other, naturally. We had candles burning, we had drank a lot of wine, and we smoked some pot. Denny and I were talking to each other right across the table from each other. We realized at one point, that John and Cass had fallen asleep in their chairs. They crashed. That's when Denny got up from the table, walked over to the sliding glass door . . . and beckoned me with his finger. No words. I got up and we hopped the little railing to the next-door apartment, which was vacant. The door was open. Denny may have opened it, I don't know. We went in there, and we made love on the wall-to-wall. And honest to god, I think that's the only time that it happened.

Denny Doherty: We were recording the first album at Western, living together at this house on Flores Street. Michelle and I are playing footsies through all of this. As I recall, Michelle and I had been mucking about ; nothing serious, and we had just signed the deal with Dunhill, I think on a Monday, and on Wednesday John and Michelle and I had a confrontation. He had come downstairs and 'caught' us . . . flagrante delecto. That was the week we signed the deal. So for all intents and purposes, it was over before it began. We had *just* signed the deal. Here it is. But, the monkey wrench had been thrown, and the group kept going on its own momentum after that. We were still living in that house when "California" came out, and we got a big hit. John, Michelle, and I got into this big confrontation. They move out, Cass moves out, I move out, and from that point on, everybody sort of looks the other way. Business as usual. John and Michelle get their little house up in Laurel Canyon. Cass moved into her place, and I moved into Sandy Koufax's Tropicana Motel and we just kept right on recording. That was about it.

Michelle Phillips: At Flores, it was still hot and heavy—it was just something that we couldn't stop. But the guilt was *overwhelming* Denny. And then he told Cass on the trip to Mexico.

Denny Doherty: I dived into a Mexican garbage dump that was underwater and came out with a Schlitz bottle sticking out of my chest. The four of us had gone down to take a little break, and we were staying in this strange apartment where the partitions

didn't go all the way up to the ceilings, so it was rather...
chummy. Anyway, I couldn't handle that scene, so one night I said
to Cass, "Let's go for a ride." We were all fucked up out of our
minds, and we drove down the coast highway somewhere—
maybe Ensenada—and on the drive I told her about Michelle and I.
Cass said, "Well, fuck all this . . . I want to go back to L.A. . . . ." I was
drunk and spilled my guts, and Cass freaked out. It was not a good
thing.

If it was known at the time, and if John had realized that his
wife was having dalliances within the group, and that I backed off
. . . Michelle had found a little independence and could go out and
have a fling with whoever she wished at that point, because her
husband had just condoned the fact that she was having a dalliance
with me, for reasons known only to himself. So she started seeing
other people, and now she's got two guys, me and John going,
(heartbreaking moan) 'Ahh, ohh . . . ' She's seeing other people
and he can't really get into it with her, I can't really get into it with
her because of the group thing, and they're husband and wife.
Meanwhile, I'm standing back, and Cass is going, "You son of a
bitch . . . " It was a rather *touchy* time . . .

Michelle Phillips: We went to Tjiuana, and I remember that
we went to a place called The Chicago Club, which was a strip
joint. I remember that I was very drunk. Everybody was very, very,
very drunk. Cass and I went into the bathroom to throw up. I threw
up, and I came back into the club. Our table was right on the
runway where these strippers were coming out. I remember seeing
the most disgusting thing: this stripper had Denny by the ears,
grinding his *face* in her *crotch!* And I turned around and I went back
into the bathroom and threw up *again!* When we came back the
next day, that was when Denny had jumped into the ocean and
came out with a bottle in his chest. But Denny told Cass, and I
remember looking back, and they were talking in the car—we
were in Harold The Bleak— and when I saw the expression on her
face, I thought, "How could he be so out of his mind to tell her?!"

Now, she didn't exactly spill the beans, although she may have
said something to John that made him suspicious. Because it was

very soon after that—after we got back to Flores—that I woke up very early one morning and went down to Denny's room, and I wasn't doing anything, I was sitting on his bed talking to him—which would not have been unusual or incriminating in itself. But I remember seeing the shadow of John coming down the steps . . . and he was *creeping* down the steps, with his hands out, and on his tip-toes . . . he was trying to 'catch' us, just to get us in a compromising situation. I knew that it was all over, and I ran out the door in my nightgown, and was walking around Flores Avenue for about two hours. I was trying to sneak back into the backyard. John and Denny were sitting in the backyard, talking, and John was saying, "I understand, Denny. I understand what a little *temptress* she is." I thought, "*Wait* a minute. Now it's all *my* fault??" They were talking very manfully, like buddies. But Denny had copped to it, by this point.

Eric Hord: Dennis had a very, very pleasing personality, which he still does to this day. Michelle had a very, very pleasing personality; she's still the same. Cass was the same, and at the time, so was John. So you have four very likeable people, and they probably thought that they were going to stay together for 10 albums! And the thing that pissed me off so much when I arrived in L.A. and found out about Denny/Michelle/etc., was that I just couldn't believe that this shit was happening after they'd sweated for so long. *So* many women loved Dennis, *so* many. You really have no idea. And then he has to go and ball Michelle. Man . . .

I got out of jail, but while I was in jail, I heard "California Dreamin'" and "Monday, Monday," and I called John. That was kind of a wake-up call for them because they thought I was still in jail. John wired me some money, and I rented this Cadillac limo, and came out to L.A. with this girl from The Village. I got into town, and I was wondering where everybody was, because I just had this one address where John and Michelle were living at that time, on Lookout Mountain. I got there, walked in, and John and Michelle were there, and Cass was there, and it was then that I found out about Michelle and Denny. But, by that point, I certainly understood the personalities that went into the whole thing . . .

Michelle Phillips: Of course, when the affair with Denny came to light, oh boy, the shit hit the fan with Cass. Because she was in love with Denny. When she was sad, and she was hurt, she was *dangerous*. And I knew it! Man . . . when I saw the look in her eye when she found out, I knew she was gonna kill me. And she said, "You can have anybody . . . why did you take the man I want?" And it was like, [shaky, nervous voice] "Yikes . . . !" It was *chilling*. She was dangerous. I mean, I said, "That's it. My life is over." I felt really badly, because I felt my friendship with Cass was over, and I thought, "What have I done?" I loved Denny, and I had a great time with Denny, but at the expense of losing Cass's friendship. I don't think I was quite aware of what this 'lust' was leading me into. But she forgave me . . .

Nurit Wilde: By the time I met John and Michelle, they had already had the little house on Flores Street, and they were all living there, the four of them, and I didn't have a place to crash, so I stayed there as well. It was where they had the picture taken for the first album, as I remember, in that bathroom. I stayed in that house on and off for a couple of months while they were making the first album. It was a great house. Everybody was really nice. John was definitely in charge, but Cass would always challenge him, whereas Michelle and Denny usually went along. Denny really followed John; Denny had the voice, and John had the creative talent. But Cass would always challenge John, but in a good way, she was a real talent. And Michelle was always beautiful, and she was John's young wife. I never thought she was terribly musical; Denny and Cass really dominated the voices, so it really didn't matter, but Michelle fit in, and so did John.

PART THREE

Bud Shank's adjustable pitch . . . John, 'The Taskmaster' . . . Where the Action is: the Sunset Strip and in Western Studios . . .

Lou Adler: They did backgrounds on "California Dreamin'," and after I doubled the voices the first time, I knew that this was too powerful to be Barry's record, that it deserved to be theirs. I had a conversation with Barry, and he said, "Go ahead . . . " John had altered the sound somewhat; if you've heard Barry's version, you can hear a little difference in what we did with The Mamas & The Papas.

Bones Howe: For "California Dreamin'," Lou said, "I don't wanna do just another guitar solo, or a sax solo. Let's do something different on this record." So, I ran down the hall and got Bud Shank, who was doing another session, and he threw on the alto flute. Remember, by this time, people like The Beatles were doing things like this on their records. *Rubber Soul* had come out, and their were other qualities that were becoming acceptable in pop music.

Bud Shank: I was doing a recording session—I have no idea for whom—at Western. I was just getting ready to leave, and Bones came up to me in the hallway and he asked of I could come in and try to put a solo on a Mamas & Papas record, and I said, "Sure." I think that Bones came up with the idea that the alto flute would be the proper instrument to put on there. What had happened was that when they had made the original backing track, they had apparently not lined it up with anything with firm pitch; it was only guitars, and it was in the cracks—really in the cracks. I listened to the song enough to learn it, then I pulled the head joint out of my also flute about an inch, and played it up a half a step, and somehow or another we lined it up, pitch-wise. It sounded kinda strange, and it really blew my mind, but that was because my fingers were going in spots where they normally wouldn't go. Now, what evolved out of that was that Lou and Bones were

Dunhill Records
(Employer's name)

Phonograph Recording Contract Blank 3499

AMERICAN FEDERATION OF MUSICIANS № 243810

Local Union No. 47   OF THE UNITED STATES AND CANADA

THIS CONTRACT for the personal services of musicians, made this 16 day of December 19 65

between the undersigned employer (hereinafter called the "employer") and 6 musicians

(hereinafter called "employee").

WITNESSETH, That the employer hires the employees severally on the terms and conditions below, and as further specified on reverse side. The leader represents that the employees already designated have agreed to be bound by said terms and conditions. Each employee yet to be chosen shall be so bound by said terms and conditions upon agreeing to accept his employment. Each employee may enforce this agreement. The employees severally agree to render collectively to the employer services as musicians in the orchestra under the leadership of Hal Blaine as follows:

Name and Address of Place of Engagement Western Recorders, 6000 Sunset Blvd, Los Angeles, Calif.

Date(s) and Hours of Employment Dec.16,65, Various Hours on personell, 8:30 P.M to 2:30 A.M.

Type of Engagement: Recording for phonograph records only. Plus pension contributions as specified on reverse side hereof.

WAGE AGREED UPON $ Union Scale
(Terms and amount)

This wage includes expenses agreed to be reimbursed by the employer in accordance with the attached schedule, or a schedule to be furnished the employer on or before the date of engagement.

To be paid Within 14 Days
(Specify when payments are to be made)

Upon request by the American Federation of Musicians of the United States and Canada (herein called the "Federation") or the local in whose jurisdiction the employees shall perform hereunder, the employer either shall make advance payment hereunder or shall post an appropriate bond.

Employer's name and authorized signature	DUNHILL RECORDS	Leader's name	HAL BLAINE	Local No.	47
Street address	321 So. Beverly Dr.	Leader's signature Street			
City	Beverly Hills, Calif.	State CR-14520	Phone		

Leader's address Hollywood, Calif.

(1) Label Name Dunhill Records   Session No.

Master No.	No. of Minutes	TITLES OF TUNES	Master No.	No. of Minutes	TITLES OF TUNES
	2:18	WE CAN WORK IT OUT		2:20	MONDAY MORNING
	2:15	MICHELLE		2:14	DO YOU WANNA DANCE

(2) Employee's name (As on Social Security Card) Last First Initial (Leader)	(3) Home Address (Give Street, City and State)	(4) Local Union No.	(5) Social Security Number	(6) Scale Wages	(7) Pension Contribution
Blaine, Hal	Hollywood, Calif.	47		447.40	35.79
Howe, Dayton B. 8:30 to 11:30 11 to 2:30 1-Dbl	Los Angeles 27, Calif.	47		61.00	4.88
Knechtel, Lawrence W. 8:30 to 2	Sherman Oaks, Calif.	47		128.65	10.29
Osborn, Joe 8:30 to 2 8:30 to 11:30	No. Hollywood, Calif.	47		203.37	16.27
Phillips, John 8:30 to 11:30 2:30	Hollywood 28, Calif.	161		61.00	4.88
Sloan, Phil	Los Angeles 48, Calif.	47		223.72	17.70
				61.00	4.88
NO ARRANGER OR COPYIST THIS SESSION*******************					

CONTRACT RECEIVED
JAN 20 1966
WARD ARCHER
ASST. TO PRESIDENT

90.01

(8) Total Pension Contributions (Sum of Column (7)) $ 76.99
Make check payable in this amount to "AFM & EPW Fund."

FOR FUND USE ONLY:

Date pay't rec'd JAN 20 Amt. paid _____ Date posted _____ By _____

Courtesy of Elliot Kendall.

Phonograph Recording Contract Blank

AMERICAN FEDERATION OF MUSICIANS
OF THE UNITED STATES AND CANADA

Nº 195932

Local Union No. 47

THIS CONTRACT for the personal services of musicians, made this 12th day of December 19 65 between the undersigned employer (hereinafter called the "employer") and _____ musicians (including the leader) (hereinafter called "employees").

WITNESSETH, That the employer hires the employees as musicians severally on the terms and conditions below, and as further specified on reverse side. The leader represents that the employees already designated have agreed to be bound by said terms and conditions. Each employee yet to be chosen shall be so bound by said terms and conditions upon agreeing to accept his employment. Each employee may enforce this agreement. The employees severally agree to render collectively to the employer services as musicians in the orchestra under the leadership of JACK SHULMAN as follows:

Name and Address of Place of Engagement UNITED RECORDS _____
SUNSET BOULEVARD Hollywood 28 California

Date(s) and Hours of Employment 4 PM TO 10 AM
12-17-65

Type of Engagement: Recording for phonograph records only.

WAGE AGREED UPON $ SCALE   SWEETENER (Terms and amount)   Plus pension contributions as specified on reverse side hereof.

This wage includes expenses agreed to be reimbursed by the employer in accordance with the attached schedule, or a schedule to be furnished the employer on or before the date of engagement.

To be paid WITHIN 7 DAYS (Specify when payments are to be made)

Upon request by the American Federation of Musicians of the United States and Canada (herein called the "Federation") or the local in whose jurisdiction the employees shall perform hereunder, the employer either shall make advance payment hereunder or shall post an appropriate bond.

Employer's name and DUNHILL RECORDS   Leader's name JACK SHULMAN   Local No. 47

authorized signature _____   Leader's signature _____

Street address 321 So BEVERLY DRIVE   Street address _____ No. Hollywood   Calif.

Beverly Hills Calif. _____ (City) (State) (Phone)   (City) (State)

(1) Label Name _____ Session No. _____

No. of Master No. Minutes	TITLES OF TUNES	No. of Master No. Minutes	TITLES OF TUNES
	"Michelle"		
	"Do You Wanna Dance"		

(2) Employee's Name (As on Social Security Card) Last First Initial (Leader)	(3) Home Address (Give Street, City and State)	(4) Local Union No.	(5) Social Security Number	(6) Scale Wages	(7) Pension Contribution
SHULMAN, JACK	No. Hollywood, Calif	47			
SHARP, Sidney		47			
SCHAEFFER, RALPH	Los Angeles, Calif	47			
BAKER, ISRAEL	No. Hollywood, Calif	47			
MALINSKY, LEONARD	Los Angeles, Calif	47			
KURASCH, WILLIAM	Los Angeles, Calif	47			
BELNICK, ARNOLD	Encino, Calif	47			
ZELIG, TIBOR	Canoga Park, Calif	47			
HYAMS, HARRY	No. Hollywood, Calif	47			
___, Norman W.	Los Angeles, Calif	47			
SAXON, JOSEPH	No. Hollywood, Calif	47			
EHRLICH, JESSE	Van Nuys, Calif	47			
PAGE, Eugene	Los Angeles, Calif	47			
De RIENZO, ALLEN	Sherman Oaks, Calif	47			

(8) Total Pension Contributions (Sum of Column (7)) $ _____
Make check payable in this amount to "AFM & EPW Fund."

FOR FUND USE ONLY:
Date pay't rec'd _____ Amt. paid _____ Date posted _____ By _____

Courtesy of Elliot Kendall.

involved with so many groups like that involving overdubs with adjustable pitch instruments, word got around town quick that you should always line the pitch up with something like a piano or a tuning fork that has a fixed pitch.

Lou Adler: It was two flute solos, actually. Bud Shank happened to be down the hall. On Barry's we did a harmonica, which we didn't want to do, but also when we found out that Bud Shank was down the hall, and we said, "Why not try it?" It was two different takes, and it jumps two different octaves, and it sounds like he jumps like an octave, but we really cut it together. I don't even know if he knows that we used two different takes!

The question of "Go Where You Wanna Go" being the first single . . . that must be the period of time when we were in between doing Barry McGuire's version of "California Dreamin'" and having finished "Go Where You Wanna Go." It's a gray area for me now, but we out put out "Go Where You Wanna Go," and I had it out maybe a week or so when we shipped it when we finished "California Dreamin'." I just though that it was a better first record. And we just stopped the presses on that, and released "California Dreamin'." It was not really 'test marketed' in Hawaii, which is what some people think, although we may have gotten out first responses from there. We didn't send it out to test it in order to put it out.

Hal Blaine: The first time they came in with Lou Adler, it was like their album cover (*If You Can Believe Your Eyes And Ears*). They were really far-out, the way they were dressed. Big, tall, skinny John, and little fat Cass. Denny looked like the only straight one, and Michelle looked like a little 16-year-old.

Phil Sloan: I was like 19 years old at the time, and Michelle was so incredibly wild, and so incredibly beautiful, that I was in awe of her. If I got a 'hello' from her, that was my day. If she smiled at me, that was enough to make all of my teenage fantasies come true!

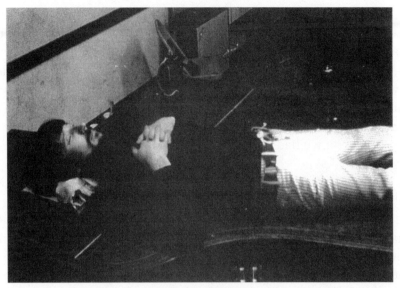

Western Studios, 1966.
Photo by Bones Howe.

Lou Adler: She didn't seem as hard, because Michelle always thought she was doing it right, so it wasn't a situation where she was arguing with you much. She didn't feel like she wasn't getting it; she always thought she was getting it. She wasn't coming so much from a musical place as the others, she was coming from a rock and roll 'street' way. She could have been a Ronette, yeah! I think she would've loved to be a Ronette or in the Shangri-La's— she was just a tough street kid.

Michelle Phillips: I was influenced by all of the girl groups, all of the Phil Spector stuff, the Wall of Sound. I grew up on Top-40 rock and roll, that's what I listened to. I think John was influenced by jazz, but I loved contemporary rock and roll music. I loved Elvis. "One Night With You" is my favorite Elvis record.

Lou Adler: I think Mitch always wanted to be a back-up singer. But she worked real hard, and John was a taskmaster with her.

Michelle Phillips: It was *such* hard work! John—the taskmaster. And nothing was ever good enough for John. John always wanted to do the next take. I would go, (tired voice) "It sounds *fine . . .*" He'd say, "No, it *doesn't.* You were flat." Whatever his problem with it was, it wasn't up to his standards. And that's why everything sounds so *great!* And that's because John made us work until he thought we got it. Of course, when we'd hear the play-back, we'd go, "My God, that sounds *great!*" Then he'd say, "*See!!* . . . I *told* you we had to do another take . . ."

John Stewart: John was just the captain of the ship. He just oozed charisma, and was definitely the leader. If he had come along at different times, he could have done Broadway, he could have been in the Brill Building with writers like Carole King and Neil Diamond, writing standards. He could write *anything,* and one of the most brilliant people I've ever met. And a musical ability that just doesn't come along very often . . .

Bones Howe: I think we know by now that there were two great soloists in that group, Cass and Denny, and I think that's what it was about. The interesting thing about having a group with voices is that *character* of the voices, the timbre of each individual voice added to the others giving you a sound that you can't dupli-cate. When Jill Gibson came in and sang with the group later, it didn't sound the same as it did with Mitchie. Now, you couldn't say that Mitchie was the best singer in the group, but her voice con-tributed something when it was added to Cass's. Those sounds together give you a sound that's unmistakable. If you leave one element out of it, it changes the sound of it, and it no longer sounds the way it does. The sound of The Mamas & The Papas is the result of those four individual voices, together. When the two guys were singing together, it was the sound of John and Denny. John's nasal sound, and Denny's beautiful, almost choirboy voice. And you had the same thing on the other side, with Cass's classic Colontro, I mean she could have been a singer in the 1930s! She had that wonderful, almost '30s-'40s style voice. Clear, and sang in tune, and had great control of her voice. And you had Mitchie, who had

Western Studios, 1966.
Photo by Bones Howe.

a fairly edgy voice, but you put those two voices together, and you had that sound, and that's what this is about. It was Cass and Denny as soloists, and also the group. You needed John and Michelle to make that sound.

Lou Adler: Denny could have been a big band singer in the '40s. He had that sort of wide-open, Western broadness to his voice. A very romantic singer. His intonation was just great. He'd get it every single time. Cass is also a throwback to the '20s and '30s; a very dramatic singer. She'd get a lot of drama out of a vocal. Michelle, she's a rock and roll baby. Her twists and turns some off of street corner type singing. Certainly not the strongest singer in the group, but definitely the heart and soul of rock and roll. John was more embarrassed of his lead singing; he didn't ever really want to sing a lead. He was a perfect quartet singer and vocal arranger—one of the best vocal arrangers, ever. I think he's right up there with the vocal arrangers for The Four Lads and The Four Freshmen.

So, you take the three leads, although most of the leads that Michelle did were duets with Cass. But John was able to use the instruments that Denny and Cass had, and narrow it down. They

Western Studios, 1966.
Photo by Bones Howe.

were very broad, and he'd narrow it down where it worked with a rock and roll rhythm section.

Steve Barri: In my opinion, and I think most people feel the same, Denny had this incredible voice, and Cass was the sound, her vocal sound was so strong. I loved her a lot. But I think that without question, Cass and Denny had the sound. John was a good singer, but I think what he was brilliant at was the songs and the arrangements. Michelle had a decent voice too, but Cass's voice was the edge of the sound.

P. F. Sloan: Cass's voice stood alone, but there was no one else's voice like Michelle's. Something about the timbre of her voice was exceptional. They didn't think so, and that's why they tried to remove her. It shows you how ignorant they were, and that was part of the Dunhill mentality. Anyone is replaceable. "She's a good looking chick, we'll get another good looking chick!" It was that *exactly*. I mean, you talk about major ignoramuses . . . *major* ignoramuses. That was the sham that they tried to put over on the American people; was that "What we have here is just another pretty face." Michelle's voice was like no other I'd ever heard, and it sends chills up your spine. The warmth of her being comes through. What the record companies didn't understand at the time—and still doesn't to the max—is that the voice is the mouth to the soul, just as the eyes are the window. All her experiences in life—pain, sadness, joy, shadows—all that comes out in her voice. To replace that with someone else is to replace history. It's not easily done, obviously.

When Denny put his voice to a song, it felt like what real aged cognac should sound like. It's the closest to a high that you could get. It just sounds real good, everything he did. It made you just completely relax.

John's voice, curiously enough to me, was the least flavorful of the group. But his mastery was to get the blend, he was responsible for the blend, and he was the one who made the vocalizations. He would tell Cass where to go up, and where Michelle would join in, and where he and Denny would harmonize. He was the master of these moving sounds that were going on: holding steady here, moving here, counterpoints. They were all in awe of his talent to do that.

John Phillips: We always rehearsed with one guitar, we never rehearsed with a band. I'd come up with a vocal arrangement, and if it didn't sound like a full record with just one guitar and four voices, it never would. That's the answer, it's gotta sound that way then. You can't expect the instruments to pick up the slack for you, and especially because none of us played, really, except for me. I just played rhythm guitar, so it's not a big instrumental thing you're looking for, it's the vocal thing. That's why we could sound as good in person as in the studio, because you had to.

Bones Howe: If you stood in front of them in the studio and listened to them sing, they sounded like a brass section. I mean, they sang *loud!* These were powerful voices. I can remember Denny, after they would sing these long passages, standing back and trying to catch his breath. They were actually seeing stars, from the oxygen depravation! And they were singin' loud. You can't always tell from listening to the records, but believe me, they were. And why? Because they had come from singing in folk clubs, where there was maybe one microphone in the whole place, and they had to blow out to the whole room.

Jerry Yester: I met John & Michelle after they had come to L.A., and the group had already been recording. In the fall of '65, the MFQ was playing The Action on Santa Monica Blvd. They came in and told us that they had gotten back from the Virgin Islands and everything, and they asked if they could get up and sing something, so we said, "Sure!" They got up and sang "California Dreamin'" and "Monday, Monday," and it was just a mind-blower. They were just using one acoustic guitar, and it was just incredible. This happened a few times at The Action, and then they came up at The Trip on Sunset and sang there, too. Those two places were the only two places I ever heard them sing and play live. It was part of the camaraderie of time, just like Crosby,

Western Studios, 1966.
Photo by Bones Howe.

McGuinn, and Gene Clark singing at the bar in the Troubadour before the Byrds started, it was part of this growing thing that was happening, and everybody was in it. We were all folkies coming into rock & roll, and it was like a brave new world, and there was a lot of unity, and that proved true after the change to rock and roll.

Denny Doherty: The Action on Santa Monica Blvd., yes. Just around the corner from Flores Street. Zappa and The Mothers were the house band, and Lee Michaels and his band were playing there, too. We got up there and sang, just the 12-string and the four voices, and did a set one night. First stage performance of The Mamas & The Papas, ever. The audience had just heard The Mothers, so they didn't know what to think. "Where the fuck did *these people* come from?" It was no big thing, 'cause the whole place was pretty loosey-goosey anyway, so we just got up and sang.

Jerry Yester: When I first heard them, I just thought it was incredible and really together. It was obviously not folk music, it was right in the pocket of folk/rock. I remember hearing them with just a guitar and realizing that any way you made that record it was gonna be a hit. You just needed to put a good band behind it and it would virtually make itself. The vocals were just really wonderful, and the MFQ were a vocal-based group, so we immediately noticed anything good vocally in a four part group. They didn't do a lot of really intricate things, but it was extremely tasty, and with voices like that it was just a mind-blower.

Mark Volman: When The Mugwumps thing ended and they came out West, they brought something with them that was very unique that hadn't really happened in Los Angeles. It was an intimate, 'sitting around with guitars and singing' attitude. That was something that happened with their record that gave you the feeling of intimacy. The kind of records that were made in L.A. before that were The Byrds, The Turtles, and The Leaves; little rock and roll bands that were the last vestiges of Beatlemania.

Jim Hendricks: After they got signed and were recording their first album and everything, we didn't see them around all that

A document/contract form is reproduced here. Its readable contents:

AMPLIFIER TRACKING INCLUDED   DUNHILL RECORDS
(Employer's name)

Phonograph Recording Contract Blank

AMERICAN FEDERATION OF MUSICIANS
OF THE UNITED STATES AND CANADA

2718
Nᵒ 195416

Local Union No. 47

THIS CONTRACT for the personal services of musicians, made this 7 day of October, 19 65 between the undersigned employer (hereinafter called the "employer") and 6 musicians (hereinafter called "employees").

WITNESSETH, That the employer hires the employees as musicians severally on the terms and conditions below, and as further specified on reverse side. The leader represents that the employees already designated have agreed to be bound by said terms and conditions. Each employee yet to be chosen shall be so bound by said terms and conditions upon agreeing to accept his employment. Each employee may enforce this agreement. The employees severally agree to render collectively to the employer services as musicians in the orchestra under the leadership of HAL BLAINE as follows:

Name and Address of Place of Engagement **Western Recorders, 6000 Sunset Blvd, Los Angeles, Calif.**

Date(s) and Hours of Employment **Oct. 7, 1965 10 A.M. to 2:30 P.M. (1 man 10 to 2)**

Type of Engagement: **Recording for phonograph records only.** Plus pension contributions as specified on reverse side hereof.

WAGE AGREED UPON $ **Union Scale** (Terms and amount)

This wage includes expenses agreed to be reimbursed by the employer in accordance with the attached schedule, or a schedule to be furnished the employer on or before the date of engagement.

To be paid **Within 14 Days** (Specify when payments are to be made)

Upon request by the American Federation of Musicians of the United States and Canada (herein called the "Federation") or the local in whose jurisdiction the employees shall perform hereunder, the employer either shall make advance payment hereunder or post an appropriate bond.

Employer's name and **Dunhill Records** — Leader's name **Hal Blaine** — Local No. **47**

authorized signature — Leader's signature

Street address **321 So. Beverly Dr.** — Street address

Beverly Hills, Calif. CR 45201 — **Hollywood 28, Calif.**
City   State   Phone   City   State

(1) Label Name **Dunhill Records**   Session No.

Master No.	No. of Minutes	TITLES OF TUNES	Master No.	No. of Minutes	TITLES OF TUNES
	2:20	SOMEBODY GROOVY			
	2:22	GO WHERE YOU WANNA GO			

(2) Employee's Name (As on Social Security Card) Last First Initial (Leader)	(3) Home Address (Give Street, City and State)	(4) Local Union No.	(5) Social Security Number	(6) Scale Wages	(7) Pension Contribution
Blaine, Hal	Hollywood 28, Calif.	47		325.40	26.03
Howe, Dayton B. 10 to 2, 1 Dbl.	Los Angeles 27, Calif.	47		162.70	13.02
Knechtel, Lawrence W.	Sherman Oaks, Calif.	47		157.61	12.61
Osborn, Joe	No. Hollywood, Calif.	116		162.70	13.02
Phillips, John	Hollywood, Calif.	161		162.70	13.02
Sloan, Phil	Los Angeles 48, Calif.	47		162.70	13.02

NO ARRANGER OR COPYIST THIS SESSION ********************************

CONTRACT RECEIVED

(8) Total Pension Contributions (Sum of Column (7)) $ 90.72
PAID Make check payable in this amount to "AFM & EPW Fund."

FOR FUND USE ONLY:
Date pay't rec'd _____ Amt. paid _____ Date posted _____ By _____

Form B-4 Rev. 4-59

Courtesy of Elliot Kendall.

much. When they had free time we hung out. They had this house that they all lived in and we used to go over and see 'em. After their first record came out, there's gonna be a certain amount change with something like that, but with Cass and Denny, our friendship didn't really change that much. Denny bought a house up in Laurel Canyon where I had an apartment which was pretty close by, and I'd go to visit him a lot.

Hal Blaine: One of the reasons that I remember them was because Lou Adler was starting to dress like them. Whatever act he was producing, he kinda dressed like. So all of the sudden Lou was wearing all the silly stuff, too. When Lou was married to Shelley Fabares, he was dressed pretty straight. And with the various different people like Rivers, etc., Lou was sort of taking on their characters.

P. F. Sloan: They were beyond Peter, Paul & Mary. The exuberance and joy that was coming from their voices was ecstatic. When you listened to them coming over the microphone, not so great. You had to hear them singing live to know there was something there.

Roger McGuinn: The Mamas & The Papas came a bit after The Byrds had "Mr. Tambourine Man," and I think it encouraged them a bit. I remember reading something that Michelle said funny like, "Well, if McGuinn can do it, anybody can do it!" I'm sure she meant it with love, though. In the scene of things, though, I was not on the high echelon of folk musician as they were, so it probably was a shock to them that The Byrds succeeded at all.

I loved their music when I heard it. I was friends with Terry Melcher, who was friends with Lou Adler, so we saw each other when we were in L.A. I'd go up to John and Michelle's house up in Laurel Canyon and hang out with them.

PART FOUR

"My god, that sounds great"...If you can believe your eyes and ears ... The Wrecking Crew and The Western echo chamber help create 'The Sound'...I saw her again last night, and you know that I shouldn't ... lookout, mountain ...

Lou Adler: Well, I think it's true of any artist during their first album, that they're recording material that they've already been working on ever since they decided they wanted to record. It's the best collection of John Phillips songs from beginning to end. Although they came up short; we ended up using "You Baby," which was a Sloan-Barri song, so they didn't have 12 songs, but the material that they had, the 10 or 11 songs that John had were all really solid. They had rehearsed quite a bit, although we did a lot of changes. Once John got used to the countermelody that I loved to do quite a lot, I would tend to ask for a counter after we'd laid down the basic tracks, I always said, "What if we try this counter?" Once he got used to that and also the process that was able to do that, he started expanding the vocal, and I'm sure that it affected the songwriting.

Bones Howe: The first album, I would say that Lou had pretty much hit his stride at that point. He had some hits with Johnny Rivers and Jan & Dean, but he hadn't connected with something really this big, and this was huge. The great thing about it was that he had a great sense about what was an album track, and what was a hit single. He had a good sense about vocals, and where background vocals worked and where they didn't. John was pretty much serving it up and saying, "Do you like this? Try this, do you like this, do you like that?" So, Lou was pretty much involved in every creative decision. It was very smooth, that first record, and it went very fast, because they were practicing every day. If they weren't in the studio, John was rehearsing with them. This was big for them, it was something that they wanted more than anything. By the way, the big bucks hadn't come in yet. They were living on their subsistence, and they were living to make this record, so they were practicing their parts. When they came into the studio, they were ready to sing. We didn't have to make lots and lots of takes to get things together, the background parts were worked out. If something didn't work, maybe Lou would make a suggestion, but for the most part, once the track was cut and the lead vocal was down, they went really fast.

Steve Barri: What Lou was able to do, was put them together with the right musicians, He just has this incredible sense of what works and what doesn't. When you were doing arrangements back then, the only way we could do it was to sketch out a chord sheet, and then the musicians would come in and you would run it down live, and try to get it to the point of having something goin'. Of course, the musicians were so amazingly talented, they lent so much to what was going on, that they made us all look good, on all the records we did, 'cause we used the same guys on all the records. Lou was one of the innovators of that kind of recording that was just beginning to be done out here. He just had this amazing sense of when a track is working, when the tempo is right, when the instruments are right. Incredible instinct. And with Bones, who was much more of a musician than the rest of us, we had to just do it on our gut feeling, he had it all. You would say to Bones if something didn't sound quite right, he might be able to figure it out musically. He might be able to relate that to the musicians.

Lou Adler: Western Studios had a great chamber. You can hear it on Brian Wilson's things, and you can hear it on the things I did with Johnny Rivers. That sound was huge. It was a tremendous chamber, but also the fact that we had to keep going down generations on their recordings because we had so many overdubs and counters, that we were creating notes that they were amazed to hear, because they weren't singing those notes, but the combination of the overdubs going down. Sometimes we'd go down to F; a lot of generations, and that was adding a lot to the appeal of it, more so than the sonic sound that we were going for.

Clark Burroughs: That studio was so wonderful. Everybody worked in Studio C; Brian Wilson worked in there, The Association, who I did vocal arrangements for, worked there, The Mamas & The Papas worked there, everybody. It was just an amazing studio. It was just so compact. The rhythm sections had a magical quality when they recorded there. It was such a small, tight wonderful sounding studio, and we just loved it. This early technology was so different from today. Back then, the technology was vocal friendly and string friendly. It didn't pick everything up, and that's what was good about it. Bones Howe used '77' microphones, The Hi-Lo's used '44' microphones—they're the same except that the '77' is mono-directional, and the '44' bi-directional, so that four singers could stand around one microphone, and get that sound. He did the same thing with The Mamas & The Papas, and that's kind of the trick. Bones was able to tweak the top end of the ribbon in order to get that crystal-clear quality, because the voices hit the ribbon at the same time, and the ribbon sort of changes shape. That's the secret of getting it on record, and Bones was absolutely masterful at that. I had worked with Bones earlier, when The Hi-Lo's were recording at Radio Recorders and then later at United-Western Recorders.

Mark Volman: Bones was an excellent sound guy. He had worked with all of those studio men who worked on their records—guys like Larry Knechtel and Hal Blaine and Joe Osborne. Those people played on the Beach Boys records, some Byrds records, and Paul Revere & the Raiders. Bones was really driven, and a great engineer, and really did a great job with them and Lou Adler.

Denny Doherty: Well, it was all new to us. Lou had The Wrecking Crew: Joe Osborne, Larry Knechtel, Hal Blaine. That was who he used, aside from any other players who happened to be in the building. Bud Shank came by and did the flute solo on "California." It was just whoever was in the building that night, Glen Campbell, whoever. It was a music factory. They'd do the tracks, then we'd do the background vocals, and then we'd work on whoever was going to do the leads. And it worked. We brought in what

Denny, John, Lou Adler, and Michelle,
Western Studios, 1966.
Photo by Bones Howe.

Bones Howe, Western Studios.
Courtesy of Bones Howe.

was already formed, a vocal quartet, to a situation where Lou heard both things. He heard us singing with a 12-string guitar, and married it with this other sound of the musicians and got the sound that he wanted to achieve. As soon as we heard the first playback, we said, "Ah fuck, yeah! I see . . . " Bones was his engineer, and who knew what was going on in the studio. I'd never seen tape that was that thick! Eight track machines, wow . . . Bones had two of these things hooked together, so we could get *sixteen* tracks.

Bones Howe: John had a lot to say about everything, being the writer of most of the songs. He was in the room when the tracks were being worked up, and John was very much a focal point, even with the vocals. He would be in the booth and maybe make suggestions to Denny or Cass out in the studio about how to phrase things or something. Everybody was listening to him at that point, on the first album. It wasn't always true with the second album. It was sort of everybody for themselves by that point. There was a very freewheeling mentality in those days. People would come into the studio when we recorded. Nowadays, there's kinda this 'lock-out' mentality. In those days, other artists would come around when you were recording. Everybody would sing and play on everybody's records, everybody would contribute to everybody's records, and everybody wanted everybody else to be successful. Lou took me over to a Byrds session, and I met Melcher for the first time. We were all contributing. I was cutting The Turtles, Lou was cutting The Mamas & The Papas, Terry was cutting The Byrds, and we were all part of the folk-rock thing that was happening, and we had all been part of the surf thing that had happened before. And it was exciting, and it was *bigger*, and that was exciting. The way the records were sounding was *big*. So there was a lot of camaraderie, it was a lot of fun, nobody took it really seriously. I often said in interviews back then, that when I was making these records, I thought I was making plastic toys for kids! I just didn't think that any of it had any real lasting value. I was just doin' it, and I was doin' it 'cause I thought it was fun, and I really loved the music.

Peter Pilafian: I came back when our baby was born and became a proud father. Russell had found a little house to rent, and a little car for me to buy for $125. It was pretty sweet, and we lived together for a couple of years. I didn't know much about L.A., so I began to work as a taxi driver, which quickly enabled me to learn all of the routs around L.A. Meanwhile, John and Michelle and The Mamas & The Papas had started to get underway, although we weren't that connected at the time right away. I remember them saying that they were recording and doing back-up vocals for Lou and things like that. I'd stop by and hang out, because that's what it was all about.

PART FIVE

Papa John & Uncle Lou deliver . . . You baby, Monday, Monday . . . Guy "I just got so blitzed" Webster snaps the 'indecent' bathtub shot . . . and then they just got more and more famous . . ."

Clark Burroughs: Lou and John were like brothers. They cared so much about each other, just fervently. Just . . . soul brothers. They worked very well together.

Lou Adler: It was one of those situations where it was like we had gone to separate schools together, and we had a lot of the same likes, sports-wise, we played a lot of basketball together and we just bonded very quickly. Denny became just a good friend through the years, but I never hung out with him as much as I did with John; although the three of us did for a while when they lived together on Woods Drive. Michelle, that just grew into something later on. Cass and I, that was a strange relationship, the most strange of the four, and not the closest of the four.

She was a pain in the ass, is what she was. She complained a lot. Once she got it, it was beautiful. John had to work really hard with Cass, because she had a mind of her own. She was extremely intelligent and quick-witted; they matched up really well. It wasn't easy. Cass wasn't easy. You know, she later recorded one album

Hollywood Bowl, August 1967.
Photo by Henry Diltz.

(*Deliver*) right up till the ninth month of her pregnancy, and practically crawled out of the studio and then had her baby. She was a very hard worker—it was just hard to get her to *work* hard. Once she did, it was just great. As time went on, as they became successful, and had more toys, and she had more other friends outside of the group, she was the first one to sort of distance herself from the group and what we were doing. But a beautiful voice and an amazing personality. She was great on stage, unbelievable as far as taking the spotlight on stage.

Joe Osborne: I first remember playing with Hal and those guys on demos for Steve Barri and P. F. Sloan. They were writing for Lou Adler and Trousdale Music. This must have been around '62 or so, and we were doing all their demos, and I think a lot of those things turned out to be the Turtles records. Bones was also involved with these demos. Not long after that, Larry started playing on some of those. We wound up working together a lot, starting around the Johnny Rivers records.

I knew Johnny from Louisiana, before we came out to L.A. We

had met when I was playing a joint out in Bosier City, and Johnny would come up from Baton Rouge and sit in with us, that's when I first met him. Johnny moved to L.A. about the same time that I did, and he was working at a club called Gazarries, this is before the Whiskey A-Go-Go. He didn't have a drummer, and he asked me to come and do a gig there with him. Not too long after that I got another call from him, and he said that he wanted me to play with him on a gig at The Whisky A-Go-Go. He said that we'd play there for a couple of weeks, just to get it goin', and we ended up staying there for two years! That's where the live album came out of that, and his first hit, "Memphis." Then it was after that, that Hal and Larry started to play on some of the things.

Larry Knechtel: I started out playing bass. I played bass in the Shindig house band in '63, as well as on a lot of other sessions, like the Byrds "Mr. Tambourine Man." By the time The Mamas & The Papas came along in '65, I was also playing piano on sessions. Generally, if Leon Russell wasn't available, they'd call me. When Leon quit to go play with Joe Cocker, I started playing even more keyboards.

Lou Adler: If you have to say, "What was the rhythm section?", it was John on rhythm guitar, and Joe Osborne on bass. He brought a lot of country to rock & roll. He'd be there at the beginning, and he'd be there at the end—no matter how long it took, he was just a very hard worker. Joe came from the rhythm section I used on Johnny Rivers records. And his playing clicked. He played with a pick. Very important. Hal was the anchor of that rhythm section, and also his enthusiasm was very catching, and a very important part of all the records that I did with him. At one point, I think he had six or seven number one songs in a row

I think if you listen to that first album, and you don't look at the names, it sounds like they're (M&P's) playing, which was very important. Even though it was basically the same musicians, the same studio, and the same engineer, you don't get that feeling on a lot of other pop/vocal groups of that period—it sounds like a vocal group that's singing. But The Mamas & The Papas sound like a rock and roll group.

Joe Osborne: I thought John played wonderfully. You can hear that big 12-string on the records, and that's John. He had a great right hand, and a great feel for the rhythm.

P. F. Sloan: His guitar playing was straight-forward and on the beat. He didn't play passionately, but he played hard, and he played direct. He fluffed up a lot, and later on, he refused to admit that he fluffed up, it was like everybody else who had fluffed up. But he was a good guitarist, and he progressed as a guitarist, especially in terms of playing the twelve-string. His grasp of chord changes became greater as he expanded musically.

With piano, John didn't really know what he wanted. He let Larry do all of his things. Larry would look at me, and I would give him cues, as to whether he was playing the right glissandos at the right moments or whatever. It soon fell into line that there would be a certain sound. Me and John would play acoustic guitars, and then I would switch to electric, and overdub electric. Sometimes Larry or Hal would overdub other instruments, but it was usually to get the electric guitar down on songs like "Straight Shooter" and "Monday, Monday."

On the records, when we went in to cut the tracks it was John on acoustic, they brought in Hal to play drums, there was Larry Knechtel on keyboards, and Joe Osborne on bass, all from the Johnny Rivers connection. I was playing acoustic guitar, because I was connected to Barry McGuire. John would play the song for everybody and we would write down the chord sheets, drum charts. Joe would get together with Hal and write out the bass lines. John was very involved in the bass parts, he definitely knew what he liked and what he didn't like.

He worked mostly with Joe, and he would say, "I want more of this . . . " etc. He made Joe stretch a bit, because with Joe playing on all the Johnny Rivers records, he had a groove, and his groove was absolutely predictable, and the sound of his bass was absolutely predictable. You can tell a Joe Osborne sound right away, and with Joe he was always hitting root notes. He had his grooves. Hal and him would groove; when the two of them played together, you just felt that there was something special going on.

But John worked very hard with Joe. He wanted specific lines, specific feels. He was rough with Joe, and Joe would say. "Who is this guy? Who does he think he is!?"

Joe Osborne: John would dictate parts. I didn't read music at all at the time, and Larry, I think, was just starting to. A lot of times we wouldn't even have a chord sheet, we would just learn the song from scratch. John would just come in and play the song. Sometimes we would just play what we played, and sometimes John would know exactly what he wanted. Sometimes he would sit for a half an hour, 45 minutes, and dictate a bass line. It was pretty well mapped out, and that was mostly John. Lou, I always considered one of the greatest producers, because he knew when to leave you alone. A lot of producers don't think that they're doin' there job if they're not telling everyone what to do. That wasn't Lou's style. John wrote the songs, and he knew what he wanted to do, and Lou sometimes would just leave and come back and say, "Are you guys ready?" Lou had ideas, too.

P. F. Sloan: Joe got the idea instantly that this was not going to be an easy three-hour date; "This is a date where I've gotta be present." See, most of these session musicians were doing five to eight sessions a day, and all of the producers wanted the best out of them, and most of the time, they were asleep. The magic of that time was, unless you had some way to reach these musicians, they were going to give you standard, and they're going to be out the door to the next one. It's not like they're playing jazz. They're playing pop/rock, and they don't always give they're all to everyone.

And it's not the money. You could give them more; it might open their eyes a bit. But in reality, there was a spiritual and personal relationship. They either liked you or they didn't. If they liked you and respected what you were doing, they'd go with you and go for it. There were some producers in those days that they'd really play for: Snuff Garrett, Brian Wilson, and Lou and John.

Larry Knechtel: We did the songs for a long time, so we got to know 'em! We'd do a three-hour session, and maybe get one song. The rock and roll acts did it that way. The regular pop acts, you'd get three or songs in the same period, but that was all arranged, with the rock stuff we were doing head charts.

Jim Hendricks: I did go to a few sessions; it was always pretty stoned-out stuff. It seemed like Lou was running the ship, recording-wise, especially when they were cutting tracks, he was very much in charge. When they got into the vocals he would defer to John a lot on that. I think that Lou's contribution was mainly the tracks, and John had to do with the vocal arrangements. I know the guys who did the tracks—Blaine, Osborne, Knechtel—and I had worked with them, and they had a lot to do with the way those records came out. Those guys had played with Johnny Rivers, who I later signed with. So, that group was really in place before The Mamas & The Papas came along.

P. F. Sloan: "Monday, Monday" was a magical session, a very easy session. As soon as Hal came up with the drum riff, which I had suggested to him from a Grass Roots record that I had made, as soon as that groove came in, it was magic. I overdubbed an electric guitar with tremolo that I had borrowed from Johnny Rivers.

Denny Doherty: "Monday, Monday": Well, it was just another song, I don't recall getting all head-up about it. I liked the opening background vocals, the 'bah-da-da-da-da-dum', I thought that was cool. But nobody likes Monday, so I thought it was just a song about the working man. I thought, "Okay, next! What's the next song?" Nothing about it stood out to me; it was a dumb fuckin' song about a day of the week! Not that I didn't like it to the point that I didn't want to record it, I just didn't hear it as a *hit single* . . . and by the time the rehearsals were over for the vocals, I thought, "Thank *god* that's over!" 'Another ninety-eight fuckin' hours with The New Journeyman!', to quote Duffy!

P. F. Sloan: I'll tell ya the payment I got, and that was them recording "You Baby" for their first album. That was the tip of the hat, because there's no reason, other then the track was already cut, and it was cheap to record. It was a demo, basically that Steve and I did. All they really had to do was put their voices on. The Turtles version was obviously faster, and done for the AM market, whereas this version was just an album track. So, that's how I got paid.

Steve Barri: I was at a lot of the sessions, but the only thing that I played on was some percussion on the song that Phil Sloan and I wrote, "You, Baby," which was basically a demo of a song that Bones wound up cutting with The Turtles. We had cut that as a demo for The Vogues, as a follow up to "Five O'Clock World," so it was a little bit different than The Turtles version. The Mamas & The Papas version of that was the demo that Phil and I cut, with the addition of John doing some overdubs. It was with Osborne, Blaine, Knechtel, those guys anyway, so it was homogenous to the sound of the record. Their vocal sound was so different from anybody else's, I thought it was the best version of all. They were a couple of songs short for the album, so we kind of lucked out, basically.

P. F. Sloan: "I Call Your Name" was kind of a throwaway cut, because those riffs that Larry plays on the piano, those bawdy, sort of ragtime-barbershop riffs, were definitely not pop. I played the electric guitar on that, sort of a wah-wah guitar before there was wah-wah, by turning the volume up and down in between strums. It gets kind of nerve-wracking, but it's fun.

Mark Volman: John was a really good songwriter who really hit his peak with one album. I mean, he wasn't like John Sebastian who wrote and wrote and was a working-class songwriter. John Phillips hit his stride one album. If you listen to that first album *If You Can Believe Your Eyes and Ears*, it was John's *one* contribution. If you go to the next album, those songs were not as great. There were sporadic moments of good songwriting, but John Phillips's contribution to the landscape of musical history was on that one album, those twelve songs.

John Phillips: I can't write unless I write about things that have actually happened to me. I'm not very good at 'situation songs', you know, "let's write a song about this, or let's write a song about that . . . " They were all so musically good, Denny, Cass, and Michelle, they always knew exactly what we were doing. When I wrote a song, and said, "Here's the new song . . ," they all felt like they had written it, too. Like, everyone doing an author's material. No one can do an author's material as well as himself. But you have four people that all felt like they had written the song, because the songs were about us, and our lives, and they recognized everything in the songs as being personal. So they sang it as they lived it.

Cass Elliot: You can be a great singer from here to hell and back, but unless you have the material, you're just standin' there. John is a great, great songwriter.

Lou Adler: Well, I had always been a song man from the very beginning. I started out as a songwriter, working at Aldon Music, a publishing house. To me, the most important thing was the song; so not only was the vocal sound so incredible, but the material they were singing was also great.

Steve Barri: Obviously, I thought John was a brilliant songwriter. As a songwriter, in those days, we were kind of taught to listen to other people's records, and whatever was happening at the time; it was a matter of copying other people's songs, and then writing something different enough, but yet sounded enough like a follow-up to a hit. We were very much into that. "Eve Of Destruction" was written because Dylan was happening, the protest thing was happening. When surf things were happening, we (Sloan & Barri) were The Fantastic Baggys, we wrote surf songs. That's what you did as songwriters. With John's stuff, when they sang it, there was *no one* else who could do this! It was so fresh, and so different, that was what was terrific about it. Sometimes you heard something that was so fresh, and so different, and so innovative, that you know that the talent is there, and you gotta take a shot. If I was a music publisher at that time, I wouldn't have known where to take those songs. They were totally fresh. It was so different, and so based in harmonies and everything, the way he John structured it, and of course with Cass's voice in there . . . it was unlike anything else.

Larry Knechtel: I thought the songs were good. Sometimes John would have us do things that were a little out of the ordinary, which is okay. But I thought in the early stages especially, the songs were excellent.

P. F. Sloan: You know, I had this lady friend of mine who had been friends with Bryan MacLean of Love and Jim Morrison of The Doors, and she used to always rant about John Phillips. She said that she always got the feeling that John's songs were contrived. Whenever he came across a heartfelt line, where it would take you into someplace, he never went there. And I think that it was his instinct for writing hit songs at the time; that he wasn't investigating his emotions, which he started to do later. As a songwriter, he was good. There was a lot of contrivance in his lyric. I think that later on, he became aware that a lot of it was contrived, for his own inner soul. But who am I to say, really? He was a very good songwriter. There are songs of his that give you chills, and you don't know why. Things like "Go Where You Wanna Go" take you places. I think that he was a spokesman for the bohemian lifestyle of freedom. He was an excellent craftsman, and a dedicated artist and musician. Truly dedicated.

David Crosby: I loved it. I don't think that it got recorded as well as it could have. There are some places in there where there are some obvious mistakes that they should have corrected. On "Monday, Monday," when the strings come back in the second time, it's just so out of tune, I couldn't believe it that they didn't get it. And a good producer would have spotted it and fixed it. But I think that they're vocal stuff was fantastic, and I think that's largely due to Cass. Cass was *the* singer in that group. Denny sang great, too, and John didn't sing bad and Michelle didn't sing bad . . . but Cass was so far out of their league that it wasn't fair. She had an unbelievable instrument.

I think John's real strength was in writing and arranging, and I think that he did a great job with that. I think that he thought up arrangements that were very clever. But to me I think that the strength of it was Cass's chops as a singer. She was just fuckin' incredible!

Bones Howe: The only thing that I ever differed with Lou about, was that I thought 'The Magic Circle' was a better name than The Mamas & The Papas. Sometime right after they signed, that name, The Magic Circle, came up, and I thought, "What a great name, and what a perfect description."

Guy Webster: Lou and I were friends back in the Dunhill days, and one day we were playing basketball, and he said, "You take pictures, right?" I said, "Yeah . . . " I gone to the Art Center, which is part of the L.A. School Of Design. He told me that he was going to start this record company, Dunhill Records, and that he wanted to see my photographs. I showed him my portfolio from school, which, I have to say, was a pretty knock-out portfolio. I had no idea about being a commercial photographer. I was an artist, and doing artwork, I had photographed some celebrities. Mostly actors, people like Jack Nicholson, whom I'd been friends with. So, Lou sees this portfolio, and asked me if I'd like to do the artwork for Dunhill. He said that he had just signed the first guy, Barry McGuire. The name didn't mean anything to me, but then he mentioned that Barry had been in The New Christy Minstrels, that sort of thing, and it rang a bell. I had already been in the music business; my dad was a songwriter and I was a publisher. P. F. Sloan wrote that song, "Eve of Destruction," and the label just took off with their first release, and that was also my first major album cover. I had done a couple of other album covers in the past, but for friends . . .

Lou calls me one day, and says, "Hey, you've got to come down here. We've got this new group, and they're coming down to sing for me a capella." So I went down and walked into the office, and there they were, The Mamas & The Papas. A very interesting looking group of people, but really no different than other hippies I'd seen in Venice or Hollywood. They stared to sing, and Lou and I just looked at each other. They could sing "California Dreamin'," "Monday, Monday", and of those songs a capella, and blow you away in an office. Lou knew he had something immediately, and I did, too.

He sort of sent me off to 'live' with them for like a day or two at this house on Flores Street where they were living. Now, I was never a dope or pot smoker; I had tried it, but it was never something that I cared much about. I was a family man. So I get there, and I grab my camera and my tripod, and we sit down, and they light a joint in the middle of the room and close the windows and doors. We got *so* blitzed. It was the highest I'd ever been in a long time . . . or ever. And we shot that cover in that bathroom in that house.

Denny Doherty: We were actually sort of hiding from him. You could hear him all over the house; "Come on you guys, we gotta get some pictures!!" We were sittin' in the bathtub, just as you see the photograph on the album cover. We were hiding from him, fuckin' with him. We were all loaded out of our minds, and we'd been up all night. "Who was this guy? Pictures? Oh, the record company sent him over . . . " We took some pictures in the back yard, and while he was loading film or whatever, we all ran back in the house and sneaked up into the bathroom and closed the door. We were all giggling, and then he opens the door, and says, "Oh, great!" and started shooting.

Guy Webster: I didn't know—I was very naive at the time— about rock and roll covers. At the time, most of them previously were pretty clean-cut stuff. There was never a mixed group of guys and girls. If I put guys into position somewhere, I didn't realize that with a mixed group it would be as intimate and as sexually provocative as it was . . . but I was high, and I was having a good

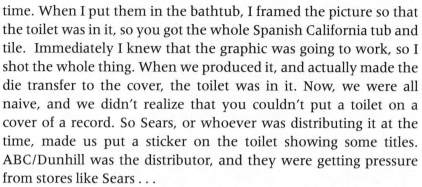

time. When I put them in the bathtub, I framed the picture so that the toilet was in it, so you got the whole Spanish California tub and tile. Immediately I knew that the graphic was going to work, so I shot the whole thing. When we produced it, and actually made the die transfer to the cover, the toilet was in it. Now, we were all naive, and we didn't realize that you couldn't put a toilet on a cover of a record. So Sears, or whoever was distributing it at the time, made us put a sticker on the toilet showing some titles. ABC/Dunhill was the distributor, and they were getting pressure from stores like Sears . . .

We started to have some fun, and then they kind of accepted me as a photographer, because I was a stranger amongst them. They were a closely-knit group of four people who lived together and lived on their own. Then here I am, a stranger in their midst . . . I remember saying to them, "Hey, this is really fun being together shooting these pictures . . . ," because the next day we went out and shot some black & white stuff in locations in the canyons and stuff and I said, "This'll probably be the last time we ever get together like this where you'll *want* to shoot the cover . . . " and they said, "What are you talking about? That's ridiculous!" and I told them that it's just the nature of the business that little petty things come in and out of relationships in groups that are together, and after a while, they don't even want to see you. I had photographed The Stones, and Brian Jones, who was a friend of mine, was kind of on the outs with the group, and nobody wanted to pose together. I'm telling this to The Mamas & The Papas, and they're like, "Yeah, right . . . " Well, the next session, it was almost impossible to get the four of 'em together. That's how *fast* the insidiousness of the business started to splinter the group; and they were a very cohesive group when they got together. But later, there was a lot of jealousy and anger, and some were making more than others, and Lou and John had the publishing, and that's where all the big money's going . . . anyway, I understood that.

Eric "The Doctor" Hord and Michelle, Hollywood Bowl, August 1967.
Photo by Henry Diltz.

Mark Volman: Lou Adler realized that there was a lot that could be done when groups like The Turtles hit with songs like "You Baby," and The Lovin' Spoonful, too, with "Do You Believe In Magic" and "Daydream." Bones and Lou were really smart guys, and a lot different than most of the rest of us who were just musicians. They were the kind of guys who would say, "Okay, here are these groups like The Byrds and The Turtles—what else can we do to make money on this?" Lou and Bones had kinda come around at the same time as the Phil Spector stuff—a combination of the sort—of '50s and '60s stuff. They saw a working ability to take a singer-songwriter like John, and turn him into a commodity where they'd say, "Well, we know they don't really play live, and we don't really care about that—we think we can make really great records with them." And they did, and they spun off all of these hit records that forced the band to start getting into the "Music Business," and to tour, and they weren't a band in that sense. They were a great act. You had this vision of this beautiful girl, you have this great guy singer who can really sing; you have this other tall, lanky guitarist who is a songwriter and is married to the beautiful

Courtesy of the Richard B. Campbell Collection.

girl, so you sort of have the two of them together. The guy with the voice, Denny Doherty, and Cass, who had this belting, Ethel Merman-kind of thing happening. Visually, it was incredible. And put them together with these great Hollywood musicians, and Lou Adler's capability by bringing Bones in. With all of that in mind, it was probably destined not to have longevity.

Eric Hord: I didn't have any idea of the run they or we were going to make. I thought, "Okay, you've got a couple of hit songs, we'll make a run for maybe a year." Actually, it didn't last much longer than that, did it?

Russell Gilliam: They were really scuffling before they got signed to Dunhill. I remember when I my son was 10 days old—he was born on November 27th, 1965—and listening to the radio and hearing "California Dreamin'" for the first time. I listened to the radio all of the time, and that was the first time I'd heard it. I thought it was *great*. But at the same time, I was so into my child. Peter had moved back with me. And then they just got more and more famous.

Chapter Four

Go Where You Wanna Go

PART ONE

"You wanna new car, kid? Go down and pick it up…"Woods
Drive & the 'fuck pit'…madness at Melodyland…"Happy birthday;
you're fired…"

Courtesy of the Stuart Rosenberg/Richie Furay Collection.

Bones Howe: We finished the first album and it came out, and
then we started the second round of recording. But by then everything was different. They'd had all this success in between—they'd
met The Beatles, all this stuff had happened. Major concerts, etc.
And they'd made a *ton* of money.

Denny Doherty: We didn't need cash. We had credit cards, or we would call over to the office and it was sent over or we would go down and pick it up. "You wanna new car? Go down and pick it up." Money didn't come to us directly as individuals, it went to our accountants. We got about $500 cash a week, and every credit card you could want. If you wanted clothes, they'd ask you which store you wanted it from, and you'd sign for it. You wanted cowboy boots, you'd go down to Rodeo Drive and come back with twelve cowboy boots and a fuckin' pair of chaps! "Just sign for it . . . " So, we never really saw any cash. The cash was being handled by our accountant, Jay Lasker's brother-in-law. Oh, please! I don't know how badly we got fucked, or when it started, but I know we got fucked . . . I just don't know who to point a finger at . . .

Bones Howe: When the money started coming in they got into this thing among them, where they would have a contest every week to see who could spend the most money on a single item. I remember one week Cass won because she had bought a Mulberry Aston Martin. Then they called Andrew Oldham in London, and they worked out this deal where they were going to buy Mini Coopers for everybody. They asked me to give my '62 Alfa Romeo Sprint Veloche to Eric Hord, and they gave me a brand-new Alfa.

Michelle Phillips: Bones was an *incredible* engineer. I think as we finished the second album, I'm not sure . . . as we were finishing one of the projects, we called an Alfa Romeo dealer just as they were closing that night. They said, "Well, just come down tomorrow." We said, "No, no, *no*, you've gotta bring it down *tonight!* We want it parked outside tonight, we wanna give him the keys . . . " It was so cool.

Lou Adler: Bones brought a real good ear to it; he brought musicianship, because he was a drummer. He was someone who never wanted to do rock & roll; when I first met Bones in the Sam Cooke days, they said, "Yeah, but he'll never do any rock and roll . . . " There were a lot of those engineers, most of them in the Shelly Mann school of, "Rock and roll is bad, and it's never gonna happen, and it's bad music." He brought an educated ear to it, he was real good for me as far as filling in holes where I came up short.

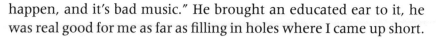

Michelle Phillips: John and I moved to Lookout Mountain in Laurel Canyon. I didn't like being treated by everybody concerned—certainly Cass—with heavy doses of disdain and contempt. John was treating me like a child that needed to be reprimanded. I don't remember how John was treating Denny; I think that he was treating Denny just *fine*. I do remember having a big fight with John, and him saying, "You can do a lot of things to me, Michelle, but you *don't fuck my tenor!!*" And, of course, when John and Denny wrote "I Saw Her Again," I was understandably upset that John was punishing Denny in a very sadistic and morbid way, by making him write and sing this song. I said, "How could you do this?, and John said, "Because I believe in turning tragedy into publishing."

Denny Doherty: So, John and I moved into this house together on Woods Drive. And the reason was that his wife and I had had a tryst, and we decided that she didn't want to live with him, and she wasn't gonna live with me. So, until things sort of found their own level, John and I were going to move in together. [serious, commanding voice], "That would be the best thing to do . . . sort of keep an eye on each other . . . " Oh, it was very strange, very strange indeed, because there would be other women around, and then we'd have rehearsal and Michelle and Cass would show up. But in the meantime, Michelle was out running around with other guys, which was slowly making John completely insane. He can't have her, and he wants her, and I can't have her, and I want her . . . and Cass is in the middle just pining away, just pissed off at everyone, and not getting what *she* wants. "Hey, the ride is on, we got a hit record, we're doin' TV, we're stars . . . you wanna go *home*?" It's very easy; we either keep doing this, or we stop . . .

Eric Hord: I got into town, moved into the pool house on Woods Drive, got some clothes, and got two new guitars. We rehearsed the tunes at 1441 Woods Drive, which is where John, Denny and I lived. John and Michelle were separated, and I was fuckin' all of the chicks that they didn't want to; the 'hangover' chicks! They had a big, sunken pit in the living room, and that was the 'fuck pit'. It was one of the best-laid out pads I'd ever seen in the Hollywood Hills. Everything was there at that house, anything you'd want—be it liquor, food, dope. There was so much liquor there, it was fuckin' unbelievable. Grass, acid, speed, everything. And if it wasn't around, John could just make a phone call and have it sent over. You know, when you hadn't lived like that for a long time—or ever —for that matter, it was real nice.

Henry Diltz: Later on, while we were still in The M.F.Q., and we filmed one of these TV shows, "Where The Action Is", down in San Diego, and The Mamas & The Papas were on the bill with us. We all knew then pretty well, especially my partner, Cyrus Faryar knew John and Michelle, and I knew Cass very well. Cyrus lived on Lookout Mountain, and I lived further down Lookout Mountain, on the Hollywood side of the hill. Michelle lived closer to the top. I just remember seeing her around a little bit.

Michelle Phillips: Well, the four of us had all been living together, and I asked John to move out, because I didn't want to live with John anymore . . . I wanted to branch out, and he was kinda . . . cramping my style. So he moved out into a house with Denny. They got a beautiful house up on Woods Drive, you know, with a sunken pit fireplace, and the pool at 105 degrees with floating gardenias. I always had this image of Martha and The Vandellas swimming in their pool with the floating gardenias, because they told me that they had a party there and that they showed up, and I was like, "Really?" . . . they didn't invite me to *their* parties! I was living on Lookout Mountain and Gene Clark was living down the hill near Cass on Stanley Hills. I had actually known Gene before, and we started hanging out with Cyrus Faryar of The

Modern Folk Quartet, and his wife Rusty . . . Henry Diltz. So we were all kinda hangin' in the canyon.

So Gene and I started seeing each other, but we were keeping it *very* quiet. Believe me, I did not want to enrage John again. Things were just settling down from the affair with Denny. So, I was seeing Gene, and John did not know. And then Gene said that he had never seen us in concert, and he knew that we were going to be playing Melodyland in Anaheim, so I told him that I'd get him some tickets through the office. But I never realized that he would be sitting *right* up front, and he was wearing a *red* shirt! And Melodyland was a theater in the round, so Cass and I went *immediately* in front of Gene, because we didn't want John to see him, so we just took that side of the stage. But, we got just a little complacent, because [lilting voice] we're singing songs to Gene . . . we're groovin' with Gene, ya know. All of the sudden, we hear this voice over the P.A. : "Get the FUCK over here!!"

So Cass and I went over to the other side of the stage and John and Denny went over to where we were, and I thought, "Oh, god, this is trouble." But we continued singing and we continued the concert, but in the pit of my stomach I was terrified. Even though John had not caught us, he 'caught' us, in the same way he had caught me with Denny. He didn't catch me in any kind if compromising situation. It was *thick* with guilt. He chased me right out into the parking lot, I was headed for my car. It was my birthday, June 4th, 1966. He came running out as I was getting into my car, and he said, "You're *fired!*" I said, "I really don't think that you have the authority to do that, John." He said, "Oh, really? Happy Birthday. Good-bye." As I drove out of there I was thinking, "Now why would he say something like that? '"You're fired!'—What does he mean by that?!" Then I found out a few days later what he meant by that, because then *the letter* arrived. He had given Denny and Cass an ultimatum, "Either you go with her or stay with me, because I'm not working with her anymore." And I understood them signing it the letter, especially Cass. This was where she could say, "Okay, you hurt me; now watch. I'm going to do something to you now that's very painful . . . " But you have a right to get back . . .

Denny Doherty: This is when John couldn't have Michelle anymore, and I had come to grips with that early on, when we, so to speak, 'split up.' She went back with John, and I'm supposed to just carry on and remove the sword from my side. So, that wasn't going to work, because Michelle and John couldn't keep it together. This was business, and we thought we could handle business. But the one straw that broke the camel's back was at the Melodyland Theater in Anaheim. Gene Clark showed up, and John said, "Fuck this, I can't handle it anymore; either she goes or I go . . . "

He just said that he couldn't create anymore, he couldn't arrange . . . the group is breaking up, with Michelle in the group . . . "The only way the group stays together is if she's exorcised from my life. I can't handle it. If you guys want her in the group, the you gotta replace me, okay?" So, it was easier to replace her . . . *we thought.* And the record company's goin' for it, management's goin' for it, and we're saying that the only way it's gonna work is if she goes . . . *somebody's* goin' . . . and it's gonna be Michelle, 'cause, "After all, it's *all her fault!*" And Lou's going, "I don't care who the fuck goes, we gotta fill in the fuckin' spot!!"

Lou Adler: I knew something was up when Michelle punched Denny at a session. I was little aware, but not as much aware as I became when I became as much of a friend as I was a producer, as years went on. There were tensions that were always there with John and Michelle. You could tell that they were talking more than just about music.

Bones Howe: I wasn't privy as to the reasons, I was just told, "She's not coming, and John and Michelle have broken up . . . " or whatever. Believe me, with everything that was going on, nothing was a suprise!

Nurit Wilde: Michelle came down to see me at the house I had with Steve Sanders while I was having the affair with John. She knew about this, absolutely. But Michelle was kind of an 'out there' kind of person; it may have bothered here, but I don't think it bothered her that much, because she was having her own affairs,

June 28, 1966

Mrs. Michelle Gilliam Phillips
8671 Lookout Mountain Avenue
Los Angeles, California 90046

Dear Michelle:

This letter is to advise you that the undersigned no longer desire to record or perform with you
in the future. Moreover, the undersigned desire to
terminate any business relationship with you that may
have heretofore existed.

To the extent there may have been any agreement
between us creating a partnership, the undersigned elect
to terminate and dissolve any such partnership pursuant
to California Corporation Code Section 15031(1)(b).

This letter should not be construed as an
admission that any such partnership exists. Nothing
contained in this letter should be construed as a
waiver, abandonment or relinquishment of any right or
remedy which the undersigned, and each of them, may
have against you. All such rights and remedies are
expressly reserved.

Very truly yours,

John Phillips

Dennis Doherty

Cass Elliot

Courtesy of Michelle Phillips.

ya know? I, all of the sudden, fell madly in love with John, out of
the blue, really, because we had been friends. We talked about all
sorts of things, we used to hang out without any mention of anything between us other than friendship, and he was the one who
initiated it. I don't know . . . when he all of the sudden said something to me, I saw him in a different light, and fell madly in love
with him. At which point, I became an absolute and complete

dishrag! I went from somebody that he fell in love with, to becoming someone that he could almost wipe his feet on. It just didn't work out. John was very controlling, and very smart. We used to have these great conversations about all sorts of things not related to the music business.

I must say, that when I hung out with him, he was not a big druggie, and I was surprised years later when he got so into it, because that didn't seem to be his focus. His whole focus seemed to be music-inclined, and power in the music business. The one thing I did not care for with John was his neglect of MacKenzie and her brother, Jeff. I think that Jeff had a hearing problem or something, and John didn't seem to want him around.

He was writing all of the time. I don't remember specific songs, but I do remember that he always had a guitar and he was always coming up with stuff. I think Scott Mackenzie came back somewhere around this time, because I met Scott through John. Scott was totally inamorate of John, he just thought John was 'it'. Whatever John said, Scott did. John was just . . . his master.

Anne Marshall: Lou Adler, a longtime friend of mine, introduced me to Denny, and he was the first one I met. I think it might have been at the Whisky or The Trip. We became instant friends, and through him, I met Cass, and of course, I liked her immediately. Then I met John through hanging out with Denny. John and Denny were living together at the time, up on Woods Drive. This was the period when Michelle and John were split up, and Jill Gibson—another old friend of mine—was starting with the group. Now, the first time I saw Michelle was at this Melodyland show, in Anaheim, and I was with John that night; I was dating him. I don't know why, exactly, it was an odd time in my life.

Peter Pilafian: I do remember when that cycle happened. I saw the drama and I saw all of that stuff going on. I don't recall being involved in it—I don't recall having a particular opinion about it, except that I thought that it was a little silly, to fire Michelle.

Cyrus Faryar: I was good friends with Gene. I remember that John and Michelle each had Jaguars, and going for a ride with Gene and Michelle in her Jag somewhere down Sunset. I also remember trading Gene one of my guitars for one of his. I think I traded him my Rickenbacker 12-string for his Fender 12-string, which I wish I still had! Gene was a very wonderful man, and rather reserved. I think that he was rather bemused by his relationship with Michelle, and her agreeability to let him squire her around. He seemed sort of taken off guard. It was as if it were a stroke of good luck that he wasn't going to question deeply or make much of. I think that he was delighted in her company and pleased to be there, but subconsciously had no expectations of its endurance. He was a very gentlemanly fellow, very reserved, and warm and friendly. And Michelle was young and vivacious, and quite volatile. There was in Michelle a quite worldly quality. She looked very slim and sweet and kind of innocent, but she wasn't, really. She was quite sophisticated and worldly. She had grown up in Mexico, and had had a childhood upbringing that was not conventional. Both her and her sister, Russell, were both cut from a different cloth. Rather bohemian. Her demeanor was not an artifice, it's just that she looked like an innocent young woman, and she was seething underneath. She had genuinely arrived at that demeanor, and there was just more to her then what you thought.

PART TWO

"Mama" Jill Gibson . . . Michelle's 'much deserved vacation" . . . No salt on her tail . . .

Jill Gibson: I found out Michelle was fired from the group at the same time I was asked to be in the group, so my reaction was focused on this request, rather on Michelle's predicament. I don't think I had seen her more than a few times, if at all, before this took place. I was excited at the opportunity to sing the songs John had written because I thought they were great songs and I loved the harmony.

Hal Blaine: Jill was Jan Berry's girlfriend, and she wanted to be a photographer; she used to take pictures. Jan had that horrendous accident, where his skull was ripped open, and to this day he's still quite paralyzed, like a stroke victim. Anyway, all of a sudden, she started goin' with Lou. It pissed us off, all of us. It was Lou's business, and yet we were sort of family. They all used to come to my home, we had parties and dinners, you know. Anyway, we were pissed. Then all of the sudden, Jill is in the band. I was especially hurt, because I was going to the hospital every week to see Jan, who was in a coma. Anyway, all this pissed me off, because Jan was crazy about Jill. Now, it's not up to me to play God and say, "Jan is a vegetable, and you have no right to run off with Lou Adler." But, she was a very pretty girl, and she became a replacement for Michelle. It didn't last very long. She wasn't really a singer. She looked nice, but . . .

Denny Doherty: She was completely out of her element, and she didn't know what the fuck she was doin' there. She was Lou's girlfriend, and she was filling a slot, like an acting gig. She was good for the part, and you don't have to skip a step—business as usual . . . take out one, insert the other, and here we go!

Jill Gibson: Lou, John, Denny, Cass, and I went to London for three weeks specifically to rehearse for the album they were going to be recording, and for the five or six upcoming shows that had been scheduled. John's music was easy to learn. I already knew some songs from the radio, so it was easy to learn everything in three weeks.

Denny Doherty: We were working on the second album, and I believe we took some of those acetates with us. We went over to George Harrison's place, and we played some stuff for him and McCartney . . . we just hung out for a while. We were going to play the Royal Albert Hall, but we weren't strong enough for that, so we just hung out. It was an uneventful time in England. It was cool meeting The Beatles. Lou set it up through the record companies, 'cause we didn't know where the fuck where we were going. I just remember getting in a limo and we were going to Harrison's place, somewhere out in the country, and there were Ferrari's in the driveway. We played him some of our stuff, he played some of their stuff, and we sat around smokin' and drinkin' until four in the morning. We did the pub-crawl, driving around in a black limo with black windows, smoking a big spliff. It was a promo trip.

Lou Adler: The politics of that had a lot more to do than with what was on the surface. Whatever John was going through . . . John's a very self-destructive guy, and he doesn't like to go down alone. He is and was a very dynamic purveyor of his ideas, where all of the sudden you think they were your ideas. He was almost magical in the way that he would do those things. He did it with Cass, even though she was very strong-willed, he did that with Denny, he was able to do that with people that were around him. Politically, whatever emotional thing that he had going with Michelle, he was able to translate into a musical, group political situation, where the other two would go along with it. I don't think that their feelings were ever as strong about it as John's were. He was so destructive, that he was willing to take a group on that second album, where they are and the success that they attained, and what they can do, and replace an important member of it, and say, "Let's get somebody else to do it . . . ." He was self-destructive, destructive, and yet so confident that musically that he could take anyone in that position and take that chance.

Jill happened to be there, he had never heard her sing. She was a very beautiful thin, tall, blonde girl. She had done some singing, but she wasn't a singer. He didn't take a girl like a Ronnie Spector or Spanky McFarlane, who were singers—it wasn't that kind of a situation. She was a girl that I was going with that looked right. We recorded Jill on six songs . . . maybe "Trip, Stumble and Fall," that sort of comes to mind. It was real hard work—she may have done some singing, but to step into The Mamas & The Papas . . . he got six vocal performances out of her, which we later replaced, some of 'em. She actually performed with them, a couple of shows. Texas, I believe.

Sandy Granger: The concert was originally scheduled for June 18th. When it was postponed until July 1st it was explained that

Live with Jill Gibson, summer 1966.
Courtesy of Sandy Granger.

John Phillips was ill. I remember that the wait for June 18th was unbearable, and when it was moved to the first . . . that was awful.

Finally the big night came and we went to Dallas Memorial Auditorium. We were *so* excited. There were about six opening acts, Brian Hyland singing "Batman" comes to mind. It took forever for The Mamas & The Papas to finally get on stage. They all came running out to the opening guitar riffs of "Straight Shooter." It was magic. First John, then Denny, then Michelle—we thought—and finally Cass. From the stage, Jill could not look more like Michelle if they were twins. Jill's hair was flipped at the ends when Michelle's would never be, but how would I know that then? After "Straight Shooter" John got busy with all the introductions. He introduced Denny to wild applause . . . then he introduced their newest member of the group, "Mama Jill." There was an audible gasp from the crowd and a few shouts of "Where's Michelle?" It was obvious she was missed. We felt cheated. John explained that Michelle was taking a "much deserved vacation" down in Mexico. That was it. The show went on. Their next song was "I Saw Her Again." John said it was so new that they barely knew the words, and that the song would be on their second album, "If You Can Believe Your Nose and Throat." Their entire set was about 40 minutes. I guess that's all they had had time to prepare Jill for. Off the stage as quick as they came, and all calls for an encore fell on deaf ears. The night was over.

Jill Gibson: I would have been more comfortable on stage if John hadn't pushed me to get stoned before going on. In spite of it, I did feel comfortable singing with the group. I felt comfortable singing, period.

I don't remember there being an announcement I was replacing Michelle. Maybe it happened, maybe I was behind stage not hearing it, or maybe it didn't happen. I remember only one time at Forest Hills, New York, where a guy in the audience yelled out, "Where's Michelle?" I think that upset John. I remember the shows going smoothly, as though people accepted me, or perhaps they didn't even realize I wasn't Michelle.

Bones Howe: I knew Jill when she was Jan's girlfriend, because I was making all of those Jan & Dean records, so I already knew Jill Gibson. Later, after the accident, Lou dated her some. I don't know if she was her girlfriend or not, but she did come to the studio a few times with Louie. She was one of the sort of the 'in-crowd' that was around, and I think that Jan at one time tried to cut some tracks, or try to make a record with her, and I vaguely remember her being in the studio before.

Whatever happened between John and Mitchie, I only got the other side of things. I'd be in the studio, and I'd say, "Where's Michelle?" and he'd say, "She not coming." Another thing is that Lou was under a lot of pressure to get the album finished because the first one was such a big hit. So there was pressure to just get the thing finished, and think the idea was just to have a voice so that we had four voices, so Jill was starting to come in. I think it was a matter of convenience, really. But as I said before, you change one voice, and the whole group changes.

I just remember that Jill came in, and John was appropriately tough on her like he was tough on everyone. In some ways, Jill had a lot of trouble blending in with Cass, because Michelle, I think had sung so much with Cass that she understood how to let Cass be the up front voice, and she just blended in with her. This was big pressure on Jill, too, and I think that she came in and tried to find a way to be part of the group in a different way.

I'm sure that there was a lot of working around the sound, you know, giving Cass more things to do, like overdubbing on herself.

Jill Gibson: Except for two songs on the album, "The Mamas & The Papas," I sang the entire second album. That would be 10 of the 12 songs. I didn't sing "Dancing in the Street."

Michelle Phillips: I had done vocals on several of the songs prior to my getting fired, and then they went in and re-recorded her . . . so I think that's very possible. There's no way to know who sang on what, because we both sang on all the parts, and it was up to Bones and Lou and John what was on the final mix. And they had a lot to choose from! When you listen to the second album . . . listen to it . . . because I swear I don't have any idea who's singing on it. There are times when I don't know if I'm singing on it, or if Cass is, and we had very different, distinctive voices. I would love to know what they are, and I'm not disputing any of it. I would take anybody's' word, because I really don't know . . . .

P. F. Sloan: When the fiasco happened with Michelle, and they brought in Jill Gibson, they called me and they wanted me to add some additional guitars, I wouldn't do it. I didn't want to be a part of it. Jill Gibson, as you know, was Jan Berry's girlfriend. Jan was exquisitely in love with her. The fact that she dumped him—and this is before his accident—destroyed him. I had nothing to do with the group while she was involved with it. I saw her a couple of times and she said hello, but she seemed like one major-league depressed lady, and the group had no spirit to it at all. Denny was

Cass Elliot and Jill Gibson, Western Studios, summer 1966.
Courtesy of the Michael Ochs Archives.

endlessly drunk. Denny was literally the most fun of the entire group. Being Canadian, he was gifted with the idea of being a humanitarian and compassionate to everyone. I don't know why Canadians are that way! They're blessed with warmth and lack of ego.

Lou Adler: Then we shot the album cover with Jill. We had already shot the cover with Michelle; we had shot that in the middle desert on the way coming home from some job. Guy Webster took her out and shot Jill and dropped her in.

Guy Webster: There was a concert that they were doing in New Mexico or Arizona. We were coming back, driving along early in the morning. I needed some shots, because concert shots are so boring, and I didn't want to do a cover with concert shots. We stopped the bus, and we shot the four of them in the window of this abandoned house. But, the break-up happened between Michelle and John, with Michelle being expunged, temporarily. My friend, Jill Gibson, became the 'New Mama'. I went out and shot one of my best covers; it was outdoors, Cass had a fan. But, they pulled it. But before we shot this other cover, they wanted to have Jill stripped in. I set it up in my garage, not in my studio, to get the proper outdoor light. I photographed Jill and stripped her in. Then, so you wouldn't see the re-touching, I put a little screen over the whole thing to give it an old-world look and to take away any rough edges, and that worked. But then we pulled that, because Michelle went back in the group. . . .

Hal Blaine: It was very nice when Michelle came back, absolutely. But it seemed to all be downhill from then on.

Lou Adler: At some point John just hurt so badly . . . I'm sure that it had more to do with their personal relationship than the group relationship. She probably came back to John and asked, and he was ready . . . that was a group that was made of chemistry. No matter how good Jill might have sounded, the chemistry was gone. The Mamas & The Papas were four unique people—not that Jill isn't unique, but the chemistry wasn't there. Plus Jill wanted out. She knew that she was in a situation that wasn't right.

Denny Doherty: As soon as we tried it without her, we all said, "Nah . . . it's not going to work without her . . . " It was just being dragged along and we were hooked on keeping it going.

Jill Gibson: I don't remember the moment when I found out, or any reaction. Michelle was constantly in the wings though, ranting and raving, struggling to reinstate herself. So, it wasn't surprising when she did. I had mixed feelings. Overall, I felt disappointed, very betrayed by John, and relieved to be out of the chaos.

Michelle Phillips: I have never tried to minimize her participation in the group, because I always felt that she did a great job, and there were times when she could hit notes that I couldn't hit. She was, in fact, a very good singer, and she enjoyed doing it. I didn't know her that well, and I didn't think that there was any kind of great betrayal on her part, because, why wouldn't she take that opportunity?

Ann Marshall: As I said, he and Michelle were split up, but it wasn't for very long—maybe a couple of months—and then they got back together. When they got back together, I guess that he had mentioned me, and he thought her and I would really like each other. Well, we became best friends the minute we met—instant best friends. When Michelle and I met, I think it was also at The Whisky A-Go-Go.

The was no fall-out from the fact that John and I had dated, because I never called him again after they got back together, and I think that Michelle admired that. I mean, I never really did dig married men, and I never made a practice of dating them. So, when they got back together, that was fine.

PART THREE

The 'sophomore album syndrome'…Rodgers and Hart and 'Why are ya burnin' that punk?'…Manzarek meets The Mamas & The Papas and Uncle Lou…

Bones Howe: We started the second album, and Lou would book the studio from four in the afternoon to four in the morning. I'd show up there in the afternoon, and sometimes the group would be there, and sometimes they wouldn't. It was very different from the first album. There was no discipline. Sometimes John and Michelle would show up, maybe Cass would drift in and Denny wouldn't show, or Denny would be there and Cass wouldn't, stuff like that. Of course, John would show up for the tracking sessions, but the vocal sessions were very loose. Sometimes I'd sit there from four in the afternoon to eight at night and nothing would be happening. Sometimes Lou would sit there with me and we'd just send out for food. Sometimes no one would show up and we'd leave.

It was the beginning of that sort of 'Rock and Roll Mentality,' and there was a lot of criticisms. John would criticize Cass and try to tell her how to sing. It was noticeably different. John would overrule Lou sometimes when he had an idea. As everybody knows, after a very successful first album, a second album is hard to do, and the pressure is very great. They had had two huge hit singles and the first album was a monster. That first album was really a benchmark, because before that, nobody had done a successful first album that was that big. It sold like a single. But I think that it turned out to be what was to become a syndrome for rock and roll, it became known as the 'sophomore album syndrome.'

It seemed to me that there was a lot of creating that was going on in the studio, whereas on the first album, they were coming in to the studio ready to sing the songs. They were all living separately by this time, too. When they were making their first album, they were all living in the same place, it was like a commune, and they would sing every day together, it was like a ritual. For sure they weren't together like before, because they weren't broke anymore! So, they weren't gettin' together to rehearse, they weren't gettin' together to write. When they would come in to lay the tracks down, there would be complications about the keys, all these kinds of things that happen when you're distracted. They were being interviewed all the time; bands would come into town. I seem to remember that Lou was friends with Andrew Loog Oldham, and I think he came into the studio with Mick and Keith. Then people would come in and videotape, there was always something going on.

In the studio there was always a lot of discussion about everything. It wasn't this smooth thing where everybody came into the studio rehearsed and ready to sing.

For me, the second album was never what the first album was. The first album was so much fun to make. The second album . . . it wasn't like pulling teeth, but . . . I've been in recording situations where people were actually yelling and screaming at each other. This was not that way, but there was a lot of contention. Denny would bring a bottle of Crown Royal in a blue velvet bag into the

Western Studios, 1966.
Photo by Bones Howe.

studio every night, and put the whole bottle away. In those days there wasn't any blow, but there was a lot of dope smoking and everything else. I mean, you don't know what you don't see. Remember that I only saw them when they got there and while they were there, and then they left, so I only saw what went on in the studio. There are other people who are better equipped to tell you whatever else went on. I do remember the Crown Royal, though. There was a shelf along the bottom of the glass that separated the control room and the studio, and Denny used to line the bottles up along the glass, so I have a visual memory of that. I remember people used to carry stuff around in the blue velvet bags, and we used a couple of them as microphone covers.

I don't remember going in and doing the album straight through. I just remember that we were doing these sessions, and they were interrupted and all kind of things were happening. It was a long, drawn-out process, I remember that, it took a long time and there was a lot of not showing up and things like that.

I don't specifically remember if we were on four- or eight-track by that time or not. If it sounds different, it may have been that between the first album and the second, I was starting to produce things, and maybe my ears were changing.

P. F. Sloan: "I Saw Her Again" was very Beatle-influenced. John felt that by this time he was in very real competition with The Beatles. He was very much influenced by The Beatles, and he was getting compliments from The Beatles. He felt that musically, this was the direction that the group should go in. I played electric guitar on the session, and it was an easy date. There was a mistake that was left in the record.

Lou Adler: On "I Saw Her Again," that's a mistake, by the way, Denny coming back in. I just left it in the mix. It was just a mistake, but when we were mixing, it felt nice to leave it in.

Joe Osborne: Is that the one that sounded like a splice? Yeah, that's some of Bones Howe's editing. He was great with a razor blade. I think he loved it, too . . . he never did like to get a whole take!

Larry Knechtel: That's probably true! He couldn't wait to get out the scissors . . . .

Hal Blaine: I remember a mistake on the ending of "I Saw Her Again." I'm not sure if that's me playing that cymbal on that part of the song. It could have been an overdub or from another take . . . ask Bones . . .

Bones Howe: We were laying down the vocals against the track and we got to that break, and they came in at the wrong place, and they all came in together, and then the track came in and they stopped and started again together. I remember punching in at the spot where the rhythm section came in, right on the downbeat. Then the voices that had led up to that point were still there. So we played it back, and I played it from before that, and of course it went, "I saw her . . . I saw her again . . . " And I said, "Well, don't worry about that Lou, I'll clean it up." and he said, "No, no, no. Don't touch it, I love it! Make sure that we don't lose that, I want to use that . . . "

P. F. Sloan: It was an easy session. Strings were added later, and I was at that date as well. It was a good arrangement, and I think that aside from some of the early Ricky Nelson stuff, I think it was the best thing that Jimmy Haskell ever did.

They were going for a top-10 hit to keep the momentum going. They were going for a hit record, not for creativity. "California Dreamin'" was a great first hit record, because it broke the mold of what a hit record should be. "Monday, Monday," as a follow-up, also broke a lot of ground. "I Saw Her Again" was in the mold. Lou Adler was an 'in the mold' kind of producer. It was not a number one record, it was a top-15 record, and that's what they were going for. As we find out, it happens to be a relevant story to their personal lives. The vocals were great, and they had a lot of fun with it. Lou put them in a double-reverb, as a Beatles thing, with the 'dut-dut-dut' harmonies on the bridge. It sends chills up my spine, every time I hear it.

Lou Adler: I think that we were trying to do what The Beatles did, by releasing singles before an album. Usually the first couple of things we cut going into an album were pointing towards a single. I just overloaded it with production; it's got everything on it that I could possibly think of, and just kept building and building. It's probably way over-produced. I don't think they thought it was the best record. When I listen to everything, it's not the best mix. It could have been another kind of a record, closer to rhythm section, more vocal record, but with the strings. To me it's not the best record.

Bones Howe: The one thing that I learned from Lou was that he trusted his gut. I learned to trust my gut from working with Lou. Some things that weren't technically perfect, lots of times would hit him in a certain way. It was like a suprise and he liked it, and those were the kinds of things that I learned. He didn't know anything about music, really, but he had a sense about what records should sound like, and he had a great sense of songs, and the ingredients that make up a record. And it was all completely subjective! A totally untrained ear. It came from listening to lot of records, and loving music. I remember during the recording of the second album, there was so much attention because the group was such a big hit, that this woman came in to interview Lou, and she asked him, "What will you do if this second record isn't a hit?" and Lou said, "Keep cutting." I'll never forget that. That's what this business is all about. That's what went wrong with Phil Spector, he didn't keep cutting. "River Deep-Mountain High" wasn't a hit, and he went nuts! He should have gone back into the studio and tried it again. It's like baseball. If you step up to the plate and you get on base 33⅓ times, you go to the Hall of Fame! Why does every record that you cut have to be a hit? That's the way I always looked at it. The pressure is huge on you, because that's what the record companies do to you. They don't hire you to make great sounding records, they want you to make hits, and it doesn't matter how great it sounds. It's sort of the unspoken direction that you go in."

The way we cut the records was great for me, because I came out of the jazz world, where *everything* is improvised. So it was fine with me that there weren't anything but chord charts. I always thought, "The looser the better," as long as you had great musicians. Certainly the philosophy that everybody had, was that if you had a really good idea, and you had a really good sense about what the song was and how you wanted it to sound, that would be the *worst* that it could be. But if you left all this room for the musicians to create, and for things to happen in the studio, it would always be better than that.

I remember that during the making of that album, that Lou a lot of times felt very isolated. John would come into the booth and talk directly to me right over Lou. Just things about the sound or whatever, he'd talk right over Lou. I remember one day, Lou just backed his chair up and sat back with his lampshade hat over his eyes, and just left John alone. And I liked Lou, he was my companion, we were a working team, and that really hurt me. I asked Lou, "Well, what do ya think?" and just kind of waved his hand in the air and said, "Well, just keep John happy." So we're into the second album syndrome where they're superstars, and they're starting to take over everything.

The big battles were always about who was gonna sing the lead, and what the lead was gonna be like, and all of that kinda stuff. And once that was done, the background vocals were like pulling teeth, because it was more or less mechanical, and like, "Okay, let's do this, let's change that . . . " Then we'd move on and overdub it and go to the next part, and it became like kitchen drudgery, getting the background vocals.

Joe Osborne: We would do the rhythm tracks before the vocals. They weren't considered demos. When we went in to record a new song, we knew that would be the record.

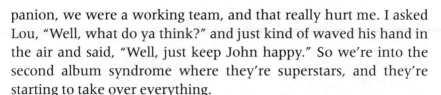

Denny Doherty: We did a Rodgers and Hart television special with Count Basie and The Supremes and Petula Clark. The idea was that we were going to record the instrumental tracks at Western, take them with us, and then sing the vocals live on the show. So we ended up using those tracks—I think there are two or three of them—and put them on the second album.

Michelle Phillips: We never had enough material, and that was a problem. We were *always* scammin'! We took a track from one of the Rodgers and Hart songs . . . I think it was one of the Rodgers and Hart songs that we did on a Rodgers and Hart special. We took the track to that and wrote "No Salt On Her Tail." I don't know whose idea that was, probably John's. He said, "Get that track out!" So he just wrote the song in the studio.

Lou Adler: That's a Rodgers and Hart song. We did a TV show, a Rodgers and Hart special, and this was a track that I believe was cut for that, and John just wrote another lyric. It was kind of an

Western Studios, 1966.
Photo by Bones Howe.

aborted attempt, and it doesn't flow quite as easily as some of his other things. It wasn't a pleasant thing, that Rodgers and Hart show. The Supremes were on there, and they didn't like the idea that they were burning incense or whatever. "Punk" she called it . . . "Why are ya burnin' that punk?!"

Bones Howe: There had been a television special, a Rogers and Hart special. They had recorded a track in the studio, and then they sang to the playback on the broadcast. John had this idea to make a song to the track. He sat down with me with the lead sheet, and we went through it bar by bar, and he told me what he needed, and then he gave me the lead sheet the way he wanted it, and sort of left me with it. I just cut a copy of the track, and then he wrote the song "No Salt On Her Tail" to fit that. It seemed to me that he already had a sense of what the song was, and had figured how to do this using the chords from the song. I remember him saying, "Is there any way we can go from here to there . . ?," those kinds of things. We just took it apart and put it back together, it was like a tinker toy. I had a lot of experience cutting jazz, and bar cutting and things like that, and it's very easy on a multi-track tape to decide where you're gonna splice things.

Ray Manzarek: It was at a session after The Doors played at The Whiskey A-Go-Go . . . it started at like, 1 A.M. or something. Somebody had heard me playing organ at The Whiskey, and told Lou Adler that there was this good organ player at The Whiskey, and he invited me to come down to play on one of their songs. There was John and Lou, and a group of musicians—they were just laying down the basic track—there may have been a guide vocal or something. The interesting thing was that I asked them, "What do you want me to do?" and they said, "Well, just go ahead and play and just improvise, and play around on it," or whatnot. So I did. I was improvising with some jazzy stuff and whatnot, and I thought I was doing extremely well. Then they said, "You'd better play it straight . . . " So the session when on for a couple of hours, and I tried to play some jazzy improvisations on it—which is what they had actually asked for . . . " Just do what you do." So, okay, what I do is sort of jazzy and bluesy improvisations. But after a couple of takes the voice from the studio says, "You know what? You'd better just play it straight . . . " I was very disappointed, and I thought, "Okay . . . we'll just play it *straight* . . . "

At the end of the session I came out and shook hands with John, and he said "Thanks a lot." and Lou Adler said. "Well, how much do you want?" This was a 1 A.M. session that went till like, 3–3:30, at least two hours, and I said, "Well, hell, just give me whatever you think is fair." And he pulled out a twenty-dollar bill. . . . Man, I thought, "My god." I didn't say a word. He said, "Is that okay?" And I looked at him and said, "Yeah, *that's okay.*" Then he said, "Ya know what? Here's another twenty!" I said, "Okay . . . " That was a little more like it; but he tried to get away for twenty!

Lou Adler: I have no recollection of that . . . boy, I doubt it. I have no memory of that. He remembers a lot of things about me, like that I had turned down The Doors, I just don't remember . . .

Clark Burroughs: I ran into John when they were recording with Bones and Lou; I think they were doing "No Salt On Her Tail"—it was midway into their fame. And I just thought, "This is great, this is making folk music hip." You really need a great writer in order to capture what's happening in the day, and that's what John did. He was just an amazing writer, and I'm still amazed at his stuff.

Michelle Phillips: "My Heart Stood Still" is amazing . . . I love that. "Sing For Your Supper" is one of my favorites, but I love "My Heart Stood Still." There is such an *energy* to that. It just builds and builds, and it's only about a minute! It's mind-bogglingly great; it's just beautiful, and is my favorite Mamas & Papas recording. The horn arrangement is gorgeous, and I believe it was done by Gene Page, who was *the* horn guy, and he did a fabulous job. He did strings, horns, everything.

Lou Adler: That would have also been for the Rodgers and Hart special. We recorded two or three things, and we had the rights to use 'em.

Denny Doherty: "Once Was a Time I Thought" was a song we had that worked up before the first album. That one was fun to do, so we worked that one up as an arrangement on the second album . . .

Michelle Phillips: "Once Was a Time I Thought" . . . oh yeah, *that's* a cool little song! We used to listen to Lambert, Hendricks, and Ross all the time. That's where the idea of the song came from. John, Denny and I used to sing a Lambert, Hendricks and Ross song . . . (sings) "My analyst told me, that I was right outta my head. But I said, 'Dear Doctor' . . . " Yeah, "Twisted"!! I was *such* a fan. I was a big, *big* fan. I remember going to London in about '69. The group was already over. I went to this big restaurant on the King's Road where everybody used to hang out, and I was introduced to Annie Ross, and I was just standing there with my mouth hanging open, and she was standing there, and she said to me, "I am *such* a big fan of yours." And I'm like, "No, excuse me, Miss Ross . . . " I didn't know what was happening . . .

Lou Adler: Yeah, "Once Was a Time"; a *great* song. I believe that was one of the songs that they played for me the first time they auditioned. I think it might've been. That comes out of that jazz-folk world that John comes from, and he probably never thought he'd ever record those on a rock and roll album. I love that song, and I love the recording of it. It's one of my favorites. The two songs that fall into that category are that and "Dancing Bear," both of which, if you played and sang them for somebody and said that you were going to put them on a rock and roll record, they'd think you were crazy. But I love both of those two songs, and that's pure John Phillips, those two songs.

Graham Nash: The first thing that I heard, of course, was "California Dreamin'" in England, and I thought it was a fabulous record. Being in The Hollies, I obviously loved melodies and harmonies and stuff. Then, later on, I came to America with The Hollies, and we were having a party thrown for us here in Los Angeles by our record company, Imperial Records. We were standing around schmoozing, and this kid came up and started asking us stuff. He was a complete Hollies fan, and his name was Rodney Bingenheimer. At that point he was this 14-, 15-year-old Hollies fan. The rest of The Hollies thought he was a nudge, you know? He came up to us at the end of the party and said, "What are you doing later?" They all kind of made some excuses and left, and I said, "I don't know, what have you got in mind?" He said, "Well, I've got these friends of mine, and they're making a record at Western Recorders, called The Mamas & The Papas." Having just heard the record, and seen the cover and seen Michelle's picture, I was *very* interested in going down there. So, I go down with this kid, wondering if he does actually know 'em, and whether he can get us in.

Western Studios, 1966.
Photo by Bones Howe.

So, we got there and got in, and we watched 'em record a song for their second album. My memory is that they were recording "Dancing Bear." I got to talking with Cass, and the first thing that she asked me aside from, "Oh, you're part of the British invasion, etc." was, "Do you know John Lennon?" And I told her, yeah, I knew them before they were The Beatles, and we had done a show with them in 1959, when they were Johnny and The Moondogs. And she said to me, "What do you think John would think of our music?" I told her, "Knowing John the way I do, he'll probably just put you down." And she burst out crying. Little did I realize that Cass has a great crush on John Lennon, and this is the *last* thing that she wanted to hear. I explained to her that John always did that at first, and he did that in an effort to keep you away until he was comfortable to let you in a little further. He would be facetious, and he would be pointed, and he would put you down. And I thought, "Holy shit, I meet this woman for the first time, and all of a sudden she's crying." Anyway, we got around that, and it was fine and we became great friends.

The next day, I think The Hollies were staying at the Knickerbocker Hotel on Hollywood Boulevard, and Cass said that she was going to come by at noon to pick me up. When I asked her where we were going, she said, "Oh, it's a suprise." So, she picks me up in a convertible Porsche, and we drive up Laurel Canyon and we stop in this garage at this house, which also has a convertible Porsche. We go upstairs, and lying on the settee is Crosby, wearing a blue and white striped T-shirt, jeans, and no shoes. On his chest is a box lid where he is, without much effort and without much concentration, rolling some of the finest joints I'd ever seen. They were almost packageable by Camel, those joints. So, she introduced me to Crosby. I obviously knew who he was, 'cause I had heard "Mr. Tambourine Man," of course. He didn't know who I was, and Cass didn't tell him who I was. But we were talking music and stuff, and he was most upset later when he found out that I was the high harmony voice in The Hollies. So, that small decision that I made in going with Rodney Bingenheimer, changed my life in a very drastic way, because had I not, who knows whether or not I would have met David or Stephen, or whether Crosby, Stills & Nash would have existed, or whether I would have met my wife Susan and had all my kids? No small decision. She started it. She knew

Cass Elliot and Graham Nash, Café Figaro, New York City, 1966.
Photo by Henry Diltz.

that David and Stephen were making music together, and she knew that David had been thrown out of The Byrds and the Springfields were breaking up, and I think she knew what we would sound like before we'd even met.

I met the rest of the band, and they were all very friendly. John was a little suspicious. I think he was having a little trouble with Michelle, who had an eye for the gentlemen. So, he was a little suspicious of me. I thought they were very adventurous, harmony-wise, and quite unique. I think that John was way up there with the quality of his music and his vocal arrangements and harmony structure. I wasn't sure that Michelle was a strong a singer as everyone else.

When The Hollies came to America on tour, Cass came with us for several dates and traveled with us on the bus. We got to Chicago, and we had a habit of going to the local radio station, and trying promote the show, etc. Cass had scored some acid from a friend of hers, at Mother Blues on Wells Street. She said, "Hey, take this." So I said, "Fine." About 40 minutes later when everything was happening, I got a call from our road manager, Ron Shields, and he says, "Okay, are you ready to go to the radio station and talk to the teenyboppers?" So I spent my first acid trip talking to 14-, 15-year-old Hollies fans on the telephone at the radio station! Quite interesting.

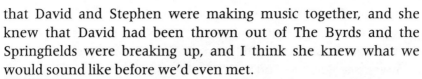

Bones Howe: Because they weren't living together, the only time that they were really singing together, aside from rehearsals at home, was in the studio, so there was a lot of emotional stuff flying around during the making of this album.

Denny was fairly loose. He came in to sing, and he had that wonderful voice. All he had to do was get out there and sing. I never had any problems getting leads from him. He was a natural, and had a beautiful, beautiful voice. The thing about Denny was that he had to get opened up, and once he got opened up, you had to get it fast. You had a window of time, because he was drinking. When he was clear, boy! You know, everybody was sleeping 'till two in the afternoon anyway. One thing that I learned about voices, is that laughing and talking were the toughest things on voices, so you wanted people to sing as early from the time that they get up as possible.

Now Cass, I think, could sing anytime. It just seemed to me like Cass walked out there and opened her mouth. It was just so natural with her.

The second album got down to the point where it was routine, and maybe that's why people wouldn't show up or whatever. "Cut the track, get the lead vocal on, get the background vocals... NEXT!" It came down to that sort of thing. Towards the end it wasn't that much fun, it was routine. We were turning a crank.

P. F. Sloan: But the second album was tight, in the can, creative, and they were breaking new ground. Adler was scared at some of the new ground that John was breaking. See, the one thing that you can count on with a hit producer, is that you're going to make hit records. The one problem that you have is if your artists get too creative on you. It's very scary when all of the sudden, your artist wants to delve into new creative areas. So, Adler had to keep reminding them that The Beatles were putting out three great new hit records every year, and that they need to think in terms of hit records, and do some creative stuff on their album, but basically stay in the pocket and do singles. And John was increasingly become tired, even after two albums, of putting out hits. He wanted to expand. Little things like "Once Was A Time I Thought" were scaring Lou. And, as John's ego got bigger and bigger, he began to proclaim that, "This will be a hit," and that became a direct opposition to what Adler knew was a hit record. That was the nature of their business.

PART FOUR

Finishing the second album ... Michelle returns ... hitting the road and becoming a "SUPERGROUP"...hidden tunnels and bad craziness at Fordham University ... toilets flushing in Phoenix... real estate, Doherty-style at Appian Way ...

Mama's & Papa's Wax Unique LP

Exclusively to *The BEAT* from Lou Adler, executive producer for Dunhill Records, this week comes news of the brand new album about to be released by the Mama's and Papa's.

The album will be the second to be released by the popular foursome, and will be entitled "Crashon Screamon Singon All Fall Down."

Although the final decision had not been made as we went to press, tentative plans for the album called for a total of 14 tracks — something which is almost never done.

Some of the selections included in the new LP will be "The Dancing Bear," sung by Denny; "That Kind Of Girl," "Once Was A Time," which will be sung acapella by the entire group without *any*

orchestration to accompany them; and "I Can't Wait."

Cass and John will sing a duet on one cut of the LP, while Cass will be soloing on two others. John has written a total of ten new songs for the album, one of which will be a surprise number. The only thing we can tell you about this track now is that it will be only one minute in length — but you will be surprised and pleased by what you will hear in those 60 seconds.

It is only just now that the world of pop has sufficiently recovered from the first onslaught by The Mama's and Papa's to be able to "believe their eyes and ears." But this exciting new release from the talented quartet should send us all reeling right back into *tubs* of *disbelief*. Another sensational album from the Mama's and the Papa's.

westminster Presbyterian Church. "To many people today, the golf course is also more popular than Jesus Christ."

The "Beatle Boycott" was begun in Birmingham, Ala., by two disc jockeys who took issue with Lennon's remarks in the Datebook Magazine article.

The disc jockeys asked listeners to send in their Beatle records, pictures, souvenirs and mop-top wigs for a huge "Beatle Bonfire." The burning was scheduled for Aug. 19 — the night the Beatles were slated to appear in Memphis, Tennessee.

Even the Ku Klux Klan is jumping on the Beatle "Ban Wagon."

In Tupelo, Miss., Dale Walton, Imperial Wizard of the Knights of the Green Forest, Inc., urged teenagers to "Cut their locks off" and send them to a "Beatle Burning" by the Ku Klux Klan on Aug. 15.

Similar bonfires have occurred across the nation, and the West Coast is no exception.

KRLA Beat, *late summer 1966.*
Courtesy of the Stuart Rosenberg/Richie Furay Collection.

John Phillips: At first, after we recorded, Cass said that she would never go on stage in the group, that she would only sing in the studio, because she didn't want to be on the same stage as Michelle. She thought people would laugh at her. It took a while to convince Cass that the quality that she and Michelle had were opposite qualities, and represented the best of each, and that she'd come out really well on stage, as was proven, she really did. She was fantastic on stage.

Denny Doherty: To go out and work on the road was just *uncomfortable.* We didn't really want to be together as a group. John and Michelle had just split up, Cass and I hadn't really gotten together, and she was pissed off because of the Michelle thing. For just the four of us to be together in a limo on the way to the airport was uncomfortable. Flying some place was uncomfortable. Being in the dressing room was uncomfortable. The group became secondary to the *soap opera* . . . as well as the success of the group. John got the idea that he had this golden goose, but he didn't know how to make it lay fuckin' eggs. To lay eggs, we had to be *what we had been.* And there was no way to retrieve that. We tried to get back together with Michelle, and it didn't work, because obviously she had come to my bed because she didn't want to be with him, and she couldn't be with me or him, so she went to be with some other people. It made me crazy, it made John crazy . . . and poor Cass was just left standing there watching two assholes be crazy over this fuckin' butterfly that was flying around. It just became an untenable situation that became worse and worse . . . and despite all of this, the world is looking at it like, *'SUPERGROUP!!!,'* makin' all of this great music. But underneath, it's like, (sighs) "Okay, let's swim through the swamp some more . . . .put your heart in your ass pocket, and away we go again . . . "

Peter Pilafian: One day I got a call from either John or Bobby Roberts, and the word was that they had gotten dissatisfied with their road manager, and would I be interested in working with them and doing that? Of course I said sure, because who wants to be a taxicab driver for the rest of their lives? We worked out a weekly or monthly salary, which I think was pathetically small, but it didn't matter. You paid the rent and had a good time. So I kind of rolled into being their "Executive Road."

I wonder if John would kind of find jobs for his friends so that we could all hang out together? It was a good situation, and I never had to do the kind of 'down and dirty, load the amps in the bus' kind of work. My job was at a essentially much higher level than that. My job was basically to baby-sit the four singers and kind of hang with them. My job was to essentially be responsible so that they could be irresponsible. I'd say, "Okay kids, come on—time to get going, time to get on the plane . . . ," that sort of thing. I would make sure that there were a couple of glasses full of Crown Royal on the stage for John and Denny to hit while they were doing their performance.

I don't think that I was a drug supplier to any extent, but there was a flow of drugs that I was part of to a certain extent. I would make all of the arrangements work; I would figure out ways to get them out of the auditorium as safely as possible.

Larry Knechtel: I did a couple of live shows with them. I remember we did one down in Anaheim, in the round, and I remember John broke a couple of strings on his guitar, and he couldn't quite get it in tune. We did something in Milwaukee in a big outdoor place, and things got out of hand. This was back when things got a little wild. The cops were dragging people who were trying to hop the fence through the dressing room! We were glad to get the hell outta there. They eventually got their own band, they couldn't afford us.

Dick Weissman: They had come into town (New York) for a show, and this was when Jill was in the band. I kinda liked Jill, actually. That might be an unpopular view. But we were just sitting in this room at a party having a drink and talking. She was very pleasant. Anyway, I was going to go to the concert, and John forgot to leave me the tickets. I went to the show and there was no ticket. So again, I said, "Fuck you . . . " and went back to the party. At this party, Peter Pilafian was traveling with them, and from what I understand, he was quite a mountain climber. And he started climbing this railing of the St. Regis Hotel, and he's like, thirty stories above Fifth Avenue. I came back to this party and walked in, and John had cocaine on the table, alcohol. John said, "I'm the perfect host; choose your poison . . . " I think I had a beer, Anyway, there's Pilafian walking on the ledge . . . and I'm losing my mind here. You have to understand that I'd been primarily doing studio work in New York, and if you acted a little weird, you didn't come back. The West Coast was a little different. So for me, this was pretty strange . . .

Michelle Phillips: I don't believe it. That was *1966!!* Nah-uh. Dick is wrong about the cocaine, and believe me, I've gotten dates and years mixed up myself a million times. Dick has seen John many times after that. I'll tell you, if John had been doing cocaine back then, believe me, he would not have stopped. If that had been the case, then there would have been cocaine all through the second, third albums, and there *wasn't* . . .

Dick Weissman: On another trip I hooked up with them, and they went to Manny's Music store, and spent about $8,000 on horns, because they decided that they were going to play a 16-bar into a song. John could play a little bit of horn, and Denny could, and apparently Lou could as well. They bought these horns, and of course, they never did anything with them. Probably left 'em in a hotel room . . .

Eric Hord: The first show that I played with the group was in Phoenix. Dennis was supposed to play bass, but The Bomber – Steve Sanders – lost his bass. But, Joe Osborne was with us too, so it was a case were Dennis was maybe going to only play on a couple of songs. Lou didn't know how the act would go over on stage. Lou knew that I could play, and I did learn all of the charts. I had to really hustle to learn those charts, because I had just come into town. But Lou felt we needed to find out how the act was going to break on stage. So we broke it in Phoenix, in the tradition of breaking in an act out of town. It was a really good crowd, and if I'm not mistaken, I think that The Turtles were on the bill too. I think we only did eight or nine songs. So we did the gig, and the audience really enjoyed us.

After the gig, we went back to the Best Western Hotel, and partied for a while. I crashed, and then woke up in the morning in a slightly blithered state. I called down to room service for breakfast. I looked of the window, and I noticed that there were maybe a hundred police cars in the parking lot! Sheriffs, marshals, police, everything. I didn't know *what* the fuck was going down! So, I got on the phone and called Cass' room, and said, "Cass . . . wake up . . . go to the window and look out in the parking lot. . . ." So, she automatically went into a delirium and took all of her stash— whatever the fuck she had, she had a lot of it—and flushed it all down the toilet. Then she got a hold of Mitchie and Denny and John, and all their stashes got flushed. Nobody was left with anything. Not even a joint! Then, I got back on the phone and called down to room service to ostensibly ask where my breakfast was, but I was really calling to ask, "What's with all of the police cars in the parking lot?" He says, "Oh, yes Mr. Hord. There's a police convention here in town and they're all staying with us at The Best Western." You wanna talk about panic? There you go . . .

Peter Pilafian: Almost every sizable venue has a system of hidden tunnels that go to and from the stage areas, and oftentimes come up a block or two away. It was amazing how frequently that was the case. I was able to engineer the departure form the stage, where we would essentially come off the stage, go down some stairs, step into a limousine, and be gone before even the applause would even die down.

Usually I would arrange for our chartered Lear Jet. I was constantly making those kinds of arrangements—getting that set-up and getting the timing figured out. We'd go back to the hotel, take a few more drugs or whatever, grab the bags, and with the right rhythm, flow into the Lear jet, then wake up in the next city somewhere.

I was pretty impressed, because John, who had spent years touring and playing in little clubs a lot, has a pretty good feel for the situation and the problems that could arise, and the pressure of doing bus tours. He didn't want to get involved in it at all. So he took an approach that I helped him facilitate and helped put things together and make happen—the approach was, if you treat yourself like a star, act like a star, and look like a star, then the public will start to assume that you are a star. That applied to things like wardrobe, clothing—everything was elegant, briquette robes and things like that. Taking limousines everywhere, the idea of always staying in the best hotels. Also, keeping the concert schedule to a minimum. We were only playing weekends, so the general routine was for the weekend, play two major dates in major cities. Back then, 8,000 or 10,000 was major. After that—fly back. That was it, three or four days. Keep it as high-level as possible, using jets and charters to stay on that upper plane. I think that it was very effective. It definitely created a mentality that they were projecting this air of nobility and royalty, which people *loved*. It was a big part of their appeal.

Of course, I was one of the courtiers or whatever, in that circus. It was definitely a high level, elegant kind of image that I don't think had ever been seen before. Certainly not coming from the music business, for chrissakes! They were obviously very civilized people as well.

Jim Mason: In the summer of '66, I was in a band on CBS called Webster's New Word. We were booked by the same agency as The Mamas & The Papas—I.T.A. We were booked as the opening act—sometimes it was just the two of us, and we would open, other times Mitch Ryder, Paul Revere, Chad & Jeremy would play. We did about six–ten shows, and they were all shows with Michelle.

When we did shows with them, "Monday, Monday" was already popular by then, and "California Dreamin'" had been a hit earlier on—they were huge. The shows we did with them were probably just after Michelle returned, although I don't remember that being an issue. It wasn't like anyone said, "Oh, Michelle's back." Eric Hord, Eddie Hoh, and Peter Pilafian were in the road band.

There was a weekend where we played in Washington, D.C., at some coliseum. It was an indoor show on a Saturday night. Then Sunday, there was a daytime concert in Baltimore. Sunday afternoon, Gus Duffy, our drummer, and I were in the car with someone else. So, we're driving from Washington to Baltimore, and we see this really picturesque flower cart, full of flowers, and there was this little old lady selling flowers. So we stopped, and I think we gave her whatever, about $100, and we took most of the flowers, and just stuffed them in the car, and we drove off to the new Baltimore Civic Center. We walked in and headed backstage with all of these flowers. Duff and I each took armfuls of these flowers and headed to Cass and Michelle's dressing room. They asked us what we were doing with all of these flowers, and we gave them to the girls and told them that they should take them on stage and throw them on stage. When they came out, they had them in their hair, and the rest of the band had them, and they threw them out at the audience. I think that this was the first time that had ever been done, but after that they did that a lot.

The shows I remember clearly were Washington D.C., Baltimore and . . . Fordham. . . .

Gus Duffy: It was a two-group concert. Fordam University probably held 6–7,000 people. The Mamas & The Papas were shit-hot—the place was packed.

Jim Mason: The last show we did with them was at Fordham University, which is up in The Bronx. At the time, Duffy and I were sharing an apartment in the Village. We were looking forward to this gig, 'cause it was going to get us off the road, and we were going to have some time off. My recollection is that we were going to get a week or two off, and then we were going to hook up again with The Mamas & The Papas and do some more dates up and down the Atlantic coast. This particular show was just us and them, and it was packed—they couldn't get another person in. I remember the fire marshal giving the student promoters grief because of all the people, and they were breaking fire codes. Anyway, the show starts, and we do our hour, and we were really tight, it was good. We also had a record out at the time. We did our set and got called back for an encore, and everybody was hooting and hollering, like 5,000 people. As soon as we got backstage, The Mamas & The Papas and all of their people started arriving, and it was obvious that they were all high or drunk or tripping . . . *something*. And when they got on stage, it was clear that these people shouldn't be on-stage; it was just too goofy. People starting hooting at the band, and after the first few songs, people in the audience started talking, and quite a few started to leave.

Gus Duffy: We went on first, we were supposed to do an hour set. Webster's was as sharp as Webster's was ever gonna get. The idea that they were Fordham and we were from Notre Dame, there was some kind of magnetism in the air. By that time that The Mamas & The Papas limo showed up, and out they tumbled, shit-faced—as they usually were. We were on our third encore and standing ovation. The audience we absolutely depleted. They tumbled on the stage, shambled around, and just got nowhere. Lou

Adler took our management aside and said, "These guys are off the tour—get them outta here." I just remember seeing him in the wings with smoke coming out of his ears. I was a little suprised, but I thought it was funny.

Jim Mason: The next day, I was at the apartment, and the phone rings early in the morning, and it's our manager. I thought, "Oh, man, what is this?—We're finally off the road for a few weeks, and now he's bothering me . . . " And he says we have to have a meeting, because you've been kicked off the tour . . . So, we all got together later that day, and he said that he had gotten a call from the agent, who said that Lou Adler wanted us off the tour because we'd 'really shown them up' over the weekend. It was really the first time that I was really made aware of the politics of the music business—because the rule is that you don't show up the headliners.

Gus Duffy: They were gods; they were in their own interplanetary universe, and they had eyes only for each other, and that's about it.

Jim Mason: In those days there was a lot less psychodrama, much less security and logistical problems. It was an easier time as far as traveling and being on the road and concert set-ups and such. Our band just traveled as a group without an entourage, aside from girlfriends. But The Mamas & The Papas, I remember that there were a lot of 'em. Aside from the four singers and the backing musicians, there seemed to be a lot of people with 'em. Obviously there was a road manager, and Scott MacKenzie was with 'em. I remember one particular show where my group was already set up and we were backstage tuning up, and they came in, and it was like "Hey guys, how ya doin'?" and it was all friendly and everything, and I thought, "These guys are already loaded." Scott came through, and he was wearing like a Dracula cape, carrying a bottle of Wild Turkey. I remember thinking that I'd never seen so few people drink so much whisky in so short a time. I'm not sayin' that we weren't doing the same thing, but these guys were big leaguers! They were getting into a lot more colorful costumes and being a little more flamboyant. The thing that I remember the most, though, was that John always managed to stop and say, "Hey, Mas, how are ya?" He remembered me from the past and we re-connected. It was nice. There was a lot of psychodrama and posturing, if you will, but when it came time for the show, they were serious, and they would run through songs and vocal exercises. There was a very serious aspect to their singing, and the public was captured by the sophistication of their singing. John was obviously the brains behind that—not to say that the others didn't make a contribution. You know, he would say, "Cass, sing this note; Denny, try this." John definitely knew how to make the most out of what they had to work with.

When I would go out in the front of the house and listen to them, I was always amazed at how close they sounded to their records. Obviously the records has a lot of double-tracking and overdubs, and that was a given for all of us who were making records. What you do live can be enhanced, and the studio really becomes your instrument. The sound they created was truly magical. I also think that the spectacle that they created as the physical 'Mamas & Papas' only embellished the effect that they created vocally. They truly seemed to be accessible. There was an awful lot of identification with the audience. Cass was attractive, but not in the same way that Michelle was. But a lot of people found Cass very alluring. Of course, John and Denny seemed to be like pretty cool, 'studly' guys, and Michelle was just awesomely beautiful. I don't recall any separation or "You guys can't hang with us," or anything like that. There was a lot of camaraderie, because they had all come from the folk world background, which was a lot more supportive of different artists and different groups than rock became. It was friendly and supportive.

I remember after one of the concert going to some club with John and Denny and some of the musicians, Eddie Hoh and Eric Hord and I think Bobby West. We all ended up at this club late at night, like a blues club—and I remember that these guys all jammed. I had only heard them in the context of The Mamas & The Papas show, but these guys really impressed me as serious players who could play anything well. John might have gotten up and sung something as well, I don't remember. Eddie Hoh had these luminous drumsticks, and at one point in the show it would go to a black-light or something, and there was just this blur of drumsticks—it was awesome, real showmanship.

Denny Doherty: We did 35 personal appearances, all together. In California it was pretty simple. We'd just shoot up to San Francisco, and then maybe up to Washington State. But when we'd go out to universities and colleges in the midwest and places, we'd take a Lear jet, and that would take us to wherever we were going. Usually the band and crew and whatever were in a propjet, a chartered Elektra, and we were in the Lear. We'd go out and do two gigs in a weekend, and that would be great. We loved it, once we were out on the stage. But it was getting from point A to point B that was a hassle. Home to the hotel to the gig and back home again was . . . well; the four of us would have to be in close quarters, as it were, that was a little bit 'iffy.' But once you get on stage, you forget about everything else.

We took The Wrecking Crew out with us a couple of times, except for Hal Blaine. We took Joe Osborne and Larry Knechtel a couple of times, but we had our own drummer, "Fast" Eddie Hoh from Chicago. Poor bugger, he died. But we had a lot of fun with him and The Doctor, who played lead guitar. He took his 'title' to heart; he had little lab coat and his doctor's bag and a stethoscope, and that's the way he would come on stage. He would tune his guitar with a stethoscope!

Henry Diltz: I just thought it was so brilliant. I was in a group that did four-part harmony as well, and that's why John and Cyrus hooked up, we were in a similar type business. We did this song called "Nighttime Girl," which was kind of a local hit, and it was 'Raga-Rock.' Jack Nitzsche arranged that for us. Al Kooper wrote that. So, we were into a folk/pop area, and that's what everybody was heading to from straight folk, to folk/rock, or pop. The Mamas & The Papas were the same thing. They had all been in folk groups,

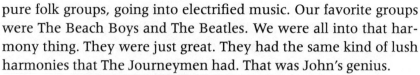

pure folk groups, going into electrified music. Our favorite groups were The Beach Boys and The Beatles. We were all into that harmony thing. They were just great. They had the same kind of lush harmonies that The Journeymen had. That was John's genius.

Cass just had an incredible voice, it just had a vibe and an energy to it. When you think about what a voice really is, when you see it in person, it really is a physical thing, you know? It's molecules of sound that go through the air that hit your ear. Of course, on a record it's once removed, but it's still a physical thing. Her voice just had an electric energy that just grabbed you and zapped you.

Michelle Phillips: I think she was the best female singer on the planet, really. You know, you can have pipes, really, really *great* vocal pipes, and I won't mention any names, but there are a lot of really big singers that have great instruments, their voices are great instruments, and quite frankly I hate the material they choose, and I hate their style. And, you know, I can't *stand* her! It's like, "Yeah, we know you can hold a note for a minute and a half. It doesn't impress me if you can't sing a lyric that really moves you. Cass could bring you to tears with the way she phrased. Brilliant phraser. And she had the pipes, and she had the soul. That combination is what I feel made her the best female pop singer in the world, when she was around.

Denny Doherty: I moved into a house on Appian Way in 1966. The guy that got me the house was our attorney, Jerry Brown—no relation to the governor Jerry Brown. He had gotten us the Flores Street house, and consequently got everybody else their houses. When we moved out of Flores Street, he found a house up in Laurel Canyon for Cass, and she liked that, and he found John and Michelle's little house on Lookout. I was staying down at Zsa Zsa Gabor and George Sanders—the guy she was married to at the time —I was staying in their pool house. While I was there, Jerry found me the Appian Way house. He said there was a house for sale up on the top of Laurel Canyon, and I went up and looked at it, the outside; I didn't know it was furnished. I said, "Yeah, okay, good. I'll get this one." It was a Spanish, Moorish thing on top of the hill. That was $55,000; house and contents. The fuckin' dining room set was worth more than the house; it was a Chippendale. I was finding Royal Dalton china and screens from the Ming Dynasty around there! Jade soapstone fingernail carvings . . . all in the house.

When the house became available, Jerry Brown said that two little old ladies had lived there since 1947 or something. The house was built for Rudolph Frummell, who lived across the street; he was having an affair with Gypsy Rose Lee. He lived across the street, and Gypsy Rose Lee lived in my house. And then when Gypsy left, Mary Astor bought the house, and she lived there until the little old ladies moved in there. These were two nurses, and one of them was married to a doctor who lived in the house, and his wife lived there with her friend; so the two nurses and the doctor lived in the house. The doctor died, and the two little old

Western Studios, 1966.
Photo by Bones Howe.

nurses stayed there, from about 1947, to 1966. Now when I looked at the house, one of the ladies had been put into a convalescent home, the one who was married to the doctor. Her name was Margret, and the other one was Lilly. The two of them lived there after the doctor died, and when that happened, the doctor's family was in line for the house. Not to Lilly; she was just a friend living in the house. The family came to California, and they were going to sell everything in the house as well as the house, because there was some really fantastic shit in the house. They could have gotten $55,000 for the house, and another $50–60,000 for the furnishings, at least.

Margaret's family had declared her 'mentally incompetent,' so she was down in a nursing home, and the family's thinking of selling everything, and they're not considering Lilly *at all*. So Jerry Brown tells me all of this, and I go in, and I want Lilly to show me the house. I probably had flames comin' out of my ears, ya' now, with a bottle of Crown Royal at my hip. And Lilly had been used to living in the quietude from 1948, and "Crazy" comes in, and "Crazy" wants to see everything in the fuckin' house. I meet her at the front door, and she's walking me down the hall, through the kitchen and out the back, where she's been living in the maid's quarters since 1948. Everything in the house has little stickers and price tags on it, every piece, every little jade carving, everything. Just like an antique store. The family's coming in and getting ready for the estate sale. Lilly is still living there; she doesn't know where she's gonna go . . .

She said, "Well, the family's coming in, and Margaret's down in Santa Monica, she's not really together . . . " So I call my attorney, and say, "What would it take for me to turn this whole thing around, so the family gets fuck-all, and I get it to Lilly?" Well, he drew up a paper, and did some investigating, and found out that Margret was not declared 'incompetent'; that family was just saying that to Lilly. I had my attorney draw up an agreement that said if Margret would sign it, everything would be turned over to Lilly. I got the paper, picked up Lilly in the limo, and we drove out to Santa Monica, out to the old folks home, Lilly took it in, and had Margret sign it. I said, "Now, Lilly . . . this all belongs to *you*º.

Would you sell it to me for $50,000?" Which she was happy to; was more money than she had ever seen, and would certainly take care of her. So, I bought the house from Lilly, and she went down and joined Margret, and I moved into the house. The family, meantime, is goin' "Where *is* everything!?" and I'm like, "Fuck *off . . .* "

Chapter Five

Mansions

PART ONE *Early 1967*

2 and 1/2 acres on 783 Bel Air Road, guarded by expansion . . . and all the bad stuff had to be swept under the rug . . . in with the Hollywood 'in crowd'. . .nothing's too good for my little girl . . . and the party rages on at Denny's Appian Way . . .

Eric Hord: Cass was pissed off at Michelle, and she was really pissed off at Dennis, but she still hung with them a little bit. But who she was *really* pissed off at was John, because he was like, "Well, we have to keep this thing going, and let's wipe it under the rug . . . " John had this thing figured out and planned from the beginning. I could really see it, because after you've been with somebody for a long time, you can say, "I know why he did this . . . I can see the modus operandi. . . . "

Michelle Phillips: Everything had to be forgotten, and all of the bad stuff had to be swept under the rug and never spoken about again, which is how we dealt with it. The big checks were starting to come in now, too. John and I wanted to buy a house in Bel-Air, so we just started driving around. We drove up Bel-Air Road, and I think that this is the first day we were driving around. We saw a 'for sale' sign at 783, but the gates were locked, and I could just *barely* peer over the gate, and we saw this lovely, beautiful Tudor house, and I said, "We have to look at it . . . " So we climbed over the gate, and were peering in the windows and I saw the house, and I said, "We've *got* to buy this house . . . " John said, "You haven't even seen the inside . . . " and I said, "Yes, I have." I could see inside, and I said, "This the house, this is the one I want."

It was on the market, I think, for $250,000. We made an offer of $150,000, with a cash down payment of $90,000, and they bit *so fast.* $90,000 in those days was *a lot* of cash. We moved in almost immediately.

Ann Marshall: Oh, it was great. Very opulent, and very beautifully decorated. They had some lovely things, and it was a very warm atmosphere, very warm, friendly, and inviting. And they invited a lot of people.

Peter Pilafian: It was like a dream come true, because they had all of this money coming in from "California Dreamin'" and everything. The house wasn't all that expensive. I seem to recall that they paid around $175,000 for it or $250,000, which was probably a cash deal. The whole thing was sort of a miracle. It was not just hitting the jackpot, it was more like having a magic genie appearing saying, "Your life is whatever you want it to be." It was much different than having a bunch of cash, much different.

Michelle Phillips: That was a fun period. For a woman, I have to tell you that there's nothing more fun than to have unlimited funds, the house of your dreams, and someone with a sense of fun, that John did have. I could have anything I wanted. We went to all auctions, and we bought a 250-piece set of Limoge china and antique crystal, we bought antique silver, just beautiful things. We also bought an antique grandfather clock. The Tiffany lamps weren't bought until my first mother's day, in 1968. I still have the large standing Tiffany with the original base and hood. We also bought another Tiffany desk lamp on that Mother's Day, and that was the one with astrological signs on it, that John ended up with. I ended up with this big one, because when I left the house, I went back one day with my friend Alan Warnick, and we took the lamp apart and we loaded it in the car and drove off with it!

We had a few old Rolls Royce's. There was a 1932 convertible Touring Car, and another 1932 Rolls Royce, with a hard top in front and open in the back. I got one for my birthday one year, a 1956 Silver Cloud, *quite* gorgeous. We were having these big parties . . . we won a Grammy for "Monday, Monday." It was when rock and roll did not win Grammy's, too, by the way. It was a whole new ballgame . . .

Peter Pilafian: It didn't seem that reality was very tangible in those days. The patterns would be from this two-and one-half acre garden in Bel Air to a recording studio down on Sunset—before we built the studio in the house—to a limo to an airport. It was all very removed from the reality of drive-away cars and four people sleeping on the living room floor and all that. John and Michelle were really riding with it. It didn't seem to make them nasty or anything. They just loved it.

Russell Gilliam: I'd never seen anybody spend more money than they did. It was just party time and spending. Anything they saw that they wanted, they bought. One day Michelle was at my house, and we were going to go over to her house, and we made two stops on the way. I had to get a little 15 cent box of goldfish food for my son's goldfish that we'd won at a little fair, and I had to wait there while Michelle bought this entire tank and a bunch of exotic fish that must have cost her $500. Then I had to stop off and buy a 95-cent play at a bookstore, and she bought about $1,000 worth of books. You just couldn't go anyplace without them *buying* everything.

I sort of got to the point where I really wouldn't party with them very much. They would call at about 10:00 o'clock at night and say, "Come on over, we're having a party . . . " and Peter would *jump* up and leave to go hang out there. He'd say, "Come, let's go!" and I'd say "I'm not going! The baby, the baby!" So I kind of backed off, absolutely. I really wasn't that interested, to tell you the truth. I really wasn't. If it was a daytime thing, we were over there, but as far as hanging out and partying, it wasn't my scene. They were getting used to having their own way, and to having people kowtowing to them, and if they wanted something, they got it, no questions asked.

Cyrus Faryar: I remember when they bought the house, and they called me and said that I should come by and check it out. Subsequent to that, the studio was built. Peter Pilafian was prominently there on the scene. The friendship at the time was very enjoyable, and their lives and successes were a pleasure. I remember Michelle got these great andirons for the fireplace that I thought were cool. They were two silhouettes of cats that were cut into wrought-iron, and the cats eyes were stones, and they would sparkle when the fire was lit.

John was a lot of fun, and an enjoyable man, and a real talent. He was an interesting mix, in a way. He was a real good musician, and a good songwriter, and a good businessman. He was friendly, and warmhearted, and generous. He loved doing what he was doing, and was inspired with great confidence. When they got the tunes together for The Mamas & The Papas, he just *knew*, he could tell that this was going to be successful. He had absolute confidence in the songs, and that they were going to make great albums. He didn't like, trumpet this around like, "What a cool guy I am" or anything. It was nice, because a lot of people were seriously ego-driven, and John certainly had his own ego, but he didn't have a banner saying, "What a great songwriter I am." He had a great deal of pride in the group, and the songs that he wrote for the group were his instruments, and he was proud of all the members, which was refreshing. It wasn't about being out in from as the solo guy— it was all about the group, and that was not common.

Peter Pilafian: We would have these really wonderful mornings in the garden, and that house had a supportive and safe feeling about it where you basically just could do anything you wanted. That house generated a very satisfying and creative magical sort of era. You felt like you were totally safe.

The expression coming out of that, jumping forward to the Monterey Pop Festival, we had the idea of getting 80,000 orchids from Hawaii, and having a hot air balloon go up over the concert when Ravi Shankar was playing, and scatter them everywhere. That was the expression, that was the feeling. Kind of like being touched with the magic. I'm sorry that John seemed to have to pay the price, like somehow he had sold his soul to the devil or something. I never thought it had to be that way. I thought the magic garden was just a magic garden. It shouldn't have a price. Michelle skated through pretty well. She's not as big a dreamer as John is, but she followed it.

The house was kind of the manifestation of being in dreamland. Which was exactly how it was built, because back in those days with the movie stars, that's the way it was, and we were just continuing it. But equally unreal, equally amazing, equally magic.

One thing that I saw that made me uncomfortable were these leeches, people that were suppliers of pool tables and services and so on, that seemed to zoom in on Michelle and John. Suddenly they were being barraged by these really smooth-talking types who were basically trying to extract money from them. It's part of the scene of having too much money, I guess. It was new and kind of off-putting to see that happen. But John was smart enough to kind of handle it, but in a certain sense, sure he wanted a pool table, sure he wanted some Tiffany lamps, and it's nice not to have to go to a store to do that. I saw that happening, but John somehow was able to keep his perspective a bit.

That was really the zenith of the whole phenomenon. The Gene Raymond and Jeanette McDonald house really was a magic garden, just like the song says. It really felt like that. When we went to look at it for the first time, when they were either buying it or just thinking about it, we went down to the basement and we found a big walk-in safe from a bank that had been the wine vault. There were sill a dozen or so bottles laying around. It was creaky and dusty, and there was just this feeling of magic, of stepping down into this magic land, like a storybook, "Arabian Nights" or something. We looked at these old bottles and were commenting on how old they were, and we uncorked some of them, and the wine had turned into vinegar. There was a brandy, though, that was uncommonly good.

Michelle Phillips: We met this guy named Steve Brant, and the minute we met him, he became a force in our lives. He was like a social director; he planned all the parties, he was just *wickedly* funny. A very slight gay guy, but he could also be very, *very* viscous, as viscous as he was hilarious. When he pointed his finger at you and he said, *"You'll never work in this town again!"* he meant it! I don't know if that was really true, but he carried a lot of weight. He knew everybody, he was like the male Rona Barrett. He invited Zsa Zsa Gabor to all of our parties,

Nurit Wilde: Cass kind of changed, and so did John, they liked the power. Denny didn't change that much, but he did enjoy it. He had plenty of money for Crown Royal! But I don't think the money changed him; he was a very easy-going guy, I felt, and I knew him fairly well. John, though, did get 'power-mad,' 'cause he was like that anyway; he was a very controlling person, and now he had real cache in the music business, you know?

John Stewart: John could be the world's greatest cynic, and sometimes he's get very serious. I always kept my eye cocked whether he was serious or not . . . Cass and John locked horns all of the time; but she didn't have any choice with John in the group . . .

Rodney Bingenheimer: I remember sending my mom a post-card after I went to one of their parties at their house, which was in Bel Air, just across the street from the house where they filmed 'The Beverly Hillbillies.' I remember Noel Harrison was there, Mick Jagger . . .

Michelle Phillips: Christian Marquand invited Marlon Brando to one of our parties, we were introduced to Roman Polanski, and it was through Roman that we met Christian, and we met Sharon Tate, Roger Vadim and Jane (Fonda), and Bob Mitchum. We met Peter Sellers, Joan Collins, who was married to Anthony Newley. There was a big Hollywood scene at the parties. Eventually I was approached about doing some acting, but John really didn't want me to be doing that. I know that Christian Marquand asked me to read for the part of "Candy," and I wanted to do it, and John said, "No, no . . . this movie's not going to be any good . . . " In other words, John would 'let me know when the right project came along . . . '

Guy Webster: I spent a lot of time at the house in Bel Air. One day, I was sitting with John, and he said, "Listen to this, you're not going to believe this group, Procol Harum..' He had this test pressing of "Whiter Shade of Pale", and cranked it *full out* on his— for the time—state-of-the-art stereo, into their big living room in Bel Air, and I was just blown away. There are just a few rock and roll songs that can just stop me cold, and that as one of 'em. We shot one of the covers in their pool ("Deliver"). That was a fun shoot. That was the last time it was easy to put them together. After that, they were on the road, and very, very busy.

John Stewart: I went to one of their parties up in Bel Air; it was just outrageous. Mia Farrow was there, Warren Beatty, all of these Hollywood types. And Peter Sellers showed up, and they couldn't let him in because there was no more room! I went up there one afternoon, and John said, "Oh, you should have been here an hour ago . . . McCartney just left." It was just like a day-to-day thing.

Roman Polanski was a good friend of John's, and his wife, Sharon Tate. A few years later, we were over at that house where all of those people got murdered, just three nights before. You don't think that gave us some cold chills? John was a frequent hanger-outer there. It still doesn't add up to me that that many people were friends with these four people in The Mamas & The Papas. Brando, McCartney . . . the world came to their house.

Denny Doherty: We didn't do that many personal appearances, but when we would go on the road, I would leave my friend Rick Steinenger at my house; and mind you, we were all in various states of comatose back then. But I'd go out on the road for three or four days, and I'd come back and they'd be a house full of people that I didn't know. I'd walk in the house and say, "Who are you?" "I live here." "Oh no, this is Rick's house." So, Rick's living in my house, he's sitting in my booth at The Whiskey. There were several different parties going on, depending if I was on the road or not. I'd get home and my party would begin, and then I'd leave and Rick's party would begin again.

When McGuire moved in with me, Rick had moved out. Cass had told McGuire the year before, to get out of L.A. "Ya know what you should do? You should go to New York and do *Hair*. And McGuire's like, "What, cut somebody's hair?!" "No! It's a Broadway show; it's great! The Smothers Brothers just did a great thing on it . . . " he went to New York, auditioned, and got the part. He stayed there for a year, I stayed here and went through the thing with the little old ladies and moved in here, the parties were crazy. Then, at the end of '66, beginning of '67—it was before Monterey and all of that shit, I'm sitting up at Appian Way on my window seat, and a yellow Volkswagen bus pulls up across the street, with a little calico kitty on the dashboard, and a guy and a girl in front, with a lot of hair. I look out and say, "That's McGuire!" He didn't know I was in the house. He brought up his girlfriend, Alanna, up to the top of Laurel Canyon, and wanted to show her the highest street in the city. I see her explaining everything to this girl, and I go to the steps and shout, "McGuire!!" He's freaked, and looking all over the place, and looks and sees me standing over on the steps. He came over, left his van where it was, and she and he and the cat and the bags walked up the front steps of the house, and stayed for a year and a half! But, things like that happened every day back then . . . it was just fuckin' magic.

McGuire helped us get our deal at Dunhill, and split for New York, came back here and lived with me when the career took a nosedive, and the party just continued and got crazier and crazier. He and Alanna eventually moved out, and then went and stayed with Scott McKenzie, and that was even crazier. Freddie Neil moved in with me for a while, and that was just too nuts, and my house turned into a shooting gallery. I moved Fred down the street to a house that Jerry Brown had, which eventually became Carole King's place . . . and the party continued at my house.

I eventually moved into the house next door, and I rented my house to Hal Ashby, who was editing *Harold & Maude* at the time, with Ruth Gordon and Bud Court. I moved into the house next door. And the party continued . . .

Barry McGuire: I lived with Denny for about a year. Denny had a lovely home, on top of the hill; probably built in the 1930s. It was a nice house, it wasn't a mansion, just a nice, upscale house. Beautiful hill. Rudolph Frummel lived right across the street, He was about 80 years old then. He wrote a standard called "Indian Love Song," and he'd get up early in the morning and play piano; very nice. He had two Steinway's interlocked, and his wife played, and they'd play duets. Talk about romantic!

Everybody would come by Denny's house: Van Dyke Parks, Peter Tork, Freddie Neil, Dion, everybody. But it wasn't as much of a wild party house as everybody seems say. Denny wasn't that much of a party guy, really, at least when I was there that I remember. Denny's a very private person. You could party, but if you got raunchy, he'd kick everybody *out*. Denny was very Victorian. I mean, we *would* do some wild stuff, like play "Whiter Shade of Pale" at 4 A.M. at full volume, but it was mostly a quiet place, it really was. Until we'd be invaded by a bunch of people who were making the rounds.

PART TWO

Cass gets ready to deliver while distancing herself from the group—"Good for her, not so good for us." . . . Third album sessions/ego shifts in the studio . . . and the hits just keep on comin' . . .

Michelle Phillips: Cass comes to rehearsal one day at the house; we used to rehearse in the 'pub room'. She was getting further and further away from us physically and emotionally. She wasn't so emotionally tied to us, which was good for her, not so good for us. John felt like he was losing control over her. You

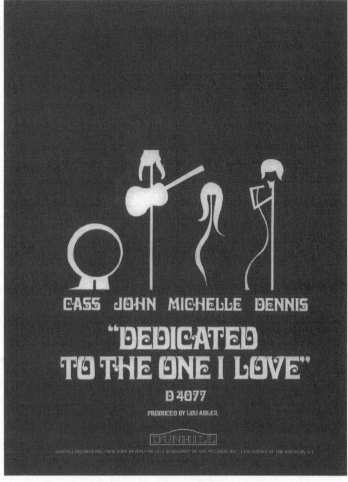

Courtesy of the Richard B. Campbell Collection.

know, she was on her diets, and John would tell her that she had to stop because her eyes were getting too close together! He used to say things like that to her. In fact, he didn't want her to get skinny; we had an *image* to uphold, 'Fat is *good!*' Anyway, we were at this rehearsal, and she kind of flippantly told us that she was pregnant. The first words out of John's mouth were, "When's the abortion?" And she said, "I'm not having an abortion . . . " and we all laughed, because we all thought that you just didn't have a baby for no particular reason, especially if you're a 'pop star.'

You know, she had a career, she wasn't married, and she wasn't really involved with anybody. But she said, "No, no . . . I'm having it." I remember all of us saying, "Why?" and she said, "Well, my doctor's actually suprised that I'm pregnant, and women my size usually don't get pregnant, and I may never get pregnant again." But, it struck a chord with me, as a woman, and I said, "Well . . . " and John said, "How are you gonna go on the road, Cass?" and she said, "I'll go on the road; I'll pull my weight, John Phillips. I'll be there." And we went on the road, and we were on the road up until about a month or so before she delivered. And it was hard . . . but you know what? I don't think she had a hard pregnancy. I don't remember her complaining about her pregnancy. I was just in awe that she was doing this. And of course, she wouldn't tell me who the father was. She called it the 'immaculate conception.' I even remember her talking about it on stage, saying, "You know, I'm pregnant. Everyone wants to know who the father is, and all I can tell ya is that this is an immaculate conception," and she used to get a big laugh from the audience.

Denny Doherty: Well, no one knew Cass was pregnant. She was already six or seven months pregnant before anyone "knew." She could have lost 50 pounds and no one would have known. I don't recall her ever announcing that, but I do remember her coming over to my house and wanting to stay and 'nest.' She was living with Pick Dawson at the time. I don't know what the circumstances were. Pickering H. Dawson the Third. I think he was from Foggy Bottom, Washington, D.C. His parents had some money, I believe. He's no longer with us. Cass moved into Woodrow Wilson Drive, and had the baby while living there.

The *Deliver* period was kind of a tense period. Jill had come and gone, Michelle had come and gone, and now she was back in the group, and John and Michelle are back together and they moved into Bel Air. Supposedly 'business as usual.' Ha-ha . . . right . . . The thing with her and I was over, and the group was supposedly continuing on. But she was running around seeing other people, and that was driving John crazy, and it became an untenable situation.

The reason that there are more covers on the *Deliver* album, was because we didn't really get back together to write anything. The first album was all done, before we went in and recorded it. The second album got done, and by the third album, things started to level out, career-wise, for the next eight months to a year, and John started doing more writing, and John and I did a little more writing, and Cass would bring in some Beatles things; those kinds of "other" songs came in and then John started writing "album-type" songs. But that was finite; it wasn't the same. We couldn't sit down and write "for the band." The magic came from him having the time to sit down and write songs that fit the group. Instead of sitting down and 'writhing songs for the next album,' it became kind of 'cardboard-y' and made up. But at that point, the momentum we'd created carried a lot of it. If we got one hit from each album, that was enough. One good single sold the album, and it didn't matter about the album cuts or whatever else was on the album. That lasted up until about 1968.

Lou Adler: If the third album (*Deliver*) was the first album, I don't know if we'd be here talking about it. Material was starting to get short, relationships in the group were starting to get more distant, Cass was very distant, and very pregnant. Like I said before, we got the last things out of her, and she crawled out of the studio and had her baby. Denny, at one point, we got the last note when we just mike'd him laying across the piano. It was a very tough album to record at that point. There was a lot more negative energy than there was positive energy at that point.

Bones Howe: The third album was obviously much worse. That was at Christmas time of '66, and I left in the middle of that album. That album was very messy. I worked on "Dedicated to the One I Love," and that was very tough to get together. Mitchie had never really sung lead before, and her part was so soft, so that was really tough. There were a lot of ideas by that album, and I think

TRIPLE SESSION 2 @ PREMIUM
TWO TRACKS 1 @ PREMIUM   (Employer's name) __DUNHILL RECORDS__

Phonograph Recording Contract Blank

AMERICAN FEDERATION OF MUSICIANS № 353773

00067

Local Union No. 47   OF THE UNITED STATES AND CANADA

THIS CONTRACT for the personal services of musicians, made this 9 &10 day of January 19 67
between the undersigned employer (hereinafter called the "employer") and _____ 8 musicians
(hereinafter called "employees").   (including the leader)
WITNESSETH, That the employer hires the employees as musicians severally on the terms and conditions below, and as further specified on reverse side. The leader represents that the employees already designated have agreed to be bound by said terms and conditions. Each employee yet to be chosen shall be so bound by said terms and conditions upon agreeing to accept his employment. Each employee may enforce this agreement. The employees severally agree to render collectively to the employer services as musicians in the orchestra under the leadership of
HAL BLAINE

Name and Address of Place of Engagement **Western Recorders, 6000 Sunset Blvd, Hollywood, Calif.** as follows:

Date(s) and Hours of Employment **Jan 9--9:P.M. to 12:Midnight Jan 10--12:30A.M. to 3:30 A.M.**
                                                                   AND 4:A.M. to 7:A.M.

Type of Engagement: **Recording for phonograph records only.**   (THIRD DATE SWEETENER)

WAGE AGREED UPON $ **UNION SCALE**   Plus pension contributions as specified on reverse side hereof.
                                        (Terms and amount)
This wage includes expenses agreed to be reimbursed by the employer in accordance with the attached schedule, or a schedule to be furnished the employer on or before the date of engagement. **WITHIN 15 DAYS**
To be paid _____
                                        (Specify when payments are to be made)
Upon request by the American Federation of Musicians of the United States and Canada (herein called the "Federation") or the local in whose jurisdiction the employees shall perform hereunder, the employer either shall make advance payment hereunder or shall post an appropriate bond.

Employer's name and **DUNHILL RECORDS**	Leader's name **Hal Blaine** · Local No. **47**
authorized signature	Leader's signature
Street address **449 So. Beverly Dr.**	Street address
Beverly Hills, Calif. CR-45201	Hollywood, Calif. 90028
City State Phone	City State

(1) Label Name **Dunhill Records**   Session No. **7057**

Master No.	No. of Minutes	1st Date TITLES OF TUNES	Master No.	No. of Minutes	2nd Date TITLES OF TUNES
	2:28	THE STRING MAN		2:16	A BIT OF FREE ADVICE

(2) Employee's Name (As on Social Security Card) Last First Initial (Leader)	(3) Home Address (Give Street, City and State)	(4) Local Union No.	(5) Social Security Number	(6) Scale Wages	(7) Pension Contribution
Blaine, Hal	L.A. 28, Calif.	47		628.35	50.27
Coleman, Gary L. 1-Dbl.	No. Hollywood, Calif.	47		353.18	28.25
Doherty, Dennis	L.A. 69, Calif.	571		314.18	25.13
Knechtel, Lawrence W. 2-Dbls.	Sherman Oaks, Calif.	47		379.18	30.33
Osborn, Joe	No. Hollywood, Calif.	47		314.18	25.13
Phillips, John E.A.	L.A. 24, Calif.	161 42		314.18	25.13
Sloan, Phil	L.A. 48, Calif.	47		314.18	25.13
8-Dbls. 1st Date Only Tedesco, Thomas J.	Northridge, Calif.	47		115.92	9.27

NO ARRANGER OR COPYIST THESE DATES.................................

CONTRACT RECEIVED

FOR FUND USE ONLY: (8) Total Pension Contributions (Sum of Column (7)) $ **218.64**
                                               Make check payable in this amount to "AFM & EPW Fund."
Date pay't rep'd **PAID FEB 1 1967** Amt. paid _____ Date posted _____ By _____

Form B-4 Rev. 4-66

Courtesy of Elliot Kendall.

that John was getting dry, and there were a lot of ideas about doing a slow version of "Dancing In The Streets." Lou had an idea to do that, and then "Twist And Shout" came out of that, I think. There was a lot of outside material on that, and if you look back, there hadn't been too much before.

Michelle Phillips: But, we worked our little asses off, and we did the *Deliver* album, which, to date is one of my favorite albums. I think that next to the first album, *Deliver* is the really *great* album that we did. I listened to the second album, I didn't really like it. I like *Deliver* and the first album. We had written "Creeque Alley," which was a wonderful, wonderful song for the album, and we were doing "Dedicated," which I got to do lead vocal on, and I really wanted to do something from that period.

I had originally suggested "I'm A Hog for You, Baby" by The Coasters. It was the B-side of "Poison Ivy." They asked me to sing a few bars from it, and I went, (straight, recital tone) "I'm a hog for you, baby, can't get you out of my mind. I'm a hog for you, baby, can't get you outta my mind. When I go to sleep at night, you're the only thing I'm thinking of . . . ," or something like that! And they looked at me like I had lost my mind. Then we tried to work up "He's A Rebel," and then we tried to do "Will You Still Love Me Tomorrow." John couldn't get a handle on those, and he had never heard these songs, and I don't think Cass had, either. Denny had, and that's because he was always a rocker. But I don't think that Cass or John had the slightest idea what this stuff was. Just number one songs in the United States! But they were into different stuff, like folk and show tunes. Then I suggested "Dedicated." I had no idea that John was going to take that song and make it, like, his own. That was *such* a beautiful arrangement of that song. It really sounded like he had written it.

P. F. Sloan: It came down to the publishing company, Trousdale. That was the most important thing in all of this. When it came down to artists, artists were not that important, they were a dime a dozen. Publishing was what was important, and it's where the money is. It was sort of, you can always get rid of The Mamas & the Papas, they weren't really that important to them. What was important was the next group that comes in that has a hit song. It wasn't the integrity of a group, it wasn't the evolution of a group, it was the songs, and they had no clue what a hit song was.

Lou Adler: "Twist & Shout" is basically "Do You Wanna Dance"—same format, same formula. Once I got through "Look through My Window," you can see that I ran out of a way to sequence it . . . but there's a solid five songs on the first side.

Is this the one where I gave the doctors credit? Personally yes, I was deep into migraines, stress throughout my body and shoulders that wouldn't move. I had plugs all over, and I had a hot pad on me wherever I was working. I was tough once! Everybody was going through it. Cass was going though her pregnancy, and not married and nobody knowing who the father was; she was keeping that a secret. All the stuff with John and Michelle and Denny . . . it was not the way to make a record, but there are five solid things on here. We were running out of material, as far as John's songs. On the first side, you have "Creeque Alley" and "Free Advice . . . "

P. F. Sloan: I remember the "Creeque Alley" session. It was one of the most complicated charts that he had ever made. It's a simple song, but a lot of things about John's songs, is that although they appear to be simple, there's a lot of 6/4, 7/4 bars and time changes that he does. I'm not talking about going into waltz time, which is pretty simple, but at this point he was getting into Lennon and McCartney and a lot of the things that were going on. They were very simple songs, but they were challenging and fun to do. When it worked, it was a great feeling of satisfaction.

Lou Adler: "Creeque Alley" is also one of my favorites, and it was written to explain to me the history of The Mamas & The Papas, because continually they were saying to me, "Oh, that was the time Cass was with Zally . . . " and things like that. So, John and Michelle just laid the history out for me. I liked that record a lot.

Jim Horn: I remember the "Creeque Alley" session. Back then, I was doing like, three and four sessions a day. Anyway, this one night, I had gotten home about 11 P.M., and Lou Adler called me, and said, "What are ya doin'?" I told him that I was just about ready to go to bed. He told me that John heard a flute on this song called "Creeque Alley" that they were working on, and would I come down? So I got in my car and drove down to the studio, and I arrived there at about midnight. They were all there, waiting' on me, 'cause I guess they wanted to see what I was going to do. John just told me to play some funky flute, so I just figured I would play something with a bluesy edge to it.

While they were getting the tape ready, I had a few minutes, so I went and talked to all of 'em. They were really great, really fun people to be around. Cass and I would talk about everything from world affairs to babies, everything. She was really well-read, really fun and a lot of fun to talk to.

I was just talking to 'em, and Michelle was sitting down reading this book, and she didn't say 'hi' or anything, and I thought, she was really into this book. But later on when we were taking a break, I sat down next to her and we just talked and talked, she was just the sweetest person, she was great.

Roger McGuinn: I have to tell you that I was astounded by the amount of disposable income that The Mamas & The Papas had compared to The Byrds, with a similar amount of success. They were living in big houses in Beverly Hills, driving expensive sports cars, and buying drugs like money was water. And we were on a kind of tight budget. Our accountant doled out a little bit here and there, but nothing like them! I was going, "Whoa, where did we go wrong!? We have these hits but we don't have the money. What's the deal here?!"

Cass and David Crosby were very close, and Cass gave David a pill bottle, I'd say it was about three inches high and an inch and a half across—like a prescription bottle—FULL of cocaine. It must have been five, six ounces. It was a lot of cocaine, and she gave it to

David Crosby to give to me, as a gesture of kindness, I'm sure. David gave it to me, and I was scared of it; I put it up in a cupboard behind some dishes or something, closed it up and just forgot about it. But then ... people would come over ... and I became very popular, ya know? David would bring people over to my house to visit, and my popularity increased at that point.

Finally I did try it, and I liked it, unfortunately. It made me feel good, and it made me feel like I wasn't shy in public, which was a problem I'd had prior to that. So, it helped with some things that I wanted to fix. I wasn't into it on any habitual basis, but I'd do it occasionally, and gradually it was all gone, I didn't jump into the coke culture at that point—this would be 1967, maybe even earlier—but I did get into it later, unfortunately. But, I stopped a long time ago; 23 years ago.

It was popular in the 1920s and 30s, but this was very early for the rock and roll scene. The coke culture didn't really start until the mid-'70s.

I heard "Creeque Alley" when it came out, and I was flattered that they'd put my name in a song. It made me happy about my association with them in the past and in The Village and things like that. It made me feel good. It's a good song, too, and a great record.

P. F. Sloan: On the first album, I was given free reign to do whatever I wanted to do as a guitarist. John would not say anything at all beyond, "I love that, Phil, give me more of that." He would show me a song and say, "Okay, come up with a lead, come up with some fills, do that thing you did with The Grass Roots, gimmie that sound ... " It was completely free reign, and you can hear the magic of that on the first album. All the riffs worked. On the second album, it was the same, except for, "Okay, come up with something new." By the third album, it was more like, "Okay, you're going to do THIS. I want you to do THAT." And I'd be like, "Okay, John, whatever you say, but there's a top part here that would add a nice dimension to ... " "You fucking know nothing. You don't tell me how to make a record ... " So that changed, and that's sad, 'cause there's no respect for the musicians.

Hal Blaine: Now at one point—and this is the only time I ever got into anything with any artist or producer—it was about four in the morning, and we'd been working all night, and everybody was exhausted. I always used to make a drum chart so that I wouldn't get lost. Aside from the fact that I was doing so many sessions, and I didn't want to get lost. John Phillips . . . he was almost like some of those country guys, he'd sing a song, and then all of the sudden he'd add a bar, or drop a bar. It wasn't always musically standard or consistent. A lot of time when that would happen, I would say, "Okay, John, are you going to add a bar?" and he'd say. "I didn't add a bar there!" I'd say "John, you did." It was getting a little hairy. Joe and Larry would sit there quietly . . . . "John, no argument or anything, if you want . . . " "I wanna do it just the way I did it!" So, okay, I'd take a second and change it on my chart. We'd run through it, and maybe for a couple of times it would stay the same, and then we'd start a take, and he's drop or add that bar again. He was, like, spinning. Then Lou might say something at that point like, "Hold on a second, there's too many bars there . . . " This would go back and forth. . . .

At one point—and we were exhausted—we started doing takes. We got to that one little spot again, and John did it again. All of a sudden, he stopped and jumped up and said, "Okay, Blaine, that was you that time!!" I came right over the drums. I was gonna *choke* this sonofabitch, it was so aggravating, 'cause I was goin' by my part. Anyway, Lou leaped out, and the other players jumped out grabbed us and calmed things down. They fed John a lot of coffee and we apologized to each other. That was the only time in all of my career—almost 40 years—that something like this happened.

Joe Osborne: John was always in charge, and he was the boss. I don't remember seeing any resentment from anybody about that. I don't remember having any problems with anyone. It was just a nice working atmosphere. I think that the thing that kept it up, and made it special, was that when we (session musicians) knew that we were working on hit records. It wasn't like, 'this isn't gonna come out, or maybe this won't make it'. You knew you were working on a hit record. It kept the adrenaline and the interest going.

P. F. Sloan: When we got down to the meat of the songs, everybody was still grooving with The Mamas & The Papas. The musicians were still happy to do it. John had to relax more with these sessions; he was very, very uptight. He wanted so many specific things to be going on. We wanted to say, "John, just relax, let us do our own thing, let us go in and put it down on tape, and you can go in and change stuff later . . ." No, he wanted it right from the beginning, he was like a maestro at this point. And studio rock and roll musicians, at this point they don't like that, they don't appreciate that. With me, of course, I'm 19 years old, and I'm happy to be anywhere in a studio making music. You could say anything to me, if you want me to do this backwards, I'll do it backwards, you know.

When we did songs like "Look Through My Window" you just knew it was happening. We were grooving, we were smiling. When it got more complicated stuff, it became like, "Okay, John's on a Julliard trip here. . . ." But then maybe a year later, the musicians would be listening to it and say, "You know, I was listening to that cut, and that's a very expert cut, I'm glad I played on that . . . John's song was very intricate, and it wasn't very easy to play at the time, and I didn't really feel like doing it at the time, but I listen to it now, and it was expertly done." So, there's a lot of kudos and good feelings about it.

Cyrus Faryar: There was one session where Cass was talking about how John had to just really work or to get that performance out of her, and he just leaned on her big time. Cass sang easily, and he had to bully her a bit to make her go beyond and really dig in and really pull out something that she knew was always there. She was kinda lazy or whatever, and he either antagonized or incited her, or gave her some shit to where she would say, "Okay, screw you, John—get a load of this!" And then she'd sing like an angel.

Denny always was a sweetheart of a guy. Back when Henry Diltz and I were learning folk songs back in Hawaii, one of our heroes was Bob Gibson. This was back in the late '50s. Later in the '60s and '70s when I lived in Los Angeles, Bob Gibson had become a friend of mine. I can't tell you how gratifying that was, because here was guy that I admired so much, and it came to the point where he would come to my house! He liked me, he was my friend, and I was so inammorate of that. One day, I looked out my window, and it looked like two bears had gotten out of a car and waddled up to the house. One of them was Denny, and the other was Bob . . .

As I said before, we were all friends first. We became friends before anyone ever got famous. In some cases, fame just destroys people, and takes some of the enjoyment of life away form them. Cass loved it, you know, but it never formed a barrier between her and her friends that I was aware of. I was particularly saddened when I heard that she died, because I saw her just before she went to Europe. I was just stopping by, and it was one of those situations where she was just extremely happy, because all of the pieces of her life were just coming together. At that particular moment, she was just cranked way up and very excited, so it was very sad and poignant when she died. Cass was very sweet, and very gracious and generous. Just a very nice woman who happened to be in a rock and roll band. John had an aristocratic streak in him, but they deserved it, as far as I'm concerned. Cass and Denny were a bit more 'down-home'.

Michelle Phillips: I just really loved the *Deliver* album, and I remember hearing it for the first time before we went on a trip to Acapulco, and I was just really happy with it. I had gotten back in the group, I was trying to get pregnant, Cass had just delivered or was about to. Life was good.

PART THREE

The Monterey Folk Festival take a left turn . . . beginning of
Monterey Pop in L.A. . . . planning and organizing the chaos . . . the
festival, the aftermath, and The Mamas & The Papas at the crux . . .

Jim Dickinson: It started out that a bunch of us were over at
Alan Prasier's house, because we all listened to music over there.
He had the same Altec 604 speakers that were in the studio. We
had just thrown a concert in the San Fernando Valley, the CAFF
benefit, which I was the head of. I was the producer, and we had
brought in Alan Prasier, who brought in Hugh Masekela. Hugh
was so excited by it, he kept telling Alan, "Do it again, do it again!"
Alan didn't quite know how we did it, and he said, "Well, let's do it
in Tijuana!" I told him that I thought that was a bad idea. Taking
thousands of stoned hippies across the border at the mercy of the
Mexican police . . . Can you say, "Drug bust?" can you say "International Incident?" I told him that he should go and talk to Benny
Shapiro and see who he talked to in Monterey, as he'd done the
Monterey Folk Festival. So, before Benny got in touch with him,
Benny was in charge . . . he hired Ravi Shankar, who he handled at
the time, for $5,000. After that, he wanted to get The Mamas & The
Papas. After that, The Mamas & The Papas and Lou Adler basically
took the whole thing over. At the time, John Phillips had gotten in
touch with me, and The Byrds hadn't been invited yet, and evi-
dently John got to thinking about that, and, as they really started
the scene out here, it wouldn't be right if they weren't included.
So, they were added sort of at the last minute, and as a result, they
really weren't that prepared for it. I was more involved in it than
they were. I got involved in it before The Mamas & The Papas and
Lou Adler got involved in it.

Lou Adler: Alan Parisiar and Derek Taylor came to us to buy
The Mamas & The Papas for a night. Benny Shapiro had put
together this sort of rock/blues festival idea for Monterey; not in
any way near way as big as we eventually took it.

Jim Dickinson: It became free, but Ravi Shankar had already made a deal, and that's why he was the only one who got paid. While Benny had been the one to get Miles Davis to call Irving Townshend to get The Byrds an audition at CBS and got us our deal . . . by then The Mamas & The Papas had happened, and as far as I was concerned, left us in the dust, and I would be inclined to agree with that . . .

Lou Adler: The Mamas & The Papas were about as broad as he was going—it was mostly the San Francisco blues-based groups and some rock and roll. But, in an attempt to bring in some head-liners, they came to The Mamas & The Papas. We just felt it was at real good chance to expand rock and roll . . . what immediately came to my mind was "Jazz At The Philharmonic," taking rock and roll to a different place. Everyone thought of Monterey as the "Monterey jazz Festival." We had earlier conversations at Cass's house with Paul McCartney about rock and roll not really being considered an art form. All of those things sort of came back to me, and John and I discussed it, and said that we really ought to do this festival for charity in order to get all of the groups. Benny Shapiro sort of bought it, but as we went on, John and I were I guess sort of overpowering, in the way our positions were starting to be in the festival. Benny didn't like that, and we bought him out. We bought him out for $50,000. John put up ten, I put up ten, Johnny Rivers, Terry Melcher, and Paul Simon each put up ten.

Alan Parisiar was very much a part of Benny Shapiro's group, and he liked what we were doing, and he stayed with it. Derek Taylor also stayed with us. This happened about six weeks before the festival. It was great working with John at that point; he was right on top of it, and it was something that excited him. Also, there was the energy of it, because we only had about six week to put it together— he didn't have time to have any of his lapses . . . we just killed it.

Arthur Garfunkel: John Phillips called Paul and I in '66–'67. They knew we were coming out to L.A. and wanted to talk about starting a festival with all free talent. And the idea that it was free talent meaning it's not a commercial endeavor, the kids are going to know that we're doing this for music's sake and for a grand party sake, was going to be the essence of the show. And I liked it a lot because I thought, take the money element away and you have something that's going to have a nice feeling about it. And we met, he and Michelle Phillips and Lou Adler, who was producing The Mamas & The Papas records, and Paul and I. We met in California and talked about this festival we were gonna have up in Monterey, and we started making a guest list of who we would invite. And we had a lot of fun coming up with the names of the people, as we knew, who the real great ones were. Otis Redding and the Buffalo Springfield, and all these artists that we knew, well never mind what the company says or what is supposed to be, we felt we knew who the genuine good record makers were. And so we had this great time coming up with the perfect guest list and seeing if they would respond to doing this great show with no pay. And everybody said yes. Everybody except Ravi Shankar, who insisted in getting paid.

Nurit Wilde: He and Lou thought up the whole Monterey thing. I flew up once with Peter Pilafian and John and Lou Adler. I kind of worked for them, but I was really hanging out. This was when they had the offices on Sunset, and I went up with them. It was very exciting and the offices were humming. I remember that everyone got really excited whenever they got somebody on board. People were in and out all of the time, and I remember there was a big thing about The Beatles, and whether they were going to perform or show up, which they never did, I remember that. And then The Rolling Stones; Brian Jones ended up hanging out at Monterey. It was a great festival; everyone was just so excited about every act. Monterey was a lot of fun. Of course, the big thing was when Janis Joplin came up with Big Brother, because before that Grace Slick was considered the big 'diva' of the up-and-coming girls that were fronting bands.

Al Kooper: I was in California actually recovering from a nervous breakdown and my local benefactor in L.A., David Anderle, dropped me off at the Monterey office knowing full well I'd jump in and make myself useful. My old friend from the Village, Chip Monck, was the stage manager, and he was pretty frazzled, so I offered to help him and that was it. I went to the office every day and made voluminous phone calls and onsite I was a liaison between the artists and the stage crew. This rock festival thing had never been done before and there were many conundrums to face, i.e., as we changed the set between acts, what was the audience supposed to do? Prior to this fest, all changeovers were handled within three or four minutes' time by emcees or comedians. Our changeovers were estimated at minimum fifteen minutes, maximum 30 minutes. We decided to just play piped music and hope for their patience. Nothing seems to have disrupted the precedent we set 33 years ago. John and Lou were on the phone constantly and Derek Taylor and his wicked sense of humor kept any difficulties from getting too out of hand. It was a great '60s experience—artists helping artists to perform art. What more can you really ask for?

Denny Doherty: So, John and Michelle are back together, and I took my wounded self back up to the hills, let the party continue and drown my sorrows in Crown Royal. "What are they gonna do?" "They're gonna do a 'festival.' "The Monterey International Pop Festival" I thought, "Fuck this, I'm not gonna work with these two now . . . " So I took off for The Islands, I went back to The Virgin Islands. For the three months they were organizing Monterey Pop, I was in the Islands. I didn't want anything to do with it. I wasn't going to go into that whole scene and watch John and Michelle be 'happy-happy'—which they weren't. I didn't want to be in that hurtful situation. So, John and Michelle and Lou organized Monterey Pop, the biggest fuckin' thing to come down the pike, and I was totally out of the loop. I was on a mountaintop on The Virgin Islands, loaded out of my skull.

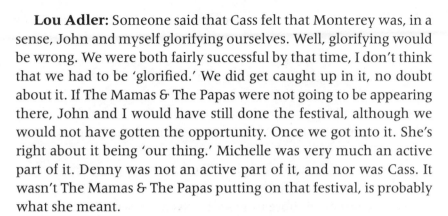

Lou Adler: Someone said that Cass felt that Monterey was, in a sense, John and myself glorifying ourselves. Well, glorifying would be wrong. We were both fairly successful by that time, I don't think that we had to be 'glorified.' We did get caught up in it, no doubt about it. If The Mamas & The Papas were not going to be appearing there, John and I would have still done the festival, although we would not have gotten the opportunity. Once we got into it. She's right about it being 'our thing.' Michelle was very much an active part of it. Denny was not an active part of it, and nor was Cass. It wasn't The Mamas & The Papas putting on that festival, is probably what she meant.

Peter Pilafian: I was on the payroll with the group, and we were all having a great time and it was very giddy, because all of this hadn't been invented before—all this rock and roll fame and fortune—it was all a new thing, especially for a bunch of folkies.

Somehow John and Lou got wind of this festival, and wrestled it away from the guys that had started it—Benny Shapiro, Alan Parisier, and those people. What they did that was interesting—because John and Lou are pretty commercially minded—what they did was to move the event out of the commercial zone, into to the social, altruistic, benevolent zone. I think it was actually set up as a non-profit organization. That was absolutely brilliant, and it showed in a way what kind of class John and Louie had. It showed that they knew what they were doing, rather than 'money-grubbing' people after hit records.

They had the big picture—and the big picture was that this was a social phenomenon that we were riding, that was more than just selling records. Selling records would come sort of automatically, and rise out of whatever was done altruistically, for the good of the social phenomenon; you know, "think big."

Lou Adler: I came up with the line "Music, Love & Flowers," but they might have added to it by calling it "The Monterey Pop International Festival." I can see how they called it a "Pop Festival," because I can't see 'Pop' being a word that Benny Shapiro would want to use, so I don't remember if they brought that in or not.

Andrew Loog Oldham was a very close friend of mine, and a very good friend of John's at that point. I had met Andrew the first time that The Stones came into town to do the T.A.M.I. Show. He was in England, and we were able to ask him and Paul McCartney what was going on there. They both mentioned The Who and Hendrix and The Animals, all of that came from them.

Brian Jones came to hang out; The Stones were never going to play the festival, and he came to hang out. Andrew was a very important part of all those things what went on with The Mamas & The Papas in England: Cass's being arrested, and all of that, Andrew was in the middle of all of that. Andrew was there when they arrived, and it was his limo, and he was a very important part of all of that. But that was a little later on.

Peter Pilafian: There was the gap between the San Francisco philosophy and L.A., and it kind of came to a head. It was remarkable that we had Janis and everyone. I know that the San Francisco gang perceived us as the 'invaders' and the 'commercial exploiters' who were kind of stomping on their turf, and they wanted nothing to do with us, and that perception continued for a long time. For years afterward, there was a big split. It was a difference in lifestyle, and it shouldn't have made such a difference, but it did. Maybe its because in L.A. we were more image conscious. We called it the 'record industry,' and they didn't call it an industry. It was in a sense, a culture clash.

In San Francisco, the most visible example of business-oriented behavior was Bill Graham, and Bill was a completely wacko, wildcard kind of a guy. I think that for the San Francisco people, they saw that as business, and the concept of doing business was Bill Graham. He was kind of a lunatic. But they were very determined that the music carry their message of how they viewed society, and they saw the L.A. people as coming from a different place, where music was just one source, and to us it included other things. But in the end, it's interesting, because look at the extraordinary popularity of The Grateful Dead. Their message bore that out, and it was real. Whereas look at the commercial side of the music business, which has gone throughout the most awful, schizophrenic changes; and you can't make any sense of it.

Michelle Phillips: I helped solicit advertisements from the record companies. I was also calling dress shops on Rodeo Drive. The record companies were not particularly eager to buy space in the program. First of all, The Monterey International Pop Festival, nobody knew what this was all about. Nobody ever did anything for free, and this was the first pop festival. Now we kind of take for granted that these things happen, but then the only thing that was even remotely like it was the Monterey Jazz Festival. So to try to get labels to buy space in a program for a pop festival was not easy to get across. In fact it was also a very foreign thing to tell the artists, that, "We're gonna fly you in but you're going to have to sing for free." I mean, they were laughing at us. (egotistical tone) "I've never played for free in my life!" These were *big* people. John and Lou were very smart, they brought people in to the board, like McCartney, Simon & Garfunkel, I think, were both on the board . . . Brian Wilson was on the board. So they—Lou and John—were smart, they built an infrastructure to drag the talent in. They got the names. It was not just Lou Adler and John Phillips saying, "Please do this." It was, "*Us guys* want this to happen." It was like the princes of rock and roll got together and said, "You do this, because this is going to be for a good cause." We didn't even know where the money was gonna go! "It's for charity!" We were going to have music schools in Watts, we were gonna have this and that. We didn't know what we were talking about. We were just, "*Please* do it for free."

But with the record companies, it was a little tough, but I had Derek Taylor to help me. When I couldn't get someone to do it, I'd say (fast-paced businesslike), "Oh, Derek wants to talk to you!" And he was like, [garbled heavy English accent] "Yes-yes-yes, and it's a good cause, you know, and-we're-all-doing-it-for-nothing. . . ." So we would cajole and push people around a little bit. But with love, ya know. . . .

Peter Pilafian: We set up offices at the Club Renaissance on Sunset, and since I was working very closely with them at the time,

Lou Adler, John, and Michelle, Monterey, June 1967.
Photo by Bobby Klein. Courtesy of Michelle Phillips.

they gave me the non-performance part of the festival, and so I became one of the producers of The Monterey Pop Festival, with the assignment of interviewing all the would-be vendors and determining how to set up the fairgrounds, booths, decorations, and so on.

I flew up to the very, very first festival that was put on—by a radio station, I believe—it might have been the Human Be-In in January 1967. I went up and got a helicopter, because you couldn't drive in, to take a look at their decorations and big floats. We got wind of all these cool statues and Buddhas and whatever, that they were creating, and they could make them and sell them to us at a pretty reasonable price.

I was dealing with a constant stream of sort-of hippie entrepreneurs, who all wanted booths at the festival. Some of them I liked, and I tended to steer towards the ones who didn't seem overly commercial or aggressive, hostile or whatever. I wanted to create a nice atmosphere. I remember one fellow named Charles Royal who came in, and we could not get rid of him. He insisted on publishing a newspaper—he wanted to publish the official Monterey Pop Festival newspaper, and distribute it around the fairgrounds. Then he wanted to drive his fleet of Cadillac limousines in, because he said that he loved parades, and so on! So I kept telling him, "No, we don't want that . . . " He showed up anyway, and by then, what could you do? It was pretty interesting.

Michelle Phillips: Monterey Pop was *so beautiful* . . . the weather was this perfect warm, June weather, like beautiful spring weather, and there were flowers everywhere. Lou had flown in 150,000 orchids from Hawaii, the policemen had them on their helmets and up the antennas of their motorcycles. It *was* a love feast. It was beautiful. Also, Monterey Pop was a very manageable festival. There were people selling their wares, their crafts. It really was like a fair, like a Renaissance Fair. Everybody was dressed up in tie-dye and ribbons and it was *very* festive.

It was convenient for the artists and the audience. Practically everyone had a seat, and if not, people were lining up against the fence, and they could see and hear. Or people were sitting outside, you could hear it outside, too. The weather had a lot to do with it too, and the fact that there *weren't* that many people . . . I don't know how many people passed through Monterey that weekend, but it was always very manageable. You also weren't having a lot of drug freak-outs. It was lovely. Also, for the artists backstage we had a buffet set up . . . we were eating lobster and crab . . . it was great! The area backstage was very luxurious.

Peter Pilafian: It was one of those things that I don't bump into these days much. It was an enterprise that had its own internal driving force, and it seemed like it was karmatically meant to be, and those of us who were jumping on the train were being driven by some other force. It didn't have to get whipped and forced into shape—it had a force of its own. We were all lucky to be part of it, and that was the feeling; it just kept growing and growing and it was hugely organic. It was guided, of course, by a lot of the right decisions, but it had an energy that . . . I just don't see that stuff anymore these days. I don't know, maybe Silicon Valley's like that now, I don't know, but that's so profit-oriented. It was the celebration of a social movement that had huge repercussions for many decades afterwards; even though it was poo-poo'd at the time for being a kind of minor blip.

I flew back and forth a few times (on the Lear jet)—it was a matter of an approaching deadline. It was chaotic; but it was productively chaotic. It was increasingly busy—people running in and out—and as the cache of the event grew, more and more groups were desperate to be part of it, and the selection had to get a little keener. It seemed that people were begging to be included. It kind of caught fire, and word got out.

The orchid thing was kind of interesting. We had this idea to bring in all these orchids from Hawaii. They were cheap. You can get 80,000 orchids from Hawaii for not a lot of money. We placed the order, and I tried to arrange a hot-air balloon to scatter them over the crowd while Ravi played. That was our vision. Unfortunately, the wind shifted, and it wasn't going to be able to go over the site at the last minute, so we had the ushers put them on the seats, so when they arrived to see Ravi, there would be an orchid there. It was one of those great afternoons where everything came together.

Backstage Owsley was walking around giving people his purple acid, and I saw Hendrix before his set take two of these, and a half an hour later he was on stage. It was pretty extraordinary—it was amazing. But with Jimi, it just powered him further into perfection, and he completely hit the groove.

Woodstock always had the air of commercialism, right from the beginning, whereas Monterey was still in the age of purity. It was a metaphor for what that era of '60s rock and roll was all about. It was peace, love & flowers, and sex and drugs and rock and roll. Monterey kind of carved in stone a statue to defy those values. It was a remarkable event, and I feel so privileged to be an intimate part of it.

Arthur Garfunkel: And that was the first festival, and since then when Woodstock came shortly after that. My attitude was Woodstock is a bit of a copy of Monterey, because Monterey was a huge success. In terms of spirit, it was wonderful. A weekend of about 20 different acts, and I had a great feeling about that. When I saw Woodstock I felt well, it's they're are already now doing the second, it's a copy, it's the East Coast version of what we did. I always thought Monterey was the one.

John Phillips: Scott inspired me to write the song "San Francisco." We were doing the Monterey Pop Festival, and the town of Monterey was sort of frightened by the thought of two hundred and fifty thousand hippies coming . . .

Scott McKenzie: Well, they were terrified. I was hanging out with John and Lou and going up to Monterey. John was on acid most of the time, and he gave a speech to the property owners and the fathers and the mothers and all the relatives of the town, the police chief, and the mayor, in which he tried to convince them to hold the pop festival there. And he did, somehow. I don't know how he did that. During this time I figured that we ought to do a song which was really written to the young people who, obviously, were coming to California that summer, and would really descend on Monterey if this pop festival happened.

John Phillips: But the idea was that they would come in peace to the pop festival

Scott McKenzie: John took it from there.

John Phillips: Which they did. There was not one arrest during the whole pop festival. (With the song), actually, I was thinking of the Olympics and the wreaths that the people wore. Garlands, yeah.

Scott McKenzie: When I recorded that song, some friends of mine all who happened to be initiated by the Maharishi and were meditating all over the place, went out and picked wildflowers in Laurel Canyon and wove garlands of flowers , and I wore them on my hair and sang the song. We did a soundtrack at Western, and the vocals at another studio . . .

John Phillips: I think it's called Sound Factory. We did some overdubs there also, on it. Lou and I produced it, put it together, co-produced.

Scott McKenzie: I don't remember it as a process. I think John and I talked about the idea of a song for a couple of weeks, at least, and then he just sort of sat down and went into his own position, whatever it was, and wrote the song. In about twenty minutes. And I loved it. We just started singing it around his house and everywhere. We'd go into Lou's office. "Here, listen to this." That's like the old days. In New York, when we first went there, you'd stop on a street corner and sing for an agent or a producer or anybody. We were just thrilled with it.

John Phillips: But the thing was, the first time Lou heard the song, he said, "God, I've got to hear this song immediately." And we went in the studio the next day, I think, and recorded it, which was a Tuesday. And by Friday it was on the radio and by Monday it was a hit. [makes exploding sound] It went all over the world.

Lou Adler: The film was really ancillary to producing the festival. It's interesting, in that we tried to get financing for the festival, so we went to ABC network, Tom Moore, a nice Southern gentleman who was president, and we made a deal that was . . . think, that Barry Diller might have come up with the idea for a ABC 'Movie Of The Week,' and this was to be a 'Movie Of The Week.' John and I hired D. A. Pennibaker; we talked to a couple of other people prior to that and we ended up with Pennibaker, who had done Dylan's "Don't Look Back." We shot it as a TV show, because they gave us the money up front, which helped finance the festival. But when Tom Moore saw the Hendrix footage . . . he said, "Take it back . . . ," which turned out to be a blessing. It turned out that we were able to put it out as a film. It didn't do exceptionally well, but over the years it's generated a lot of income, but as a documentary. Woodstock did really well, but 'Monterey Pop' didn't do that great.

The Monterey Foundation is probably more active now than it

was at the beginning, because the funds that it's generated have been continuous, and they seem to grow as the years go by. Mostly, it's the deals that we've made on the audio rights through licensing to compilations and the studio packages that we've put out through Rhino, there was one on Liberty/United Artists, one on Warner, and we have an override on the Hendrix. . . . recently we did a VH-1 'Lost Performances,' and there's an hour of that that's wonderful.

We build a floor at the L.A. Free Clinic, and there's a thing called "Black August,' which in exchange with Cuba, people can hear the Hip-Hop pioneers . . . We give money to the R&B Foundation in New York, and we picked up some of Mary Wells's hospital bills. It's entirely arbitrary, and we don't have to go through a lot of channels to make our decisions. . . .

John Phillips: It was a non-profit organization. It still is and still has—well, there had been very good revenues from the movie. See, what we did, we called acts all over the world that we thought were the right acts for the first pop festival in history. We told them that no one was getting paid. All they would get would be the expenses from where they were, expenses while they were in Monterey, and plane tickets to their next job. And for that they signed away all their recording rights and movie rights, and every right to any income from it, and it all went to the Monterey Pop Festival fund, which still exists and still gives out scholarships and supports old rock and rollers and sick people in the music industry and things like earthquake relief. We built the Free Clinic in L.A. The one in San Francisco, also. Lou's mostly responsible, Lou Adler, for really handling all the ins-and-outs of getting these things together. After the concert itself, I was so exhausted. Michelle was a great part of that concert also. Should have been a co-producer, actually. She worked night and day for months.

Larry Knechtel: We played with them at Monterey, but we were also playing with Johnny Rivers, Laura Nyro, Scott McKenzie. It was neat being at Monterey, but those things are kinda foggy . . . . I had a great time, though. I had never seen Otis before that.

Richie Furay: It certainly was a big event, and I was excited about it, but Neil had just left the band (Buffalo Springfield), and that probably knocked some of the wind out of our sails. It sure seemed pretty organized. Also, the confines of it—it was on pretty limited grounds, and that had something to do with that as well. It certainly was an adventuresome move to do a show on that level.

Henry Diltz: I was asked by John to shoot The Monterey Pop Festival. I remember that before they went on, they were downstairs in this dressing room area warming up. I remember Hendrix was on the other side of the room eating fried chicken. He had a little entourage with him, people like John Entwhistle and some others. On the other side of the room is The Mamas & The Papas and Scott McKenzie and some other people, and they're doing their warm-up exercises, holding their tongues while making these sounds, you know, gibberish, babbling, while they grabbed their tongues. All those pictures went to Dunhill Records, and I don't remember what happened to them, for obvious reasons!

Joe Osborne: I was in Monterey. I also remember a show we did in Anaheim, and then we went to Arizona or someplace. I did about three or four live shows with them, but nothing on a regular basis. It was a lot of fun. I don't remember any problems, really.

Most of the people on that show who later became famous, weren't known at the time. It didn't mean thing at the time, seeing Jimi Hendrix or Janis Joplin on stage, they were nobody at the time. It was just a lot of people, and a big outdoor venue, and a nice gig.

John Phillips: The only real down side of Monterey Pop Festival is that we were the closing act of the whole festival. It took us three months to put it together and we had no rehearsals or sang at any time during that three-month period. Denny was in the islands and he showed up ten minutes before we were supposed to go on stage. We thought he wouldn't show up at all. I thought we sounded really bad that night, which was a letdown for me, because after all the work we put into it, I wanted it to sound wonderful and it didn't.

Denny Doherty: Cass called me while I was in The Virgin Islands and said, "You know, next weekend, we're closing The Monterey Pop Festival. You'd better get home. We gotta do this." I said, "Don't worry, I'll be there." I got home the day before, got in my Cadillac, and drove to Monterey with a buddy of mine, Owen Orr. At about 9 A.M., Owen said, "What time do you have to be there?" I said, "Well, I dunno; we're closing the show tonight." "We gotta fucking get *going!*" He said it was an eight-hour drive, and I thought it was just a couple of hours up the coast, just up from Santa Barbara. He said, "No, no! We gotta *go . . .*" So, we drove for eight hours up the Coast Highway #1; I didn't know about Highway 101. So, it took at least the whole eight hours. By the time we arrived, it was getting dark, and we just followed the crowds and the noise and the lights. I had no ideal what had been going on, how long it had been going on, who was on the bill. It was the big 'poobah,' the big 'do' and I didn't know. So I thought, "I'll be there, do my thing, and then go home . . . " I had no idea what they had created.

When I got there, I found out that The Who and Jimi Hendrix were going to play, and then we were going to close the show. I found the stage, climbed up, went around the back, and you had to go back down into the far corner to go backstage. I turned to the stage at exactly the same moment that Keith Moon held up the victory sign, stood up on his drums, and kicked them over, and they exploded. I don't know what kind of charge he had in there, but he kicked the whole fucking thing over, and it all exploded, as Townshend was putting his guitar through the amplifier. The whole stage was being destroyed. I thought I'd walked into a riot. I didn't know *what* was goin' on! "What the *fuck* is this?" 'cause I'd never seen The Who do anything. I didn't know they destroyed the stages . . . and Pennibaker is trying to film this, so these guys are all running around trying to save their mikes and cameras and equipment and stuff, and The Who is destroying the stage. I disappear down the hole, and I find the gang downstairs, and the noise upstairs subsides. I change into the caftan that I'm going to wear, and we're supposed to do a sound check and warm up with "Dedicated." All of the sudden, this fuckin' racket starts up on stage again! I'm goin' "What are they doin' *now*?!" "Well, The Who's finished, and Jimi's on stage . . . " "Jimi who?" No, not *The* Who, they were just on stage. Jimi *Hendrix . . .* " Now the place is really goin' fuckin' crazy, and the feedback is so loud, that windows are rattling and light bulbs are popping. I go up the spiral staircase, peer my head out to the stage, over the drums that they're using, and Hendrix is lighting his fucking *guitar* on fire! "Wait a minute, who the fuck is *this* guy!?" Apparently, Hendrix and The Who flipped a coin to see who was going to follow each other. So Hendrix won, he's on stage setting his stuff on fire, and this guy comes up and says, "Okay, you're on!" "Huh? We gotta follow *this!?*" So, when you hear those live recordings—which are fuckin' abominable—the reason is: all of the stage had been destroyed by The Who and Jimi Hendrix! We came out and used whatever was left! We came out, did our set, finished our set, I came back to the hotel, and eventually drove back to L.A. Who knew I was involved in a fucking milestone?

At the hotel, which was the Carmel Highland Inn, I think, I was in someone's room. The door was open, and a huge truck backed up right up near the door of the room. The back gate came off, and it was The Who, again! Playing on the truck, with a generator. Full blast! This party was not gonna stop at *all*. I was walking back, kinda hugging the building, trying to get back to my room, and I'm looking down near the sidewalk, and the rooms had the curtains that went from ceiling to floor. I walk by one room, and I see Mickey Dolenz's face pressed up against the glass, down on the floor, smilin' and sound asleep. I don't know how many other bodies were in there, but the hotel was full of everybody from Monterey Pop in various stages of celebration and decomposition. I don't know where Cass or John and Michelle were. . . .

Chapter Six

Farewell to the First Golden Era

PART ONE

The spirit of Monterey at The Hollywood Bowl . . . The secret
studio without a variance . . . private rehearsals in the front room
. . . tearing out Jeannette MacDonald's cedar closet . . . Paul Simon
and "12:30" . . . The new Dunhill contract, and "Mama Michelle"
reads it . . . Dunhill says farewell to the first golden era and cashes
in their chips to ABC . . .

Hollywood Bowl, August 1967.
Photo by Henry Diltz.

"Farewell To The First Golden Era"
Notes by Derek Taylor
Autumn 1967
(Used by permission of Universal Music Group)

"All the leaves are brown . . . and the sky is gray . . . "

. . . The opening words of "California Dreamin'" speak of a summer past and it's sad that the high Summer of the wonderful Mamas and Papas is over; it's melancholy that we may not see them again for a long time.

Michelle and John, Cass and Denny are leaving America soon and will pass through London in their way to the Islands which punctuate the Mediterranean and Aegean seas where they will seek to rediscover the unity, the sense of fun and the inner strength which took them from a cheerful valley of poverty and struggle to the broad, sunlit uplands of fame and success, of world-wide recognition and widespread acceptance as incomparable contemporary minstrels.

It was in the Virgin Islands, sunworshipping and lazing around in the early 1960s that the four of them planned how it would be when someone gave them the key to unlock the musical treasure chest which, their experience and instinct told them, they surely possessed.

The key came in Los Angeles from Lou Adler, the producer who recalls being introduced to them by Barry McGuire, and who, when he first saw them, couldn't believe his eyes and who then, when he heard them sing, couldn't believe his ears. Nor, could any of us believe our eyes and ears, for it seemed too much of a bonus in 1965, that exiting bountiful year, to realize that on top of all the other musical adventures and explosions were the Mamas and Papas. Looking back from now, it's unbelievable that in pop-terms there was ever a time that there wasn't a Mamas and Papas.

The group felt that by leaving America for a time and by traveling though Europe—and who knows how far beyond—together, the four of them will be able to find each other again. By remaining a unit and yet by separating themselves from familiar environments, they feel they may—now being now and then being then—rather than recapture the old magic, fall into a new alchemy.

It's impossible to accept that we will not again enjoy that lovely line-up—honest, happy, hippy Cass in an enormous dress, billowing, feathering and soft-shoeing across the stage in her boots . . . lovely Michelle enraptured by John, her lean and long husband, group leader and composer of the music. And Denny with the cheerful, hooded, wicked eyes, owner of that light baritone—or maybe tenor, depending on your ear for pitch—which has threaded its way through so many songs. While they're away, we will miss them.

Through "California Dreamin'" to "Monday, Monday," "Words of Love," "Look Through My Window," "I Saw Her Again Last Night," "Dedicated to the One I Love," "Creeque Alley" to "Twelve-Thirty" (the story of the journey from the streets of New York to the California canyons—a record which went into the top ten) through the marvelous Monterey International Pop Festival, through countless magazine articles, numberless television appearances and through a continuing involvement in the local Los Angeles "scene," we have grown to prize them highly and love them dearly.

It is two years since "California Dreamin'" became a reality and the Mamas and Papas, owners of a brand new recording studio built in the Bel Air home of John and Michelle—a home once owned by Jeanette McDonald—and there is no reason, beyond sentiment, to mention it—were to have recorded their fourth album of original songs. Three album songs were already finished, but they have found that they can no longer carry on without the search for peace and new artistic expression as a group. Eras are only eras; they are not the end of time.

John York: The last gig that I remember with them was The Hollywood Bowl in August of '67. That was an amazing evening. Hendrix opened, and he had just left The Monkees tour. It was a wonderful evening, because they had Hendrix open, and then they had a Beethoven string quartet—which was just exquisite, and The Mamas & The Papas played.

I just remember only one rehearsal, and it was for the gig. They

Michelle and Cass, backstage, Hollywood Bowl, August 1967.
Photo by Henry Diltz.

were just so wonderful to the musicians. It was at John and Michelle's house, the old Jeanette McDonald house. We rehearsed in the living room, and it was a lot of fun. There was never any pressure, and we had a very respectable rapport with them. Again, we had a lot of freedom, so there wasn't any 'critical commentary.' Once in a while, Cass would come over to me and say, "Hey, there's a cool bass line on the record, would you make sure you play that?" Out of all the different groups I'd played with, the one thing that stands out in my mind is how well they treated the musicians. They were wonderful.

That gig at The Bowl, they had talked about it as the last show, the swan song of the group, so we knew that was the end, and that's why we rehearsed. I remember the party they had at their house after the Bowl gig, and they had a huge billiards table in one of the rooms, and we were sitting around the room watching the game. I don't remember who was playing, but Hendrix was sitting right next to me, and some guy was shooting pool. Everybody was watching Hendrix all of the time, anyway, because he was just blowing everyone's mind, but nobody had seen him up close like

Jimi Hendrix and Michelle Phillips, backstage, Hollywood Bowl, August 1967.
Photo by Henry Diltz.

that, and you could feel everyone watching him. This guy was shooting, and really intent on his shot, and he draws the cue back, and just SLAMS Hendrix right between the eyes. The whole room, everybody stopped—you could almost hear people breathing, waiting for Hendrix to react, and he didn't do or say anything, he just sat there, and everyone went on with whatever they were doing.

I remember at that Bowl gig, at one point in the show John was introducing all of the musicians. The stage at The Bowl is pretty big, so there was a lot of space between all of the players. I don't remember what state of mind he was in, but he gets to me and says, "And on bass we have John . . . " and he's looking at me, and he walked over to me and says, "Man, you'll have to forgive me, I'm really stoned and I can't remember your last name." So I said, "It's okay; no problem, man, My name is John YORK, like New York." So he walks back to the mic, and by the time he gets there, he forgets again!" He says, "John . . . John . . . The Piper's Son," from that old rhyme. And the whole audience just burst out laughing.

August 24, 1967

Mr. Don Morris
Local 47
817 N. Vine Street
Hollywood, California

Dear Mr. Morris:

                                    394716,394717
Enclosed please find contract #412582,394715,412581
                              9103,9104
covering session # 9093,9098,9102 held on 8/11,199,14,15

at Western,Sound Studios   . The leader is

M.Deasy,J.Kolbrak,H.Blaine,P.Sloan, the artist is

P.F.SLOAN,MAMAS & PAPAS,JIM VALLEY,BARRY MCGUIRE

Please return approved copies for my files.

Thank you.

                            Sincerely yours,

                            Rick Ward

RW:CP
ENC.

Courtesy of Elliot Kendall.

Peter Pilafian: At some point, John called Jay Lasker at Dunhill and said, "Sorry, we're not going to give you another album unless we re-negotiate our deal." He could throw his weight around, because they needed another album. Meanwhile, the syncophants would come and sell them rugs or whatever.

John kinda wanted to reel it in, and I think that he didn't want to pay all of this big money to United (recording studio). He also wanted an environment that was super-friendly and intimate, where he could just take whatever time and ambiance that he wanted to bring that incredible four-part harmony to fruition, and not be constrained by a commercial environment. I don't know if studios cost that much those days, I don't know if the money flow was a problem. I think it was more that he wanted to create an ambiance that was just about music, and not about over and over again about, "We're going into overtime, and the engineers or musicians have to go home," etc.

Hal Blaine: They built a completely secret studio. It was a wonderful thing. It was fun because it was so easy going, so laid back. There was always a kitchen, so there was always some food to grab on a 'five,' you know. The L.A. County, or Bel Air Patrol were always coming around, and there always seemed to be a lookout, watching. You couldn't have a recording studio in a house in those days. Downstairs we had instruments set up, bullshit instruments, we didn't rehearse down there. And if we were recording, there would be a lookout for any cars that looked like they might be building inspectors, they would give us the holler, and we would all run down to the living room and kind of act like, "Well, we're The Mamas & The Papas . . . we're rehearsing with our band . . . " They would always go away scratching their heads, because there would be all of these cars and cartage trucks parked outside. They would sing a couple of bars of something, and you could see these inspectors looking, checking for any kind of wiring or some sign, because it wasn't code, you couldn't have a recording studio in a house in those days. But, they couldn't figure anything out.

Michelle Phillips: Well, we couldn't get a variance from the

Michelle and Cass, Hollywood Bowl, August 1967.
Photo by Henry Diltz.

city of Los Angeles to build the studio. But did that deter us? Nooo! We went in there and we tore out Jeannette MacDonald's cedar closet. Actually, the studio itself was built into the attic. The cedar closets were built in the '40s. They had lowered the cathedral ceiling in the living room and built the cedar closet over that ceiling. So, instead of a cathedral ceiling, the ceiling was high, but it was flat at the top, and we turned the cedar closet into the waiting room. The studio was in the attic.

Hal Blaine: When the studio was built, everything was done in between the walls; there were no wires or cables showing at all. In order to get to their studio, there was this beautiful staircase, which I believe was walnut paneled. Just gorgeous. When you walked up it, there was one panel that you pushed, and that led you to the studio, which was another staircase, which led to another wing, which had been Jeanette MacDonald's cedar clothing closets. They had pulled all that out, and built their recording studio. Lou, somehow, had gotten a hold of the board at Western. All of a sudden he became the engineer. He had been on that board so much you know. But he wasn't an engineer, really. I used to laugh sometimes, because we'd rehearse a tune sometimes, and Lou would say, "Okay, let's make it." And we'd do it again to record it. Lou would be futzing with everything, and of course, he wouldn't get it! I'd say, "Lou! This is fuckin' F Troop, man!" This is when that television show was very popular, and the characters in the show would make all these mistakes. They ended up putting that on the fourth album: "Engineered by F Troop." It was hysterical.

Michelle Phillips: Everything that had to do with the studio and the waiting room had been bootlegged. The studio looked beautiful. We bought a table that looked like a coffee table, but you could take everything off of it, and it was a game table, and then you took everything off of that and it was roulette table under that. I think it was craps on the top, roulette on the bottom. It was just great. We were very big on toys. We had antique slot machines, music boxes . . . we liked old things. The studio was state of the art, and we had big pillows made at Profle de Le Monde . . . big huge paisley pillows that you could lie around in at the studio. We had every type of instrument. We had finger bells, and violins, and guitars and drums . . . all kinds of drums. Every time we saw a new instrument, we would pick it up for the studio. I had a little baby's push toy. It was a little roller, and a stick that you would push, and when you pushed it, it would make a little tinkley sound, and we used it on "San Francisco," and you can hear me playing it at the very beginning of the track. Of course, we used the music box at the end of the *Deliver* album, "John's Music Box," and John got the credit for the publishing! That's an abuse, I'm sorry! Instead of turning 'tragedy into publishing,' that was turning '*nothing* into publishing!' In the studio, we had a big hookah and big basket of pot next to it, and that studio was a *den* of *inequity* and fun; we had a lot of fun up in the studio.

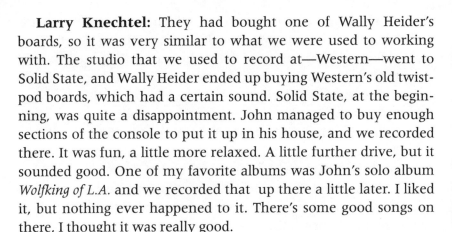

Larry Knechtel: They had bought one of Wally Heider's boards, so it was very similar to what we were used to working with. The studio that we used to record at—Western—went to Solid State, and Wally Heider ended up buying Western's old twist-pod boards, which had a certain sound. Solid State, at the beginning, was quite a disappointment. John managed to buy enough sections of the console to put it up in his house, and we recorded there. It was fun, a little more relaxed. A little further drive, but it sounded good. One of my favorite albums was John's solo album *Wolfking of L.A.* and we recorded that up there a little later. I liked it, but nothing ever happened to it. There's some good songs on there, I thought it was really good.

Lou Adler: Well, the nightmare of that was their own studio. For me it was an unbearable situation. It's nice for me to be able to go to work, "We're going to work, we're going to the studio—that's the ambiance, we're working . . . " It was never like that at the Bel Air house. As great as Peter Pilafian was, he was trying to make whatever equipment was up there work, and it wasn't the ideal situation for recording either from a working standpoint or from an engineering, or electronics standpoint, any standpoint. They'd literally get out of bed and fall into the studio, or fall out of the studio and fall into bed. Michelle, in the middle of the thing, she'd decide that she wanted to make a meal for everyone. It was a nightmare working there.

Now, the evolution of a studio in a house—nowadays everybody has a studio in their house—most of them are digital systems. We were recording analog, and supposedly we should have had the best board and all of those things, which we didn't have.

Michelle Phillips: I know that there was very questionable stuff going on. Abe Somer, the attorney, represented everyone. As far as I can remember, Abe represented The Mamas & The Papas, represented Lou, represented Dunhill, P. F. Sloan. He was like the Mafia 'consiglieri.' He was the lawyer to the family. He was the

Dunhill consiglieri. So, no one questioned it. "The deals are being made in your best interest. [Italian accent] Don't question it . . . ." We were happy; we had an album that went straight to the top of the charts. We were stars. This is what we all had wanted. Cass was happy, and John was happy and Denny was happy, and I was happy.

But, later on . . . we didn't know that we were signing an extension of our contract so that we could be sold to Dunhill. Those negations had been going on for quite some time. But we didn't find out about the sale of Dunhill to ABC until we read it in the trades, in *Cashbox*. After that happened, ABC had the whip out and were demanding more product. Jay Lasker became president of ABC as part of that deal, and it *emboldened* him so much. He puffed *right* up. He was just such a monster, and I hated Jay. You know, they all fucked us over. You can get fucked and then you can get *fucked*, and we were getting fucked and not being kissed. At least Lou was kissing us!

Now, when we went to sign the contract, I actually *read* the contract, and I found something very unusual. There was a clause that said something to the effect of, "If the group breaks up, John may be allowed to be called 'Papa John,' Cass 'Mama Cass,' etc. . . . but Michelle may not use the name 'Mama Michelle'" . . .

Remember that Abe, Jay, Lou, and John were all part of those negotiations. They knew it was in there. It was something that they were *giving* Jay. Jay obviously put it in there, and they all said, "We didn't see that . . . " They *never* expected me to read that contract. I'd never read a contract ever before in my life. But something . . . the vibe in the atmosphere in that room, and the fact that I had not been allowed to attend the negotiations for the last month. . . . I was told that was because of the fact that Jay and I fought so bitterly, and that I was five months pregnant. But there was something in my instinct that told me that I'd better sit down and read this contract. The atmosphere was thick as a *knife*. When I came to that part, I re-read it a few times to make sure I had read it right! I looked up at Jay and said, "What the *fuck* is this?!'" Jay looked at me, shut his briefcase, and walked out of the room. Abe was running after him, and I was running after *Abe*. I *had* to hear what he was going to say to him. Abe said, "Jay, where are you going? These negations aren't over . . . " Jay said "They're over, because Michelle looked at me like I was a piece of shit." and I said, "Well, if the shoe fits . . . '"or something stupid like that.

John and Michelle, Bel Air, 1967.
Courtesy of Michelle Phillips.

PART TWO

The final Sullivan show ... Europe on a million dollars a day ... madness on the S.S. *France* ... Cass gets arrested for stealing blankets and chats with Scotland Yard ... Lou Adler sticks his head in an ice bucket, and The Mamas & The Papas begin to disintegrate ...

Peter Pilafian: We had this idea to go to Europe on the S.S. *France*, so John booked first class tickets, and we headed over there. As I recall, there were the four singers and Lou and myself and Abe Somer. It was a fairly quick, four- or five-day trip across the Atlantic.

Michelle Phillips: Well, we got to New York, and we played Carnegie Hall, and then we performed "12:30" on the Sullivan show, and now we were going to go to England on board the *France*, which was a luxurious ocean liner. The people called us the next day, and said, "We're thrilled that you're coming with us ... would you like to make some reservations?" We sailed a couple of days later, and we stopped in Boston and John and Denny got off the ship and scored us some pot, because we didn't have time to score any pot. And we were going to England, where they didn't have any pot, just hash. We had some tabs of acid with us, too, and some uppers and some downers. When we got on the ship ... we were really big stars by the time we got on that ship, I've gotta tell you. After Sullivan, we were so recognizable that when we walked into dinner on the *France*, that first night ... it was super-duper first class, and we were wearing our robes and our silks, and when we went to dinner, the entire dining room gave us a standing ovation. It was pretty impressive. These were old, staid passengers, on an old, staid ocean liner. The captain invited us to sit at his table ... we were having a fabulous time.

Peter Pilafian: It was a suprise after this wonderful trip across the ocean and first class dining, and two waiters for every table, and wine stewards. I started to notice that the people in the conventional class seemed to be having more fun, and parties and everything! 'Cause the first class people were pretty stuffy, and that's where we were. So I bribed one of the stewards to give me a passkey to let me into the regular passenger area.

Michelle Phillips: Towards the end of the trip, we lost a stabilizer. I remember that we were high as kites, and we all had our lifejackets on. I was crying, and I was drunk! I thought it was gonna be the *Titanic*, like, everything's so wonderful . . . and now it's gonna end! When we docked in Southampton, our party was being separated from the rest of the travelers. We knew something was up, but we didn't know what. Then one of the pursers came up and said, "We just want you to know that there are police waiting for you at the bottom of the gangplank, to arrest Cass." Now, at some point in the trip, Cass and I had sewn all of the pot and the uppers and the downers and the acid into the lining of our coats. And done a very nice job, I might add. We had put them in baggies, and then put them in the lining of our coats, and we sewed it up.

Now, when they told us that the police were waiting for us, John went to Cass and said, "Go to the bathroom take everything out of your coat and flush it . . . " and I said, "What are you talking about?" and John said, "She *has* to *do it*. She's going to be *arrested*." And she was gone for an awfully long time, and finally John came up to me and said, "Go *get* her . . . " I went to the bathroom, and she was on her hands an knees, and there was pot from one end of the bathroom to the other, and she was trying to . . . she had dropped it *everywhere*, and it was soggy and wet, and she was trying to pick it up and flush it down the toilet and it wouldn't go down, it was staying on top. I was trying to help her, and John stuck his head in the door and said, "You too, Mitch . . . " and I said, "No." Then he said, "You heard what I said, *you too*" and I said, "*No!!*" he just pointed his finger at me and said, "Just get that out of your coat *this minute* . . . '"So, I'm tearing it outta my coat and flushing it down the toilet. I was *so* angry, because I knew that this was overkill, and that they weren't going to search me.

But it was just as well, because I almost got arrested, too, we all almost got arrested. When we came down, we tried to just get them to go away, and then when they wouldn't, they insisted on taking Cass, and John said, "No, Cass, just get in the car. Andrew Oldham had met us with a fleet of limos, and John said, "Don't go with them, just let's go." Then the police blocked our exit, and they called for a matron. They got a woman who was bigger than Cass. She was as big around as Cass, and twice as tall! And we had a tug of war in these Rolls with her pulling Cass at one end, and we were pulling Cass from the other. It was insane, I don't know what we thought we were doing; she was under arrest for *something* . . . anyway, I think it was because they didn't have a warrant, that John said, "Let her go." The police said, "Mr. Phillips, we don't *need* a warrant. This is not the United States. She's under arrest, and she's to come with the bobby now . . . "

So, we followed her to the jail, I fainted outside of the jail, I was crying. John, Denny, and I had a press conference, I think that day. The following day we had to go to court. Now, Jill Gibson was along . . .

I was very upset that Jill was along. I didn't see how Lou could do this, to rub her in my nose like this. When we were going off to court the following day, and I saw that Jill was coming to court with us, I flipped Lou the bone. When we were in court, I was just *glaring* at him. They let Cass off, as you know . . . they had no charge, really, they wanted to know where her boyfriend was, Pic Dawson. He was money laundering in Europe, and I think he was dealing drugs, and he was traveling on a diplomatic passport—his father was a diplomat—and he was just being an all-around bad boy, which was Pic Dawson to a tee. He was bad news. Cass bought him a Harley-Davidson, I remember. But anyway, she didn't know anything, and she went to court the next day and the judge said, 'You may leave this court with no stain on your character.' We walked out of court, and there's a picture, actually, a newsreel of the four of us walking down the courthouse steps, and we're eating something . . . it was the pot cookie that she had in her purse, and we were kind of getting rid of the evidence.

Graham Nash: When they came over in 1967, Cass and I

Courtesy of the Bill Wasserzieher Collection.

rented a giant Rolls Royce put in a case of ginger beer and a bottle of gin, and we went to a late-night concert that The Hollies were giving at Oxford University, and of course, by the time we got there we were *quite* merry.

Peter Pilafian: It seemed that there was a huge amount of publicity involved, and it was very public. I can't imagine that they would have gotten anything out of her—I always thought that it was some sort of publicity grab. The English government wanted to make a stand against all of these horrible rock and roll people who were taking drugs . . . to send a message to the kids that this was not okay . . . we don't condone them or their drug-taking activity. That's the way it looked.

We hung out in the Hotel Zorasank in Paris, which is a very fancy hotel. We were just enjoying things there. John arranged for about four or five hookers to have a party with us. It was pretty amusing, the attempt to stage an orgy, I guess. It was pretty funny, and experimental more than anything else. Abe Somer had a desire to go to Israel, and I went with him there. This was just after the Six-Day War. After that we hooked back up with the group.

Michelle Phillips: But, but this time, everything had fallen apart. Cass left immediately. She had said, 'I'm outta here!' I'll tell ya how she left . . . I had something to do with that. When I flipped Lou the bone, when we were walking out of the courthouse, Lou turned to me and said, "You know Mitch, you better think about why you're so hostile to me and to Jill . . . " and I said, "Yeah, I will think about it." And we all walked away. And, I thought about it, for about fifteen minuets, and I walked downstairs to Lou and Jill's room, and I said, "Well, I've thought about it, can I come in?'" The tension in the room was just about as tense as you could imagine, it was just the moment of truth. Here was this girl, Lou's girlfriend, who had replaced me in the group, who caused me so much pain; even though if I had been in her position, I would have taken the job, too. Lou had caused me so much pain . . . I had not been allowed to say one *fucking word* since it was over and they let me back in the group; I was not allowed to bad-mouth Jill. Not allowed to bad-mouth John, Denny, Cass, and they had put me in my place, and I was in my place, and goddamit, I was just going to endure whatever it was that they wanted to do. And I said, "Ya know what Lou? I've *thought* about it, and the reason that I don't like her do be on the road with us, or to be on vacation with us, or to be on our business trip with us, is because I don't like having it being reminded all of time to me that she was my replacement. And second of all, I don't like the fact that you're *with* her, in the first place. Because I love you, very much, and I know that it's not fair for me to say this, but I don't want to see you with other women. Don't do it in my presence."

He walked over to the ice bucket, where the champagne had been, and stuck his head right in it, and I walked out. Jill didn't say a word. It was *pretty* shocking. I was married, I was pregnant, and I had just about had enough. And Lou *was* mine. See, the truth was, that I really felt that Lou was mine. What he wanted to do on his own time was fine, but when he was with me, I didn't want him flaunting this girl in front of me that had represented the most brutal pain that I had ever experienced. Frankly, when I got the group back, I felt that I got Lou back, too, and Jill just had to go . . .

Lou was the one who was constantly buying baby clothes for Chynna, long before we knew it was a girl. He gave her a beautiful owl from F.A.O. Schwartz . . . he was more like my husband than John was. John had already been though it before, and was not particularly excited about it. Lou was *very* excited about it . . .

When I did this, Lou and Jill got out of the hotel. They left. I went downstairs to Scott's room, just kind of sleeping. Anyhow, it got around really fast, what I had done. John left, everyone left. Everyone left, except for me and Scott in the hotel. Denny may not have left, but I think he did. Cass went to Paris. Lou and Jill disappeared, and Abe Somer and Peter went to Israel. That's when Cass said, "Fuck you guys. I can't take this drama, this 'Michelle drama.' I can't stay here anymore. Good-bye." Denny may have stayed in his room, watching TV like, "I'm minding my own business, I'm tryin' to mind my own business . . . I've had my scene in this movie before . . . "

Denny Doherty: We were in London, and John and Michelle had gone off to Marrakech, and I stayed in the hotel in London with the waiter bringing me gimlets—Rose's lime juice and gin—to my room. Eventually I came back to L.A., and when John came back, he had bought this huge, three-foot, four-stemmed hookah pipe, with a bowl like a cereal bowl, that you could put an ounce of shit in. This had to come with us on the road, and on the road we were traveling in the Lear jet, with a three-foot fuckin' hookah pipe, full of Harvey's Bristol Crème in the bottom, instead of water. One day we took off in the Lear and John put a handful off grass and hash in the pipe, in the bowl, which had a cover so it wouldn't spill. So we're all honkin; on this hookah on the four stems; everybody had a line, after takeoff. Now the Lear jet has no door between the cockpit and the cabin, just a little curtain that they would pull closed if they wanted any privacy. After a few pulls on the pipe, the captain thought there was an electrical fire! Of course, they're getting a contact high from the pipe, and they don't realize it. They're freakin' out, and we're saying, "No, no . . . it's just this blend of Turkish tobacco, don't worry 'bout a thing!"

I walked my way up to the cabin, and started talking to these guys who are flying this Swedish plane. I asked them, "What does she do, what do these controls do?" They explained that it was a Swedish fighter plane, and that it did 670 MPH, and if they took it over the apex, we'd all be weightless. "Really? Could *we* do that!?" So he says, "Well, you all have to strap yourselves in, 'cause we don't want anyone to get hurt." So we all look at each other and say, "Yeah, we'll strap ourselves in . . . right . . . " So the guy takes the Lear jet over 70,000 feet, and we're all floating around the cabin, weightless. I used the line in my play, but Cass said that it was the first time in her life that she didn't weigh a thing! But while we were over the apex, everything in the cabin was weightless, but when we crossed that and came back down, *everything* came back down! Luggage, drinks, magazines, everything . . .

John Phillips: Actually, we became much closer to the English groups than the American groups. I don't know how that happened, but we were much closer friends with The Beatles and The Stones, for instance, than we were with The Byrds or Buffalo Springfield. And Morrison. I knew Morrison quite well, but I didn't know the other guys in the group or anything. But John and Paul and Ringo and Mick and Keith and all that. We were all like best buddies. And it was always that way.

Michelle Phillips: We knew Simon & Garfunkel. As a matter of fact, they opened up for us the night I was canned, at Melodyland. Yeah, we liked them. We liked them a lot. Yeah, John really liked Paul; there was a real thing there. I remember them coming to the studio when we were doing the vocals on "12:30 (Young Girls Are Coming to the Canyon)," and Paul was just *falling* all over himself, saying, "I *love* this song! oh my god . . . " He stayed there for hours while we were doing the vocals.

And the house, the house was beautiful. We had so much fun in the house. We built the studio, and we had friends coming over, I remember George Harrison coming over, and we would play and record, and Ravi Shankar, Paul (McCartney), just lots of musicians. It was a fun atmosphere. We had lots of parties, pool parties, and barbecues down by the pool. Just enjoying being rich hippies; we were enjoying our new life.

Peter Pilafian: Back in those days, I seem to remember feeling the best thing we could do was to take some psychedelic drug about one a week to keep a clear head and get a good view on reality. I kinda miss those days, actually! I remember about a year going by during this period, and realizing that not a day had gone by that I hadn't taken some sort of drug. In those days, marijuana was pretty much common, and I remember the feeling was that you had to be a little bit careful about getting arrested. Like a lot of people at the time, I remember moving a few bricks or whatever, to take care of my own supply or make a couple of bucks—nothing major. I remember once buying over eight or ten kilos, and when I left the apartment I was at, and leaving with all of these shopping bags, I experienced a level of paranoia that I'd never experienced before! I was certain that every third car had an FBI agent in there.

Everyone was smoking one thing or another, and pills would

Photo by Henry Diltz.

come and go. There would be some speed around. People would try this or that. The Mamas & The Papas were kind of part of the sub-culture where we were experimenting with various things, and we'd try all kinds of things. I remember one evening John got a tank of nitrous oxide, and we set it up in the studio, and that was kind amusing for a couple of days. As far as cocaine use, it seemed like it was in and out. In the course of an evening, someone would lay out a couple of lines or whatever. But what I recall was that in our gang, cocaine never got out of hand. I remember, because I was particularly sensitive of other people who might have had a big habit, and they were particularly nasty people. It was very clear to me that people who were using cocaine a lot were not fun to be around, and I didn't want to be like that or be around that. I could see the results. My recollection is that while it was around every now and then, it never got to be a big thing during this period that the group was together.

Michelle Phillips: I did not know of any other drugs that Cass did, aside from the stuff we were doing like acid, grass, etc., and I went absolutely kicking and screaming defending her, because I

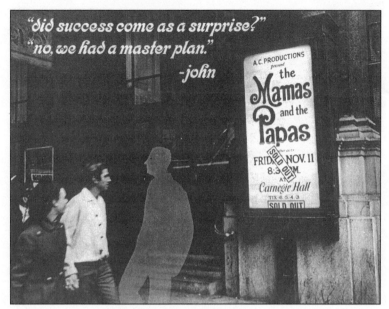

From tour program, 1967.
Courtesy of the Robert Stoico Collection.

had *never* known. Since then there are people who have told me that she was, and that they had firsthand knowledge of it, and I was shocked. I didn't believe it when they told me that about *John*. We never did hard drugs together. Never. It was the furthest thing from our life, and when we did acid, we did it purely for fun, and we smoked pot. I don't remember us *ever* doing any cocaine together. In fact, I *know* that the four of us never, *ever* did cocaine together. There was never any cocaine at any session. There was a lot of alcohol, a lot of Crown Royal, a lot of pot, and a lot of Marlboros, but never any hard drugs. We never recorded on acid, never performed on acid . . . although John Phillips says that he did. But if he did, he did it alone, and very quietly. We were very businesslike. I mean, we blew a lot of money in the studio, but we were not a 'drug-crazed,' problematic group. We worked our *asses* off, and there was no room for heroin or cocaine.

John Stewart: He could charm anybody . . . he was brilliant. But I missed John long before he died. I missed him in Bel Air.

Chapter Seven

Too Late

Cass, Woodrow Wilson Drive, 1968.
Photo by Henry Diltz.

PART ONE

The Papas & The Mamas early 1968 sessions . . . "Dream a Little Dream" . . . The Beach Boys 'party' at the home studio . . . John's bow and arrow act . . . Cass flies solo with Dunhill's blessing . . . "Too late to try to understand . . ."

Peter Pilafian: Cass pretty much always had her own life. When we'd do sessions, all the rest if us would hang out whether we were recording or not. But Cass, as soon as the work was done, she'd leave and go off with her friends. I guess that she was part of a different mentality or something. She may have leveraged her way in, which was perfectly accepted, but it wasn't organic. We were all very sad that Cass seemed to like heroin. That was a very private part of her life that I didn't know very much about. She would sort of go away and do that and come back for sessions.

The recording sessions would usually start very late in the day, and the consumption of alcohol and drugs would start several hours before the recording session; so that by the end of it after we laid down a few tracks or whatever, everyone would pretty much be out of their minds and not able to do much else. It was a combination of the drugs as well as the creative process.

We ended up with a pretty cockeyed schedule where we were recording around 10 or 11 P.M., and they couldn't always do that with a commercial studio all the time, it was a little hard to do that. So he decided to build the home studio, and it was just a matter of spending some money. We had a new board; it was a German board, as I remember. It was all new stuff, I think, although it may have gone through the channels of the guys at Western. I came in as sort of a construction manager, I just kept an eye on things and made sure things were put together so that they'd work and made sure that it was laid out. We had this light scheme of three or four different colors on dimmers and that sort of things. I became the house engineer.

The way it was set up was that it was behind a secret panel that had been part of the upstairs hallway. It was something that you wouldn't notice. If you were walking around the house, there were two bedroom wings in the upstairs with wood paneling molding down a hallway. There might have been a bookshelf or two or a lamp fixture, but it would never occur to you that there might be something else up there. But the builders put this secret panel that you could push on and open. Originally it had been an attic and storage—a space. It was in the upper framing of the house, and it was actually quite enormous. It was a big house, with a big peaked roof, and there was a lot of space up there. That became refurbished, and you'd go through this secret panel into this almost magic world. Suddenly you'd go from this old, warm, traditional wooden house into the modern world of a recording studio. There was kind of a lounge downstairs with a sofa and whatnot, and then you'd go up to the upstairs where there would be the studio itself, with modern, recessed lighting. It looked very much like a modern, commercial recording studio. For an echo chamber we brought in a big Studer plate echo box, that required some space, either in the closet or out in the barn area.

Joe Osborne: It looked like a studio, it had a control room separate, and it was set up just like a regular studio. "Dream A Little Dream" came out of that studio, but I don't remember any other hits that came out of there. But it had a sound. I heard some tapes of some things that never had come out, with Larry, and they and me had the same sound as Cass's record, so it did have a distinctive sound.

I never did like that atmosphere, though. You know, when you go into a session, let's go in to work, and leave the lights up. Sitting around and hanging out . . . you lose the momentum, and you get sleepy. I never did like that. You go in in the afternoon, and you're still there at three A.M., that's why it (*The Papas & The Mamas Present*) sounds so tired. We had done very long sessions with The Mamas & The Papas, and other people as well, at Western, but it was all a working attitude, not just hanging out.

Denny Doherty: The fact that the studio was there to begin with was amazing, because you have to go before the Bel Air housing commission before you drive a nail into a wall there. But John was like, "Authority? No . . . " The commission people would come by periodically and see the construction trucks in the driveway, and all kinds of shit; workers coming up the driveway. But there were unable to find anybody or anything going on. They didn't know about the secret panel . . .

You'd come into the house at 783 Bel Air Road and enter the foyer. On the lefthand side was a stairway going up to the second floor. At the top of those stairs, you'd make a left to go to the master bedroom suite. But if you pushed a panel on the wall, there was opened up, and there was a great, big wide door that had been Jeannette McDonald's cedar closet, which had all of the gowns that she had ever performed in. But you couldn't see the room from the outside, and you couldn't see it from the inside, for the beautiful, walnut paneling on the inside. But if you pushed it, 'click-click,' you could get a truck through there, and this became the studio. So, whenever the Bel Air Commission would come by, John or somebody would ring a bell or whatever and he'd say, "Quiet, shut up!" and stop pounding nails, and the Commission would come through with their pads and forms and ask, "What are you doing in here?" "Nothing, nothing." They're looking around for sawdust, drills, tools, anything that they could write up. Meanwhile, there was a massive undertaking going on up there . . . So, Jeannette McDonald's cedar closet became a studio over time! And we were recording at night, whenever we could. It was good, because we were never walking into anyone's session. It was like, "When do you want to record?" "Whenever you can get here . . . "

Peter was the engineer, and he had his dog around, which was a big standard poodle who was injured, walking around with a full leg cast through all of this. At one point, John was yelling at Peter, "I thought you were an engineer!?" "No I'm not, I'm a mystic . . . "

So, we recorded the fourth album in there though a whole lot of craziness.

Peter Pilafian: I'd go up to the house every day. John loved to have things brought to him, so that he had this sort of benevolent kingdom that you could just live in. He'd walk around in his robe, and have coffee out in the garden, it was very nice. The dogs and kids and transients would come and go, and maybe show John a new pool table or something. It was pretty heady. John was really into it, and of course Michelle was going along for the ride and loving it. They really played the nouveau-royalty. It was benevolent, and there was the feeling of ease and safety and comfort that seemed to be a part of it. There wasn't the desire to sort of order people around.

Nurit Wilde: I did hang out at the Bel Air house, and they had a very big party that I went to there. That's where I met Steve McQueen, who was there with his wife, Neilie. Huge party. The place was huge, and that there were a lot of people that you'd seen in films. Offhand, I can't remember anyone but Steve McQueen, because I liked him, and there he was! They had peacocks running around, it was incredible watching them fan their plumage. They were beautiful, and the place was beautiful.

Peter Pilafian: John and Michelle were enjoying being the kind of king and queen of the manor, and they loved that life that they created. It was extremely safe, as that song "Safe In My Garden" will reinforce. That was the feeling.

Denny Doherty: Well, John's got the studio up in his house, and he's happy, Cass and I are just showing up whenever. This is after Monterey, and John and Michelle are back together and they're going to have a baby and "everything's wonderful." But she's still out fuckin' around on him, and he's trying to get her in line. He'd drag her around to all the rooms in the house and say, "This is the nursery! This is your bedroom!" It didn't help, and it didn't work. The whole fourth album to me was, "Let's just get it done . . . "

"For The Love of Ivy," that was going to be for a movie, "For the Love of Ivy" with Sidney Poitier. I think John looked at it as "For the Love of 'I.V.'! Anyway, it didn't get used for the soundtrack, because it didn't have anything to do with the main character, 'Ivy,' who was a maid in the movie. It ended up on our album instead . . .

Jim Horn: I think the most fun was recording up at the house, because it was so relaxed. You didn't have to worry about getting started right away, or if the engineer was going to get tired or whatever. It was just like when I went up to George Harrison's house to do The Traveling Wilbury's record, the same vibe. You could always go down to the kitchen and get something to eat or some tea, they had it right there. It was always fun going up to these guy's houses and recording. They were all really nice people, John especially. He always had really great ideas. I loved the way he would double up their voices, not too many people in pop music were doing that at the time. I think that the sound they made was really special, and those songs of John's were a lot of fun, they were really great. The lyrics were really cool, because back then we were kinda coming out of the rock and roll-Elvis Presley era, with a lot of real simple kind of bluesy songs. Finally someone came along with really fun songs and great songs. I had also been working on The Beach Boys sessions, and between John and Brian they were coming up with some great songs. I really like the fact that they were writing their own songs, that was cool.

Peter Pilafian: The Beach Boys came up to the studio one night. We were making great use of the studio, and I think it was the first home studio in Bel Air. The concept was pretty new, and it was kind of a breakthrough, and word got out. It wasn't intended as a commercial venture to be rented by anyone, but John knew people in the very tight community. So, I guess Brian wanted to try it out and give it a whirl. They came up, and we had it all pre-pared—we wanted to run it like a proper studio. They wanted to just kind of sit in the room for a while, and that they wouldn't record anything for a while, they just wanted to just get the feel and meditate. So, we kind of left them in the room. We checked in every once in a while to see if they wanted to roll any tape or any-thing, but they were just kind of sitting around and enjoying. As I recall, after about six hours they emerged, and we hadn't rolled any tape. They said, "We're just not in the groove today, and we're not going to record anything. But thanks . . . " and they headed out.

Marilyn Wilson: I think that Lou Adler asked Brian to partici-pate, or come down to some of the sessions. John and Lou Adler had Brian come down and play on this baseball team that they had. I think that they played at Beverly Hills High School. Brian was the centerfielder, and they always wanted him, because he was the best player on the team. Every time he got up to bat, the outfielders would all spread out, because Brian would hit these homers. He was really good.

But this is also where Michelle and I met, because we were both standing there with our babies. Michelle *still* makes fun of me, and she still cracks up, because Carnie was this little baby with a bald head and a pink ribbon on her head that looked like it was attached with tape or something! But Carnie and Chynna went to the same Santa Monica Montessori school, and they were always in the same class and became friends. She's so funny and so 'out there'; she always made me laugh. Myself being so conservative, we're quite different, but our friendship is based knowing each other for who we are, and it's all real. Deep down inside, she is just warm and giving, and I just admire her a lot.

Larry Knechtel: "Dream A Little Dream," I liked that. Cass sat on the piano when we did that. I always had a little bit of old ragtime in me, I guess.

Lou Adler: Knechtel had three hands, we always thought. There was one coming out of his chest or something! He would play stuff that we couldn't believe that a guy with just two hands could play. He was the opposite of Hal, as far as personality, his head was always buried in his keys, but very, very important. Stuff that they did on "Dedicated To The One I Love," where Hal and Larry were playing together, is just fantastic. Everything he played was right.

Michelle Phillips: Well, "Dream A Little Dream" was part of our fourth album, and it was recorded because I had known one of the writers of the song, Favian Andre, when my father, sister, and I lived for a short period with him in Mexico. Favian, I don't know if he was teaching . . . I think he was just hanging in Mexico City, and my father and him were just kind of expatriates that knew each other. He may have had something to do with Mexico City College, where my father was going. But, he died, I think, on New Years Eve 1967. He fell down an elevator shaft, drunk out of his mind. Anyhow, that was the story that we read, and my dad had told us that Favian had died. So, we just started talking about him and what he had written, and "Dream A Little Dream" came up, and we started singing it. Of course, we were always looking for material like *sharks*. So, we worked it up. It's a beautiful arrangement, beautiful backgrounds . . . wonderful performance, and Cass wanted to perform it from the very beginning. This was *right up* her alley. Now, "Words Of Love," for instance, she didn't want to do the solo on that. We *forced* her to do it. That's when John stood her up on the piano in the studio and made her sing it. Anyway, we recorded it, and Cass had already been talking about going out as a soloist. She had been talking about this for a while.

All along, any time there was any hint of trouble with the group, Dunhill was going to Cass and saying, (rubs hands excitedly) "You can do your album, you can do your *own* album . . . you can be a single; we'll support you . . . " So they were always dangling that carrot in front of her, and they knew that she was a more reliable source of product. Because she had the energy, she had the will . . . and she didn't care *what* she sang . . . and they didn't either. I'm surprised that she didn't do an album of show tunes. She would have eventually, of course.

Denny Doherty: It was a hit for The Mamas & The Papas before Cass 'went solo.' It happened to come out at the same time that Cass was going out on her own. The record company said, "What's getting a buzz off of the last album," and that was it. That's the way that worked. It was an album cut for us that came out as her first single. Jay Lasker . . .

I think that "Glad to Be Unhappy" was leftover from the Rodgers and Hart special, at the time when Michelle and Jill Gibson were changing places. That was kind of a strange time: Michelle was going. Jill was coming and going. It was a state of flux. "12:30" was a song that John started writing in New York, around 1964–65. The song was about a church steeple outside of his and Michelle's apartment that they were tearing down, and the clock stopped at 12:30. Then we moved to California, and all he had was the first part of it, and then he wrote the second part about "young girls are coming to the canyon" when we moved out to Laurel Canyon. So the first part was New York, and the second was Los Angeles. It wasn't recorded as a single, it was to be an album cut, from what was to be the fourth album, although it came out on the "Farewell to the First Golden Era" hits album.

Eric Hord: The thing that keeps it going is money, pure and simple. Everything can be going to shit—which it was with The Mamas & The Papas, but if there's an opportunity to go and make another record and keep that money rolling in, well . . . that's different. It got to the point where people would say, "fuck this, fuck John, I sing in these records, let him work it around my schedule." Now Dennis wasn't like that; he's compatible, and he's a team player . . . but Cass really wasn't, and she *knew* she could make it on her own, and she just got tired of dealing with the nonsense that was always going down . . . and let me tell you, it was *always* going down.

Peter Pilafian: John would push the envelope. I remember that John had some kind of bow and arrow kit. I don't remember what the tips of the arrows were made out of, but John would enjoy shooting them straight up—which as you know is a bit of a game of chance as to where they would come down. It's an interesting metaphor, and of course the arrows never came down on anyone's head, and nobody ever got hurt.

The parties were pretty wonderful and lavish, and getting pretty loose. It seemed like fortune was smiling upon everybody involved. Nobody was talking about their I.P.O.'s and what their stock was worth or make some merger. Everything was just rolling. I don't recall any sort of envy. These days everyone is sort of lusting after money, and they're envious of anyone who had somehow done a bigger deal. I don't recall anything like that. That was a magic era, and in the golden bubble, and the life up there in Bel Air sort of exemplified that for a while.

I think that John was pretty aware of how delicate it was, and I think that he got caught a little bit in the pressure of making it keep happening, and the pressure to keep writing hit songs. Very difficult. I guess that he and Cass didn't see eye to eye about things, although god knows why Cass would ever have a problem. Her talent was comparable to John's; she was a singer, John was a writer. It was very strange. Things got tense, and I guess the fourth album got shut down in the middle. It just wasn't working.

Courtesy of the Richard B. Campbell Collection.

PART TWO

Cass and John, the dueling Virgo's . . . Cass's picnic with Eric Clapton; the spirit of Laurel Canyon . . . Marlon Brando's brief visit during the end of the beginning of the end . . . some final mansion masterpieces . . . "A visit to paradise is limited by nature . . . "

Michelle Phillips: She never wanted to write . . . she was very, very bright, and she was very good with words, too. I'm very suprised, but I think she didn't want to put herself in that position with John. I don't know why, but they were always butting heads, you know. They were two Virgo's. She resented him a lot. She admired him, but the fact that he was very pushy kind of put her off. You had to do it his way, it was his music, and you know, "No, Cass. Don't sing it that way." She'd get exasperated because she wasn't used to having a leader of a group, somebody who would give you a part and say, "Sing it." and she'd say, "I can't sing that." and he'd say, "Yeah, sing it." He would make her sing higher and higher and higher, which is what made a lot of the sound, everybody singing at the *very* top of their range. But there was a lot of humor between them. They used to make each other laugh, a lot. They respected each other a lot. But they were always butting heads . . .

Henry Diltz: Later, I met this fellow named Gary Burden, who was a designer, and he was designing Cass's house, making renovations, etc. She said to him, "Hey, I need someone to design my album cover, why don't you do it?" and he said, "Well, I'm an architect . . . " and she said, "Well, it's the same thing, it comes from the same place!" So, he went for it, and right around the same time we became partners, and he said, "Hey, do you wanna take photos." So that's how that worked out. We ended up doing the *The Papas & The Mamas Present* album first. We went up to John and Michelle's place and took those photos. Cass had this great picnic in about '68 for Eric Clapton. He was just near the end of Cream, he was here on tour, I believe, and he really didn't know anybody, and so she invited him over to the house and had a little backyard barbecue. She invited David Crosby and Joni Mitchell, who he had just discovered and was showing her around. Mickey Dolenz came over with his 16 millimeter Bolyou camera. I keep asking about that film, and he tells me that he filmed French fries, and things like that. He was filming a plate of French fries that was next to Eric Clapton. That was his lunch! Gary Burden, my partner was there with his wife and little girl. Joni and David and Eric sat out under the trees and played guitar. Eric mostly sat and listened. That was Cass, and that was what it was like.

Out of all of 'em, I knew Cass the best. She was just an incredible, wonderful lady. She was like the lady who was the friend of Alice B. Toklas, who wrote "A rose is a rose is a rose . . . ," and she had Hemingway come over . . . Anyway, she was a social catalyst, she was very funny, very witty. She was just a great person to hang out with. In the sixties, everyone was goin' to each others' houses, all the musicians. You might go over to someone's house, smoke a joint, talk, you know. Someone might play some new songs, or you might all go down to a club or something, go get something to eat at Ben Franks or Barney's Beanery. The day would take off, and you'd never know where it would go. And you'd see all these people on the way, and that's when I started taking all these pictures. But often at Cass's. I'd go over there and see John Sebastian and Eric Jacobson hanging out, and people in the swimming pool.

Jerry Yester: Cass was just a regular ol' gal, she was good people. When she was hangin' out with a lot of people she was obviously having a good time, but aside from that I would say that she was demure.

P. F. Sloan: Cass never really paid any attention to me at all. She always wanted to know what I was doing there. I had talked to her one time at The Beverly Hills Hotel shortly before her death, and I asked her, "Cass, why was it that you never said hello to me?" and she said, "Oh, Philip, you had no idea what was going on with the group. I always thought that you were the most precocious person I'd ever known in my life." And I just lit up. If I was at a party at Denny's house, basically Cass would never come up and say hello. With John it was the same thing. Denny was the one, really. He'd put his arm around me and say, "This is *my* man!" He was ever full of good feelings. A real blithe spirit. Denny was the most funny, unaffected, most easygoing guy. Always talking in different voices. Fun-loving. He always made me feel very much at ease.

Mark Volman: Cass was kind of a loner. I think that Cass was kind of a loner in life a lot. She had a child right away with Owen, and that became the center of her life. There was also all of these sort of personal things going on with Cass on the outside that no one could figure out, about her men, and who her husband was, who was Owen's dad. I remember going up to parties at Cass's with my wife and daughter, and there were always all these people running around. Henry, Gary Burden, Glen Frey and Don Henley when they were called Longbranch Pennywhistle. Also Warren Zevon, who was writing a lot for The Turtles, he had his folk duo called Lyme & Cybelle. So all of these people that we sort of knew from The Turtles, were some of the people that ran around at Cass's.

The rise and fall of this group truly revolved around the rise and the fall of the personalities. They were really personality-driven. The success of the band, if you look at it, was because of the distinct personalities, the four of them. Not just to the sound, but to the visual, which was a really big thing at the time.

It wasn't a matter of them getting along as a four-piece group, it was the inner-relationships. The problems that John and Michelle were having, Cass's problems outside of the group. Denny was sort of his own problems, but I think that because he was Canadian, he sort of kept his thing separate from the Hollywood thing. The inner struggle was because of the personality problems of each of them that would arise, and the eventual losing of members—Michelle leaving, Cass dying. That was it. It wasn't like you could repair or replace Cass. The Mamas & The Papas were this image, this thing. It was maybe like you'd say, "John, Paul, George and Ringo"—you couldn't replace John Lennon when he died. And it was pretty much the same with The Mamas & The Papas. The interesting thing is, is that this happened around, what, five hit songs?

Guy Webster: We were friends, and we were all pretty much tuned in to the same ascetic wavelength at the time. I always liked them and hung out with them at recording sessions and so on, and I was very close to all of them. Cass and I had a very close friendship I think. I did a fashion show with her, where we did fashion photographs for the *Los Angeles Times* fashion section. First time ever that a rock and roll woman, or even one overweight was used as sort of a fashion spread. Cass and I became close because being a photographer, I think she wanted me to record a lot of her personal life and what was going on with her and her baby. My wife had a baby at the exact same time as Chynna was born. So, I photographed Chynna the day she came home from the hospital. I also shot Michelle and Chynna for a famous fashion layout with the baby carriage. That was done at the house in Bel Air.

Cyrus Faryar: I was at their home studio one night, and there was this little anteroom between the studio—like a lounge, and I remember sitting there, and right across from me was Marlon Brando and some other gentleman, and they were speaking French. I remember quietly thinking to myself, "This is interesting . . . " A lot of the 'illuminati' of the trade would show up there, because parties were a good way to get yourself seen and to be omnipresent in the rock and roll firmament. If you were at a party, and say, Mick was there, your value increased, I don't know.

Donovan: I remember sitting in Joni Mitchell's canyon house ('Our House' song by Graham Nash when he and Joni lived together) and we were watching the Disney 'toon,' 'Wind in the Willows.' Toad was up to his tricks again, going for the thrill, regardless of expense and consequences. Cass screamed, "Yeah Toad—you're just like us." Cass knew we all were pushing the envelope higher and faster into the night. We lost Cass along the way. But her honey dripping voice still thrills.

John, 1966. Drawing by Donovan Leitch, from his poetry book Dry Songs and Scribbles *(Meadowlight Publishing Company, 1971).*

Henry Diltz: Earlier, in '67, I was staying in Greenwich Village staying with The Lovin' Spoonful, and taking pictures of the group, because their producer was my old roommate, Eric Jacobson. During that summer, Cass came over with The Hollies, about three or four of 'em, and came over to Zal Yanovosky's apartment. She said, "Hey, I want to bring some friends over." And that's the way she was, and she arrived with all these English guys that didn't know anybody, and we had a great little impromptu party in the afternoon, hanging out and telling stories and laughin,' you know. A lot of 'instant friends' and Cass, once again, was the catalyst to that. I met Graham that next day, and I shot an album cover for The Hollies. And then Cass introduced Graham to David later in L.A., and that's the beginning of the whole CSN thing. Cass was very instrumental in making these things happen. Cass was an exceptional person, and a great lady. I'd put her on the level of the Kennedys, she was really as great a person in the music world as the Kennedy's were in politics. In terms of the music world, being funny, being witty, being talented, being smart, she was just a great person, and we all just miss her a great deal. I can't imagine what it'd be like if she were around. Things would be way different, because people would have met more people. She was just a blast, a wonderful person.

Lou Adler: There were some good things on the fourth album. "For The Love of Ivy" was possibly for a film of the same name. "Nothing's Too Good For My Little Girl," that was written by Ned Wynn. He was just a good friend of this group that John and I started hanging out with along with Terry Melcher. Ned's father was Keenan Wynn, the actor. He just came up with this song, and I think it's the only song he ever got recorded.

"Meditation Mama" was a song that John and I wrote together. But on here, there's hardly any John Phillips. "12:30" was actually the last great single that they did. That was John's way of appeasing the group and Dunhill, for giving "If You're Going to San Francisco" to Scott McKenzie and Ode. I think that "12:30" and "Dream a Little Dream" were recorded at a real studio, and the rest of it was recorded up at the house. "Mansions" was a nice lyric . . .

Peter Pilafian: "Mansions," ah yes. This is a door opening to what could have been the next era of The Mamas & The Papas. John's use of that moving parallel in the octaves is sort of a break-through. It's a little dark, but it's *so* nice. The absolute perfection of the vocal rendition is so astonishing . . . there isn't anything today that has that extraordinary perfection. Those four voices are in the most extraordinary, celestial, resonant harmony. You *never* heard people sing like that. It's like a masterpiece that belongs in the Sistine Chapel or something. It is absolutely extraordinary. Just listening to that, I realized what we were doing there day after day, night after night after night. Unbelievable. Absolute masterpiece, and driven by a musical inspiration and songwriting inspiration of the same level. God, to take those four voices and have them resonate in that extraordinary level of perfection, it's fantastic. It's too bad John had to pay the price to the devil for doing that.

Michelle Phillips: Yeah, I remember that, that was an epic arrangement. Doing session after session of vocal tracks. That was like the *Gone with the Wind* . . . or the shower scene on *Psycho!* So, we're trying to finish the album, and it's taking *forever* to finish the album. "Mansions," for instance, we probably took a week and a half, two weeks, just doing the vocals on that *one song*. No one liked to do that, no one like to work like that. They'd wake me up in the middle of the night when I was pregnant and ask me to come in and make me put another part on. It was brutal.

Peter Pilafian: "The Right Somebody to Love," which Michelle sings, that sounds like a little 12-year old girl singing, and nobody will criticize her for it. It's a sweet idea, and it is what it is. Listening to this reminds me that the reason for building that studio in Bel Air was in order to sing with complete purity and lack of defensiveness, and without even a whisper of the outside world trying to criticize or to attack the art. I think that's what was going on.

To have me as an in-house engineer, I wasn't the best engineer in the business, but the thing is, is that I was family, and there was a total feeling of openness trust about that.

We would spend hours and hours and days and days doing vocal overdubs. The musicians would lay down their tracks, and then they would leave, and we would stay and do the vocals—which seemed like the real work. John and Lou and I and the group would sit there night after night finessing those vocals out. I don't remember the level of productivity, but it seemed that if we got one take of one song, then it would be a good evening.

It got to be where I'd show up every day in the late afternoon, around five, six. John and Michelle would just be getting up. They'd be sort of regaining consciousness, and breakfast would be arranged somehow, and Esperanza, their housekeeper, would cook eggs or something like that. Meanwhile, I'd be getting the studio ready for that evening's session. We'd have whatever scheduled, and we'd sort that out, the usual stuff, getting the tapes ready and the mikes set up. And pick up the debris from last night's debauchery. Into the early evening Cass and Denny would come by, and there'd be some friendly stuff, a glass of wine or something. Then we'd sort of drift upstairs, and Lou would show up and we'd

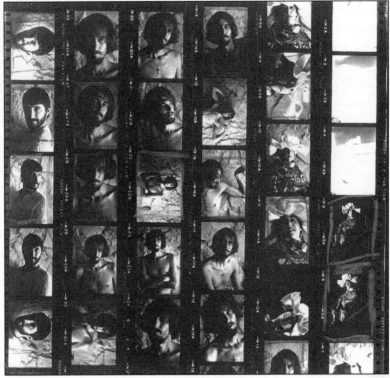

Bel Air, 1968.
Courtesy of Michelle Phillips.

start putting things up and listening to a few things, so it'd might not be until ten or perhaps eleven that by the time we'd actually start working and laying down the vocals to the tracks we'd been working on. There'd be the Crown Royal, and the dope, and whatever drugs of the evening would come out, the coke or whatever was around. So the hours would sort of wear on, and we'd sort of peak between two and four in the morning. That's my recollection, anyway. It was a timeless environment, of course, because we had dimmers on the lights and no windows. There were no union engineers or anything telling us it was time to quit. I ran the place, Lou was the producer, of course, and he and I ran the control room. We were all family, and it was part of the package. Nobody was on the clock.

We'd go at it. John would just finesse and stroke and go back

Courtesy of the Richard B. Campbell Collection.

and forth. He was wonderful with the singers, with the group, and he would cajole just these extraordinary performances out of the group that they would never have been capable of otherwise. And I'm sure they got a little tired of his perfectionism maybe, but he's a Virgo and he's entitled to be a perfectionist (laughs). We'd just work and work until we'd eventually fall over in a stupor at four in the morning or something. I'd go drive home and recover and then the next day, come back and do it again. That was our schedule, and that's how we made that album.

For John, every song took a tremendous amount of attention. He wasn't just crankin' 'em out—it wasn't a volume situation. He was making masterpieces, and he knew it, and that's the way he approached it.

He might stay up all night writing. "Safe in My Garden" was like that, and hangin' out with Michelle, and the beautiful ambiance there, just kind of letting the reverie flow. I really feel like they were very much in love then. They were very happy. It sure seemed like they hit a stable patch there. It's kind of sad that it didn't last longer than it did, but of course, a visit to paradise is limited by nature I guess, I don't know. . . .

Chapter Eight

Look through My Window

Courtesy of the Richard B. Campbell Collection.

PART ONE

Get on your pony and ride . . . . The Mamas & The Papas end the ride . . . John's P.D.R . . . a gathering of flowers and the end of the '60s . . . and the innocence is over.

Michelle Phillips: By 1968, we knew that we weren't going to go out and perform, certainly, so we knew that the group was over. And frankly, my dear, I didn't give a damn. It was fine with me. It was fine with Cass. I was fine with Cass going out as a single. I was about to have a baby, I had a beautiful house. The group can just go away. . . .

I felt that we were beating a dead horse. Not *dead*, but I wanted to go out with something that we could be proud of. Everyone was proud of the group, and I wanted to end it like that, on an 'up' note. It seemed like a perfect time to do it. John kept saying that he wanted to write for films. I pretty much thought that I was out of there, too, meaning the marriage. I knew that I was really not in love with John anymore, and there just didn't seem to be any point, once we were finished. And after I had Chynna, our marriage *really* started to fall apart. It was during the Daisy period . . . Mia (Farrow), there was another girl named Winona, there was another girl from the canyon. He was having affairs. In his . . . not in his defense . . . but I just think that he needed to feel loved, and I don't think that I gave him that. I think that he felt that The Mamas & The Papas was over, and that was a big blow to him, because he didn't really *know* that he could pull it off again, and if he could have another big success and I think that scared him. He started to really delve into drugs more.

I remember that we had a friend, and he found a big box of pharmaceutical drug samples, and he brought it over and he gave it to John for Christmas. It was a *big* box, *full* of samples. John would take them, not knowing what they were. I remember that year I gave him a *P.D.R.* (*Physician's Desk Reference*), because I was so afraid that he would kill himself. He would take *anything*. If it was a pill, he would take it. That was another thing, and that was another one of my justifications for leaving him, was that the

Photo by Bones Howe.

house was *so* unsafe for the baby. There were drugs *all* over the place. You couldn't walk twenty feet without finding a 'bennie' or something on the floor . . . or a hundred-dollar bill, for that matter! John was always known for reaching into his pocket for something, and leaving a hundred-dollar bill on the floor. It was a very difficult time, and it wasn't a very happy time. He was having an affair with Mia Farrow right under my nose. Mia couldn't care less. Mia would pretend to be my friend, and then she would disappear into the desert with John for eight hours. And then he was keeping a girl named Winona, and I would wake up at 5,6,7 in the morning, and he wouldn't be home. I remember once, when he came home at 7 or 8, I asked him, 'Where have you been?' and he said, 'You aren't going to believe this, but there was this big full moon out, and I just had to stare at it, and I got off the motorcycle and I laid down in some ivy, and I fell asleep . . . .and I *just* got up . . . ' I said, 'John, you expect me to believe *this* story!?' Sometimes that's the only thing you can do; just tell the most *outrageous* lie, and then let it hang there!

Up until I had Chynna . . . I felt like I was the only person taking care of Chynna, because he was sleeping all day, and I was up with her all day, and then I was too tired due to The Daisy, and I couldn't go, and the paths were going in different directions.

Michelle Phillips: Cass and I, after Chynna was born, particularly, were good friends. I think that when Owen (Cass's daughter) was first born she felt a bit isolated, a little on her own. But she was thrilled when I was pregnant, and it was great. All of the sudden we were buying baby clothes together, and "goo-goo gaga" with the kids, you know. And we hung out together quite a bit towards the end of her life, we hung out together a lot.

The last Mamas and the Papas album, that I count, *The Papas and The Mamas Present* . . . it's got some good things on it. I don't think it's as buoyant as the other albums. We were running out of steam, I think. There was some good stuff on it, but you didn't get a string of hits off of that album. It didn't have that kind of material on it. John's writing was starting to get a little introspective. It's not my favorite album . . . There was nothing left to do! When you've got somebody writing for you and they play you stuff and you say, "*Yeah!* What's my part!?" I guess that excitement was gone by about the third album, *Deliver,* which was a good album. But by the fourth album that spark just wasn't really there anymore. The thing was, we could always sing. Whatever we sang, we sang the hell out it, ya know? But we weren't writing any hit songs, and that's real important. You got to keep those hits comin' . . .

We broke up when there wasn't anything left in the pitcher. I think that in the two and a half years that we were together, there was *so much* created, that there just wasn't anything left, you know? It's like we were *wrung dry.* You know, as I look back on it, I kind of feel sorry for John, because he was expected to keep writing those hits. He was like a machine, and for two years, he did do it. He kept it up.

But there are so many variables. We used to say that if we had taken that time in 1967–68 and gone back to the Virgin Islands, bought a house on the beach and recharged our batteries, we might have been able to do more. But that wasn't going to happen. Cass was already very much out on her own, she wanted to go out as a single. She really didn't want to continue with the 'drama' inside the group. And there was a lot of drama . . .

Denny said something in a documentary, that he felt that if The Mamas & The Papas had recorded the songs that were on John's first solo album, that it would have been the best album . . . It would have been a *terrific* album! You see, by that time, John had the opportunity to recharge his batteries. He was writing great songs . . .

Clark Burroughs: My wife Marilyn was in a Jeff Corey acting class with Sharon Tate. They weren't great buddies, but they knew each other from this class. Sharon and John also knew each other, so we were sort of connected that way. Sharon's husband Roman Polanski used to always come up to John's house to hang out, and we would see him from time to time there. One evening, John called and said, "Hey, why don't you come up, there's a party up at Roman's place. Sharon's gonna have some people over, and they'll be some singers, and we're gonna listen to the first stuff from Crosby, Stills & Nash." He didn't say "Crosby, Stills & Nash," he said it was Steve Stills's new band with David Crosby and Graham Nash, and that Cass was hanging out with them, and she'd been helping out with some of the vocals. It was an incredible evening; a beautiful balmy mid-summer evening, and everything was just wonderful. I remember that when "Wooden Ships" came on over those big speakers, everybody just fell out. John was there, but I don't think that Michelle was.

It was a wonderful little studio that they had upstairs, which was later bought by Sly Stone. Not very much came out of it, but I did recognize a couple of cuts from it that had that sound, because it was an attic that had sloped ceilings, and it gave it a tight, compacted, sort of flat sound as far as the vocals were concerned. By flat, I mean no chamber at all, it was really, like, dry. Their fourth album bears this out.

Denny Doherty: I never did know what our status was with Dunhill at this time. They didn't talk to me, I didn't talk to them. I went in and recorded my solo album—"Whatcha Gonna Do"—for them, and I think Michelle also went in and tried to cut something for them as well . . .

I left L.A. in 1970. Just before this, Don Sterling, who was our accountant, called me and said that he could no longer handle my accounting, that it was "too out of hand." He sent all of my records and everything over to me in cardboard boxes, and it stayed in the corner. One day, McGuire was looking through everything and said, "Here's a cashier's check for $10,000!" It was at a time when I was looking to get out of town and this house anyway, so, I took the ten grand and left. I told my real estate man to rent the place out; I'd be back. My friends and I were going to buy some land in Florida. We ended up in Fort Lauderdale, drinking for about a month and a half, and went through all of the money. Then I heard that my mother was dying, and I went up to Nova Scotia. She passed away, and then I went back to L.A. . . .

Jay Lasker contacted me then, and we negotiated my 'get out of my contract' solo album, which became *Whatcha Gonna Do*. Bill Symzeck was gonna produce it, as he was sort-of the 'house producer' at Dunhill. He had done B. B. King's *The Thrill Is Gone* album and some other things. I started working with a couple of producers named Lambert & Porter, but it didn't work out because it was too formulated, and I was pretty scattered. But Symzeck was looking to move along from the blues, and work in more of folk/rock/country mode, which is where I was at. We met, and started working together. He didn't know what he was getting himself into; I had The Doctor coming in, and 20 other people, dogs coming in the studio. The Doctor was playing country guitar, and we got Buddy Emmonds to play pedal steel. Russ Kunkel was playin' drums, all these great players. Bill had never been exposed to any sort of folkie/country players. So, we finished the album; it didn't really do anything here, but went to #7 in Japan. But, there were really no great expectations. I was just finishing an album to get out of Dunhill. This was to finish up my involvement with them, and to put a cork in the bottle . . . or so I thought . . .

PART TWO

Michelle's unreleased Kristofferson singles—"I think you've lost the thread . . ." . . . The "reunion" album . . . the 'people like us' get sued for a million dollars.

Michelle Phillips: You know, I came back from Peru, when I went there to do Dennis Hopper's movie (*The Last Movie*) in 1970, I had met a young songwriter named Kris Kristofferson, whom nobody had ever heard of. I came back and I asked to have a little meeting with John and Lou. I went to the meeting with my guitar, and I played them two songs. I told them, "I just want to do a single, I've got two sides to a single." They said, "Let's hear 'em," and I sat down and played them "Help Me Make It through the Night" and "Me and Bobby McGee." They both sat there, and this is exactly what they said: Lou said, "Don't you think it's a little country, Mitch?" I said, "Well, whatever it is, I think they're hits." And John said, "Well frankly, Mitch, I think you've lost the thread of things." So I got up and said, "Never mind!," left the meeting, and within six months they were both #1 records! Dunhill was furious that that John's solo album wasn't a Mamas & Papas album, because there was the material, and we owed them an album.

Denny Doherty: Everybody thought they were out of their contracts, obviously, and we weren't. Everybody was fine individually to do whatever we wanted, but was had a collective agreement that we hadn't met, and they wanted one more album. At the time they were selling Dunhill to ABC, part of that deal was that they'd get one more Mamas & Papas album.

I went to the mailbox one day, and in there was a letter saying that I was being sued for $250,000. I called everybody else, and they all got one too. So, we were being sued for a million dollars for "not delivering product." So, with all of the bumps, warts, and shit that we'd been through with relationships and everything else, we all had to go into the studio together. "This is gonna be fun! Isn't it?" Cass had her nurse with her in the studio, John and Michelle weren't together; she was with Jack Nicholson, and John was with Genevieve by then. It was all just fuckin' weird. The vibe of the group is definitely not on that record; it was like white bread. The idea was to get past it. We had to, or we were gonna be in court for god knows how long.

Michelle Phillips: That album sounds like exactly what it was: four people trying to get out of a contract. We had *no* material . . . It was awful! It's tragic . . . But you know, even if we had had that material from John's solo album, there was just so much water under the bridge . . .

People Like Us *album cover outtake, Los Angeles, 1971.*
Photo by Henry Diltz.

PART THREE

Cass's final stand in London . . . "You don't really need the nurse on this tour Cass, you can take care of yourself . . . *right*, Cass ?" . . . glory at The Palladium . . . "This was Cass hitting the jackpot" . . . it's her great big heart that gave out . . . and for the thousandth time, it was not a ham sandwich . . .

Peter Pilafian: That house lasted only two or three years, until it generated into debauchery. I got the impression that the fourth album was going to be our last album. It devolved, and things seemed to get more and more decadent, and John was getting weirder, and Cass had that unfortunate attempt at opening in Vegas soon after. What a shame, because she could have been a big hit. I guess she had a self-destructive streak.

She had some people around her. But she brought 'em around. She was a brilliant talent. There were so many people from that era that were burning themselves out, and burning their candles at both ends, and Cass was one of them. It went sort of hand in hand, the self-destruction and the fame. It was as if the voice was a crying out as the artist was drowning out from a disaster of their own making.

Nurit Wilde: Before Cass died, I had a friend named Peter Meyerson and we were driving around one day, and we decided on the spur of the moment to visit her at her house on Woodrow Wilson. Peter had a son that was born on almost the same day, same year as Cass' daughter, and they used to have birthday parties for the kids. Anyway, we knew that she was going to England soon, and we decide to visit her. We got to her house, and she was with that guy Lee Kefir, who I thought was a bit of a bum. Cass would get herself involved with these guys who would kind of hang on because of who she was and the money. I do remember— and Peter and I commented on this later—that Cass was in a great frame of mind. She had been rehearsing, and said that she was going to have dancers on stage and backup singers. She was so looking forward to going on this trip to England. She was happier than I'd seen her in many a year. She said that she was leaving the day after tomorrow, and it was the last time that we saw her alive . . . So, my last memories of her were very nice, because she was so excited, as she was finally going to make her career as a solo artist.

Eric Hord: Bobby Roberts was managing—or mis-managing—Cass at the time she died in London in the '70s. She was supposed to have a nurse with her on those dates, when she was alone back in her London apartment. But none was provided, courtesy, perhaps, of the Bobby Roberts agency. I think he was just trying to save some money, and probably said to her something to the effect of, "You don't really need the nurse on this tour Cass, you can take care of yourself . . . *right*, Cass?" And she probably said, "Sure." But she needed somebody with her, taking care of her.

Michelle Phillips: Cass had gone to England to play The Palladium. I think she was concerned at how she was going to be received as a soloist; she had not really done all that well here. She called me after the second show, and she was deliriously happy. She called me crying with joy, and she told me that she'd had standing ovations both nights, and that both of the shows were sold out. So this was Cass hitting the jackpot and this was Cass finally being acclaimed for her music, her performance, on her own as Cass Elliot, not "Mama Cass." I think she was billed as Cass Elliot. Earlier when she played as Caesar's Palace, they did the old 'switcharoo' on her. She was supposed to be billed as Cass Elliot, and two hours before the show, they changed the marquee to "Mama Cass," and she was really, really pissed off about that . . . But here she was, calling from London, laughing and crying and bubbling over with excitement. She was, I think, on her way over to Mick Jagger's birthday party.

The next day, I went to lunch at Warner Bros., with David Geyler. Larry Gordon, who was a film producer, and who produced my very first film, *Dillinger*, came up to us. He came up to us and said, "Michelle, brace yourself, I have some very bad news. Cass has died." I just remember getting up from the table very quickly, having the chair fall out from under me, and I just walked out of the commissary and went over to this little square of trees outside the commissary, and I was just shocked. I guess I just had to take it all in. How could she be dead after this wonderful success and finally achieving what she always wanted? She achieved it, and now she was dead. It was just unreal to me. I sat under that tree until David came and got me. I was going with Warren Beatty at the time, and Warren was filming *The Fortune* over at The Culver Studios. I don't remember exactly how this happened, but David took me over there, so that I could be with Warren. I don't remember exactly what happened after that, I just went blank. I was with Warren for a while, and as it started to get a little later in the day, I said that I had to get home, because I didn't want Chynna to hear about this from the television or somewhere. I had already heard that she had apparently choked on a ham sandwich. When I got home, Chynna was standing in the yard—she was about 6— and I got out of the car, and she came up to me and said, "Mommy, mommy, Cass died!" and I said, "Yes, I know." She said, "She choked on a ham sandwich." I said, "Well honey, we're not really sure if that's what happened; we're gonna have to wait and see to find out the true story." I went in the house, and I was so shaken, I couldn't speak. I remember the two of us just sitting there, and she started to shake her head and went, "Died of a ham sandwich!" And for the first time, I burst out laughing, from the way she said it, which was like a she had a collision or something with a ham sandwich!

Anyway, it took a little while to get a coroner's report, and the report said that she died of a massive heart attack that she suffered in the middle of the night, and that it was so massive, that she probably didn't even wake up. Anybody that knew Cass, knew that she never went to bed without a little snack nearby. That's where the ham sandwich came in, because they did find a half-eaten ham sandwich on a tray near the bed. She was staying at Nilsson's apartment. But that story persisted forever. As a matter of fact, that was one of the reasons that I wanted to write my book, because there were certain things that I wanted to straighten out, and one of them was that she didn't die of choking on a ham sandwich. I don't know why it bothered me so much, but it did. There were other reasons, too, like MacKenzie Phillips, whom I love dearly, but she was not my daughter, she was my stepdaughter, and I was getting asked about that all of the time.

But that was the sad story of Cass's demise. Her body was flown out here, and there was a funeral for her at The Hollywood Cemetery. Carol Burnett was there, they were very good friends. By this time Cass had a whole new retinue of friends that I didn't know that were there. But she had gone on with her life, and her life did not consist of John, Michelle and Denny any longer. I think it was hard for me to realize that at that point, like, "Who are these people?"

Cass and MacKenzie Phillips, 1968.
Photo by Henry Diltz.

Denny Doherty: I was living up in Carmel, and I got a call one morning that she was dead. She had been in London, playing The Palladium, and that she was dead; that was all I heard. No cause of death, or any details. I then headed for Los Angeles to see what was going on. By the time I got there, they were bringing Cass home for the funeral. I spent a couple of days in L.A. for the funeral, sat with her mother, and that was it. What are ya gonna do? Michelle and

Cass's funeral, 1974
Courtesy of the Michael Ochs Archives.

John showed up in their black suits and they were in mourning, and fuckin' Peter Lawford and I showed up in denim.

David Crosby: I share a lot of things with John, in that he went through a lot of things that I did. But I gotta tell you, my biggest thing with John now is that I'm kinda pissed at him. In his book, he says that I turned Cass on to heroin, which is not true. That's a fucking lie. Cass and I did a lot of drugs together, and we did do heroin together. We did coke together, and we did every drug in the world together, but she had done heroin a long time before me. So, that was just a lie ... she was doing heroin long before I ever did it with her. No, I did not turn her on to it.

Denny Doherty: The first thing that I heard, and that every-body suspected in our circle, was drugs, that she overdosed on drugs. And I'm sure that's what the rest of the world thought.

Cass Elliot, London, 1974.
Photo by Les McCann.
Courtesy of Nash Editions.

"Where did she die?" "In London, in an apartment, an old shooting gallery in London." It had been Harry Nilsson's place, as well as Keith Moon's. It was a well-known druggie hangout, and that's where she was living. That's what I heard, that she was in Keith Moon's place, and that she died. What else are you gonna think? Then I'd heard that she had a heart attack, and eating a ham sandwich. We found out that she was found in the middle of the night or early in the morning, and it was too early for a coroner's report. But then, they couldn't find a cause of death, any "obvious cause of death other than natural causes." When they don't say natural causes, they think foul play, in order to cover their asses in a criminal investigation. Then they pick it apart and take it from there to find out what really happened. But since it was Cass, and she was a big name, and they heard 'foul play.' Well, what do you think 'foul play' means? It can mean anything from murder to OD'ing on heroin. Everybody was speculating on everything in the world. By the time we got the coroner's report, it was 'heart attack due to fatty tissue around the heart.' And the press was running with "heroin overdose at Keith Moon's apartment," of course, and she had a history of using heroin, and blah blah blah. Yeah, well, she was too fat and her heart quit. But, when we finally got the coroner's report, there were no drugs found, and it was "cardiac arrest due to fatty tissue surrounding the heart." Her heart just gave out. God love her.

PART FOUR
The "Denny" television 'reunion' ... 'Mitch, don't worry ...' horror on the Halifax/Dartmouth freeway ... "Needless to say, we got back to the studio, John did the shit, we did the show, and they left ... "

Michelle Phillips: I talked to John, he was in New York, I was in Los Angeles, and I told him that if he took any drugs across the border, I would kill him. I told him, 'If you come into Halifax with any drugs, I will not go on, I will not perform. He said, 'Mitch, don't worry ...' Then, when I got there, I took one look at him, and he was gray. He said that he didn't take any drugs ... maybe *that* was the problem. I remember it was a big joke, because they put us in adjoining rooms at the hotel. I remember the whole time, wondering if he was doing drugs next door. . . .

Denny Doherty: I got home in 1977, and I got approached by the CBC, and they said "Oh, you're back; god, Denny, you saw the elephant and everything ... " So, my idea was to have grand piano, drum riser, and some furniture and have guests in that could talk about how we all came together. I could have people like Sebastian, McGuire, and Zal come down. People like that. The only thing was, being a CBC show; it had to have 80 percent Canadian content. Taxpayers were gonna fund this show, not Americans.

Anyway, John and Michelle came up to do the show. Michelle was in L.A., and John was in New York. She got him to promise that he wasn't using, and he swore up and down that he wasn't. Okay. On those grounds, Michelle will come up and do the show. Now, it should have tipped her off, that rather than her meeting him up in Halifax, he flew to Los Angeles, to get a ride from Michelle, and for him to get the attention off of him 'traveling alone.' Because he was using. And by the time they arrived in Halifax, she was furious. Apparently, on the way to the L.A. airport, John threw some of his paraphernalia—a bent spoon—out into a ditch.

She agreed to do this, and had to walk in on his arm. They arrived in Halifax to do my show, and the first show went really great. John had something stashed someplace, and he was able to maintain. The first show went so well, that they agreed to stay over and do another show. Halfway through the second show, the producer came over the PA and said, "Denny, could you come up to the booth, please?" I go into the booth, and John and Michelle are out with the band, waiting. In the booth there's a bank of about 20 video monitors, and the producer says, "camera three, could you do a close-up of John's breast pocket?" They do a close-up, and the producer says, "Den, what is that?" and it's a hypodermic needle sticking out of his pocket. "What's wrong with this picture, Den?!" I went down and took John into the hallway, and he took it out of his pocket and slammed it into his leg, and then tossed it into the trash. Oh, my, my, my. Later, we were doing the end-of-show rap time, and I went to the producer and told him that we weren't going to get the show finished unless we got John some medication. John needed some Dilaudid, which is synthetic morphine. There was a place on the seedier, other side of town that I thought we could procure what was needed. We found the last six Dilaudid pills that were in existence in Halifax county, and we went through those rather readily. We went to this nightclub of rather 'nefarious reputation.' Down on the waterfront, if ya know what I mean. I found an old friend who was out of jail, and explained what was going in, and a little rat-faced guy comes over and says, "Follow me . . . " We go get my car, and John comes with me, and we're both in makeup and costume, and the guy says, "Ya gotta go over to Dartmouth . . . " They call it Dartmouth. We get what we need to get and are leaving, and about seven or eight Mountie police cars sur-round us and say, "Don't move!" I'm thinking to myself, "I'm dead . . . " The dealer and his girlfriend are in the backseat, John and I are in front, and I know the Mounties recognize me. They ask me where we were goin,' and I tell 'em we're on our way back to the CBC Studios, and we're doin' a show, blah-blah-blah, and by now they've got flashlights in out faces, and apparently we aren't the people they're looking for anyway. This was some bust that was supposed to go down any minute, and *we're in the way!* We got outta there real quick. We were the wrong car, but I didn't give a fuck, and we left. We got a free one there . . . if they had taken us out, and spread us out on the car and went through everyone's pockets, they'd have found the shit, and we would have all been busted . . . my life was flashing before my eyes, this was IT. Need-less to say, we got back to the studio, John did the shit, we did the show, and they left . . . it's on tape somewhere . . .

PART FIVE

The Rock and Roll Hall of Fame, pain . . . and just a little bit of shame . . . Rest in peace, Papa John . . . A return to The Strip . . . The Mamas & The Papas Spanish rise to the occasion at The Roxy for Papa John and the legend . . . The Mamas & The Papas legacy . . . once was a time I thought . . .

Michelle Phillips: When I realized that we'd be eligible for induction for The Rock and Roll Hall of Fame five years earlier, I hadn't really sat down and done that math, because I thought it was a no-brainer. I did. I had also known that John had made a lot of enemies in this town and New York. So, I started to lobby for it to happen. I spoke to Jan Wenner, who told me that it was going to be a hard sell with people that John had pissed off. And I said, "That should not be the criteria for being inducted into The Rock and Roll Hall of Fame, *if* as you guys say, "It's not all politics." So next time I saw Ahmet, I sat down right on his lap, and said, "Ya know Ahmet, I wanna be in The Rock and Roll Hall of Fame. And I

Michelle, John, and Denny, West Los Angeles, 1986.
Photo by Henry Diltz.

know that everyone hates John, but that's not fair to me and Cass and Denny." We sold the amounts of records, we had the hits, we had the legend; we had all of the criteria. "If it's not all about the politics, then I'd like to see our name nominated next time around." Ya know what? Jan Wenner and Ahmet Ertegun can get *a lot done!* So, we were nominated the first year, and I really didn't know how it worked. But, you get nominated the first year and you don't get in, and then you get in the next year. But, we should have been nominated five years before. But anyhow, it was fine. I was very happy when we were inducted. I really didn't know how we were going to handle it, because John apparently wasn't speaking to me. And ya know what? It was just total bullshit that John wasn't speaking to me. Whatever John and Farnez's problem was with the whole fucking world, was what this was about. You know, they didn't talk to any of the kids, they didn't talk to anyone.

Denny Doherty: The Rock and Roll Hall of Fame came about because Michelle shamed them into it. Jan Wenner, the guy who produces *Rolling Stone*. Let's shoot back to the Monterey Pop Festival, backstage. Clive Davis and Ahmet Ertegun are back there having bidding wars on all of these groups, including Janis Joplin. Jan Wenner wasn't doing *Rolling Stone* quite yet, but he and Lou and John were arguing, because all of the Bay Area folk were pissed off at the L.A. people for stealing their thunder, putting on this big festival and beating the big gong for themselves. They also made some insinuation that the money wasn't going where it was supposed to, and that there was some financial hanky-panky going on. So Jan, John, and Lou all got into this big screaming match and accusations; throwing dispersions on each other. And over the years, Jan Wenner was saying, "No, we're not going to vote to put The Mamas & The Papas in The Rock and Roll Hall of Fame; that prick Phillips. Fuck him . . . " Now, this was never proven; this is what Michelle told me. Because she was there and I wasn't. But there was always animosity between Wenner and John and Lou. John also had bad dealings with Ahmet Ertegun. So guess what? They're all the guys who vote for The Rock and Roll Hall of Fame. And they're not voting for us . . .

Michelle's calling these guys up and saying, "Why aren't we in The Rock and Roll Hall of Fame?" "Well, ah . . . it has to be 25 years since, ah . . . " "Well, we did that." "Well, ah . . . you have to have a certain number of sales . . . " "We did that." And that's how we got in; it was long after we should have. But the whole thing at the Waldorf Astoria in New York was a circle jerk, as far as I'm concerned . . .

Michelle Phillips: When John Phillips (and the rest of us) made the film deal with Fox years later, I extended the olive branch to him, and asked him to join me as an executive producer on the film, as I did with Denny. Which he accepted immediately. But then when the time came to talk about how we were going to be credited as executive producers, he wouldn't be on the same 'card' with me, on the credits that roll. We were going to have a card together as executive producers, the three of us. Then I heard, "John won't be on the same card as you." I said, "That's fine . . . he can go on with Denny, and I will go on with one of the Fox producers, I don't care" But to make matters worse, he didn't want to be on the same card with Denny either! Denny is a man who named his *son* after John. Who spent ten years of his life going on the road with John, to keep John afloat. Denny did a lot for John out of friendship. And when I heard this, it made my blood curdle, and I thought, "Those two people, John and Farnez, are so wicked. They are just wicked people. Anything I can do to get this project done and get out and away from them, and not to have any more business dealings with John or Farnez, it cannot be soon enough for me . . . " They burned their children, they burned everybody in their path. I'm relieved, that now after John's death—now that we are talking about John in the past tense—that I don't have to have anything to do with them ever again. That's how I feel. I feel that John turned into something so *bitter* and so sick, that I couldn't and didn't want to have anything ever to do with him.

Now, before John died, I did go to see him in the hospital. I'm very glad that I did, because at first, Farnez didn't want me to go, and she made it quite clear that I was not to come. There was a part of me that wanted to go; to say goodbye to the man that I once loved very much. To a man that changed life forever. But there was also a part of me that said, "I'm not gonna go up into the ICU and make a big scene!" So, I waited. And Denny Doherty and Lou Adler said to her, "Look, this is really wrong. You should let Michelle come and say goodbye. So, she finally allowed it, and I went in one night when she wasn't there. He looked kind of shocked to see me, but he held my hand, and we talked. He could barely talk at that point. But I thanked him, and then after a few minuets it looked like he was dozing off again, and I said, "John!" And he opened his eyes, and I said, "Do you want me to come back?" And he reached over and kissed me, and said, "Yes." And that was our last exchange, I felt good that I had done it, and then after that he really went downhill. And I didn't slip him anything, either! But, we made peace.

Michelle Phillips: When Lou called me and told me that he was going to do The Roxy Tribute for John, he said, "Ya know, everybody's gonna sing, Mitch . . . you should really get up there." I said, "No. No way I'm gonna get up there." He said, "Denny's gonna sing, Barry McGuire's gonna sing, Scott's gonna sing, John Stewart's gonna sing . . . " I said, "Well yeah, let 'em sing. I'm not gonna do it." "MacKenzie's gonna sing, Spanky's gonna sing . . . " I said, "Nah; let them do it . . . " But once it started, it was just impossible to resist . . . it was so much fun. It was just so much fun to see those people. I hadn't seen John Stewart since probably '68 or '69. But, my rock and roll side was tapped.

Michelle Phillips: It was a huge part of my life, and yet it was a bubble. I think that great things are. I think that they aren't things that go on forever and ever. They are an experience that hopefully you can share with the world—and hopefully you can—and then to have it continue for years and years and decades afterwards is extremely gratifying. Every time I do hear a song, it takes me back to that crazy, crazy period that lasted only a few years, in reality. The group was in fact only singing together for two and a half years! So, it was an amazing experience for me, and I know how many people it touched, even today. People say to me, "Ya know, I came out to California when I heard that song . . . "

Mark Volman: Their legacy is intriguing to look at, because it sort of revolves around the song "California Dreamin.'" It revolves around the dream that it conjures up for everybody that has never been to California. Like the way Brian Wilson gave California a sound, they gave California a vision. That one song kind of gave us the landscape of Southern California.

Michelle Phillips: I know that the group touched millions and millions of people, and not just 'hippies.' Our audiences were always very funny; we saw a young crowd, there was a middle-aged crowd. They just liked the music. It wasn't just a little hippie, teenybopper appeal. It was across the board. People thought we did something very special vocally, and John and whoever was writing with him—and he did have people writing with him, on occasion!—thought that the songs were special. And there you are, you see . . .

Al Kooper: I enjoyed the production on the M&P records. The harmonies were fat and double-tracked nicely. The arrangements were great and most were strong songs. They sounded great on the radio!

The Mamas & The Papas borrowed equally from The Beatles and Beach Boy legacy to create a unique American sound that represented California world-wide in the summer of 1967. Their powerful harmonies and strong songs have survived any one-hit wonder status and will surely live forever in the annals of pop music history.

Kim Fowley: It boils down to: they had a great sound, great songs, a great image, and they had a great career. And isn't that fine? The tragedy of The Mamas & The Papas was unlike the Beach Boys or The Four Seasons, because they chose not to continue their magical sound, so they didn't have the longevity. It's a shame that they didn't continue. But that tragedy makes them exotic. And quirky. And everyone can read this book and wonder "what if?"

Jerry Yester: I think that they embodied something else of that period, and that was having no idea what was happening to them. I'm sure that some of them look back on it now and say, "if I only knew then what I know now," that kind of thing, because so much of it was thrown away by them, and by people like them at the same time. Not many people handle it very wisely or appreciate it. I think that John's story is one of the saddest there is; all the stuff he's thrown away. It started out from the whole acid period, which began as something very spiritual, but them quickly turned into an orgy. Back in the MFQ, we had heard about acid, and we knew it was coming and we studied it, because it was for enlightenment. That spirituality very quickly became a party, and the wedding of

thunderpussy—this horrible, wretched thing that eventually spawned the Manson family. I think that aspect of The Mamas & The Papas reflected that part of society helped give them life.

Cass Elliot: I think that we were the freshest sound that I've ever heard. I don't think that The Beatles, collectively vocally, are as good as The Mamas & The Papas were. Individually they each have something going. Paul is one of the great all-time singers, and John is a fantastic singer, and even Ringo is emerging as a singer. But collectively, I don't think there's been a group . . . Crosby, Stills & Nash comes closest to what I consider to be the perfect vocal sound. The Mamas & The Papas had a sound that electrified us. Just making the music turned us on. We would sing all day long until we got sleepy, and then the first one up in the morning would wake everybody else up, and we'd just sing, and we just loved it. I think that that kind of love, coupled with the intensity that we devoted to it, kind of made a magical vibration which stimulated a lot of people.

Donovan: The music of The Mamas & The Papas reflected perfectly the sense of adventure which the American bohemian felt, a true Americana journey across that great continent from New York to San Francisco, and rolling down to Tinsel Town, where we all met and became part of a great fraternity of music, philosophy, and angst. California Dreamin,' indeed.

John Phillips Eulogy

I met The Mamas & The Papas in 1965 in a studio at Western Recorders when they had just finished singing their first song, "California Dreamin'." I opened my eyes and looked at them; I had the title to their first album: "If You Can Believe Your Eyes and Ears." I asked what it would take to sign them and John answered: "a steady flow of cash from your office to our house." (Of course, at that time they didn't have a house.)

John would become the tallest rock star. And he would become and do a lot of things very quickly. He went from corduroy hats to chinchilla hats, from a small house to a mansion in Bel Air, from rags to DeVoss, and a '61 Buick to a Rolls Royce.

John had a great sardonic sense of humor. Ask Terry Melcher. In 1987, at a tribute to The Monterey International Pop Festival, he asked Terry to sing background on "California Dreamin'" with Scott Mackenzie. During rehearsal, he said to Terry, "You sing so well, why don't you sing the verses while I sing background with Scott?" Later that night when they were on stage, Terry only got to "Stopped into a church" when John interrupted him and said: "You know Terry, I've heard you sing it better than that. Let's start again." Terry started, John stopped. John repeated: "You can do better than that." After the third time, Terry got the joke.

John loved recording and being in the studio. He was a taskmaster. You can't ask Cass, but ask Denny or Michelle about the time Cass, nine months pregnant, crawled out of the studio, after John got the last note he needed from her. And when Denny, who had passed out on the top of the piano, finally opened his eyes, he awoke to Bones, our engineer, lowering a microphone over his mouth to get the last note that was needed from him.

But John drove himself as hard as he drove anyone. Along with

Brian Wilson, John was one of the greatest vocal arrangers of the last fifty years. And, he was a great songwriter. Andrew Oldham, an old friend and English gentleman who produced most of the Rolling Stones records, sent me the following words of love regarding John that sums it all up beautifully:

> There are only a handful of writers that capture a moment in time. John Phillips was a true Captain America of song. The Mamas and Papas led the movement that seized the mantle of pop as an American art.

Anyone who ever had a relationship with John Phillips experienced a roller coaster ride: scary, wild, and the thrill of a lifetime. Thanks for the ride, John.

LOU ADLER
March 24, 2001

Tribute

JOHNNY ALWAYS
PUSHED THE LINE.
THE SURVIVAL LINE
THE MUSIC LINE
THE DRUG LINE
THE MIDDLE LINE
THE PARTY LINE

HE WAS ALWAYS THE BRIGHTEST
ONE IN THE ROOM
HE ALWAYS OWNED THE ROOM
I NEVER SAW HIM WORRIED
I NEVER SAW HIM NOT HAVING FUN.

HE WAS A MAGNET FOR THE ELITE
MOVIE STARS
BEATLE STARS
ROLLING STONES STARS
LSD STARS.

I HAD SOME OF THE BEST TIMES IN MY LIFE
WITH JOHN PHILLIPS
WRITING "CHILLY WINDS"
IN A ROW BOAT IN THE SAN FRANCISCO BAY
WRITING "OH MISS MARY"
IN NICK REYNOLDS'S HOUSE IN SAUSALITO.
BOTH BECAME SIGNATURE SONGS
FOR THE KINGSTON TRIO
AFTER I JOINED THE BAND.
WHEN THE BEATLES HIT

PHILLIPS LISTENED TO THEIR
FIRST ALBUM WITH EARPHONES
FOR HOURS AND THEN
ANNOUNCED TO DENNY
AND MICHELLE, "I'VE GOT IT"
AND PROCEEDED TO WRITE
HIS OWN BRAND OF FOLK ROCK.

WHEN HE CAME BACK FROM THE VIRGIN ISLANDS
HE AND DENNY AND MICHELLE
WALKED INTO MY OFFICE AT THE
COLUMBUS TOWER
IN NORTH BEACH
AND PLAYED ME
"CALIFORNIA DREAMIN'"
I LITERALLY FELL OFF MY CHAIR
AND THAT WAS WITHOUT CASS
I HAD NEVER HEARD ANYTHING
LIKE THAT IN MY LIFE.
I SAID YOU SHOULD GO TO
L.A. AND SEE LOU ADLER
LOU HAD THE SAME REACTION
AND THE CRAZY RIDE
THE MAD RIDE
THE MULTIMILLION-DOLLAR RIDE BEGAN.

"MONDAY, MONDAY" WHICH PROVED A
STORY SONG DIDN'T HAVE TO MAKE SENSE
TO BE a HIT.
"I SAW HER AGAIN LAST NIGHT," "CREEQUE ALLEY"
"IF YOU'RE GOING TO SAN FRANCISCO"
FOR HIS LIFE LONG FRIEND SCOTT MACKENZIE
HIS BRILLIANT SOLO ALBUM. *WOLF KING OF L.A.*
HE TOLD ME HE CALLED IT THAT JUST TO "PISS PEOPLE OFF"
IN THAT BEAUTIFUL ALBUM
HE REVEALED THE SOFT SIDE OF JOHNNY
AND HE NEVER LIKED IT.

HE DIDN'T LIKE PEOPLE KNOWING THAT SIDE OF HIM EXISTED.

JOHNNY ALWAYS PUSHING THE LINE.

JOHN TOLD ME ONCE THAT HE USE TO LIKE
TO TAKE LSD AND DRIVE WITH THE TOP DOWN
THROUGH NEW YORK.
THIS WAS A METAPHOR FOR HIS LIFE
WHAT WOULD TERRIFY OTHER PEOPLE
WAS JOHN'S KIND OF FUN.

HE COULDN'T FIND IT IN FAME,
SO HE LOOKED FOR IT
IN DRUGS AND BOOZE.
BOY HE WASN' T ALONE ON
THAT ONE.
THERE'S NOTHING IN FAME AND MONEY
EXCEPT A HIGH ROLLING COASTER
WITH A DOWNHILL RIDE FEW SURVIVE
NOT EVEN JOHNNY PUSHING THE LINE.

JOHN'S LIFE IS WHAT LEGENDS ARE MADE OF
BUT NOT WHAT HEROES ARE MADE OF.
JOHN COULD BE THE NICEST GUY
IN THE WORLD AND NOT THE NICEST

HE WAS A DUDE
A KAT
A BLUE BLOOD
A JUNKY
A GENIUS
AND A FOOL.

HE WAS LIKE THE LYRICS

TO THAT KRISTOFFERSON SONG,
PARTLY COOL AND PARTLY FRICTION.
HE RODE IT OUT WITH A "WHO CARES?"
ATTITUDE THAT WOULD MAKE
BONNIE AND CLYDE ENVIOUS,
IN THE MIDDLE OF A NEW SOLO
ALBUM AND ONE WITH
KEITH RICHARDS.

FROM VIRGINIA, TO NEW YORK, TO L.A.
FROM THE SMOOTHIES
TO THE JOURNEYMEN,
TO THE MAMAS & THE PAPAS.
FROM HITS
TO DRUGS
TO BOOZE
TO REHAB
TO LIVER TRANSPLANTS
TO TABLOIDS
TO A HEART ATTACK
JOHN ALWAYS HAD HIS FAMILY
WHO WERE ALWAYS MAD AT HIM
AND ALWAYS LOVED HIM
AND ALL HIS FRIENDS
WHO ALWAYS FELT THE SAME.
HE LEFT BEHIND
A WORLD THAT KNOWS THE WORDS
TO ALL HIS HITS
AND A BUNCH OF PEOPLE
HERE TONIGHT
WHO DON'T WANT
TO LET HIM GO.
WHERE EVER JOHNNY IS RIGHT NOW
YOU CAN BET
THAT JOHNNY'S PUSHING THE LINE

AND YOU CAN BET
HE'S HAVING A REAL GOOD TIME
AND JOHNNY WAS A FRIEND OF MINE.

JOHN STEWART
read at the John Phillips tribute
The Roxy
West Hollywood, California
March 29, 2001

Discography

ALBUMS

If You Can Believe Your Eyes and Ears
(Dunhill D50006)
February 1966
Produced by Lou Adler

NOTES: This album had the group's name listed as The Mama's and The Papa's. Except for some related single releases, the apostrophes were never used again. If you listen to the latest compilation CD *All the Leaves Are Brown:The Golden Era Collection* (MCA 088 112 653-2), and turn your balance level all the way to the left channel at the beginning of "California Dreamin'," you can distinctly hear Barry McGuire sing the opening phrase, "All the leaves are brown." [*Editor's note: His version appears on his follow-up album to* Eve of Destruction, This Precious Time *(Dunhill D50005). The Mamas & The Papas appear on almost all of the tracks on this fine album, which almost serves as warm up for their debut. Extremely hard to find, it is indeed worth seeking out. The album's sterling P. F. Sloan title track is available on* Creeque Alley: The History of The Mamas & The Papas *(MCAD2-10195) —M.G.*]

SIDE ONE

"Monday, Monday"
"Straight Shooter"
"Got a Feelin'" (Doherty/Phillips)
"I Call Your Name" (Lennon/McCartney)
"Do You Wanna Dance" (Bobby Freeman)
"Go Where You Wanna Go"

SIDE TWO

"California Dreamin'" (Phillips/Gilliam)
"Spanish Harlem" (Leiber/Spector)
"Somebody Groovy"

"Hey Girl" (Phillips/Gilliam)
"You Baby" (Sloan/Barri)
"In Crowd" (Billy Page)
All songs written by John Phillips, except where noted.

Cass-John-Michelle-Dennie A K A *The Mamas & The Papas*
(Dunhill D50010)
September 1966
Produced by Lou Adler

N O T E S : Denny's name was misspelled on the album cover. The album cover photo was changed to include Jill Gibson, but none of the album covers were actually printed showing Jill. The pre-release album covers that showed up on billboards around the country did have Jill in Michelle's pose. Take it from one who was there, this was the most anticipated Mamas & Papas album ever, and it went gold before it was released. [*Ed. note*: As mentioned in the text, Ray Manzarek plays organ on "No Salt on Her Tail." Also, part of the album was recorded while Michelle was temporarily replaced by Jill Gibson, who does appear on several tracks. —M.G.]

S I D E O N E

"No Salt on Her Tail"
"Trip, Stumble & Fall" (Phillips/Gilliam)
"Dancing Bear"
"Words of Love"
"My Heart Stood Still" (Rodgers/Hart)
"Dancing in the Street" (Stevensen/Gaye)

S I D E T W O

"I Saw Her Again" (Phillips/Doherty)
"Strange Young Girls"
"I Can't Wait"
"Even If I Could"
"That Kind of Girl"
"Once Was a Time I Thought"
All songs written by John Phillips, except where noted.

Deliver AKA *The Mamas & The Papas Deliver*
(Dunhill D50014)
March 1967
Produced by Lou Adler
NOTE: The title is a reference to the birth of Cass's daughter, Owen Vanessa.

SIDE ONE

"Dedicated to the One I Love" (Pauling/Bass)
"My Girl" (Robinson/White)
"Creeque Alley" (Phillips/Gilliam)
"Sing For Your Supper" (Rodgers/Hart)
"Twist and Shout" (Russell/Medley)
"Free Advice" (Phillips/Gilliam)

SIDE TWO

"Look Through My Window"
"Boys and Girls Together"
"String Man" (Phillips/Gilliam)
"Frustration"
"Did You Ever Wanna Cry"
"John's Music Box"
All songs written by John Phillips, except where noted.

The Papas & Mamas Presented by The Mamas & The Papas AKA *Papas & Mamas*
(ABC/Dunhill D50031)
March 1968
Produced by Lou Adler

NOTES: Most of this album was recorded in the Phillips's secret attic studio at their Bel Air residence. The overall sound and feel of the album is quite different from their earlier work, but it has aged surprisingly well.

SIDE ONE

"The Right Somebody To Love" (Shirley Temple)
"Safe in My Garden"
"Meditation Mama (Transcendental Woman Travels)" (Phillips/Adler)
"For the Love of Ivy" (Phillips/Doherty)
"Dream a Little Dream (of Me)" (Schwante/Kahn)
"Mansions"

SIDE TWO

"The Right Somebody to Love" (second verse) (Shirley Temple)
"Gemini Childe"
"Nothing's Too Good for My Little Girl" (Ned Wynn)
"Too Late"
"12:30" (Young Girls are Coming to the Canyon)"
"Rooms"
"Midnight Voyage"
All songs written by John Phillips, except where noted.

SINGLES

NOTES: The very first single is rumored to be "Go Where You Wanna Go."
The legend is that it was released as a promotional copy in Hawaii where it
was quickly dismissed by the program directors in power. Lou Adler quickly
pulled it and sent out another song. The rest is history. [*Editor's note: See Lou
Adler's quote in Chapter Three—M.G.*] "Glad to be Unhappy" was never on a
legitimate album. It was recorded along with "Here in My Arms" for the television special featuring Rodgers & Hart tunes. "Unhappy" saw the light of day
when "Arms" never would.

"California Dreamin'" b/w "Somebody Groovy"
(Dunhill 4018)
December 1965
(Debuted on the Billboard charts January 8, 1966—peaking at #4 during its
17-week run)

"Monday, Monday" b/w "Got a Feelin'"
(Dunhill 4026)
April 1966
(Debuted on the Billboard charts April 9, 1966—peaking at #1 [for three
weeks] during its 14-week run)

"I Saw Her Again" b/w "Even If I Could"
(Dunhill 4031)
June 1966
(Debuted on the Billboard charts July 2, 1966—peaking at #5 during its 9-
week run)

"Look through My Window" b/w "Once Was a Time I Thought"
(Dunhill 4050)
September 1966
(Debuted on the Billboard charts October 22, 1966—peaking at #24 during it's 7-week run)

"Words of Love" b/w "Dancing in the Streets"
(Dunhill 4057)
November 1966
(Debuted on the Billboard charts December 3, 1966—peaking at #5 during its 12-week run. The B-side, "Dancing In the Streets" charted on its own, reaching # 73)

"Dedicated to the One I Love" b/w "Free Advice"
(Dunhill 4077)
January 1967
(Debuted on the Billboard charts February 22, 1967—peaking at #2 [for three weeks] during its 12-week run)

"Creeque Alley" b/w "Did You Ever Wanna Cry"
(Dunhill 4083)
April 1967
(Debuted on the Billboard charts April 29, 1967—peaking at #5 during its 9-week run)

"12:30 (Young Girls are Coming to the Canyon)" b/w "Straight Shooter"
(Dunhill 4099)
August 1967
(Debuted on the Billboard charts August 26, 1967—peaking at #20 during its 6-week run.)

"Glad to Be Unhappy" b/w "Hey Girl"
(Dunhill 4107)
October 1967
(Debuted on the Billboard charts October 28, 1967—peaking at #26 during its 7-week run.)

"Dancing Bear" b/w "John's Music Box"
(Dunhill 4113PS)
December 1967

"Safe in My Garden" b/w "Too Late"
(Dunhill 4125)
May 1968

"Dream a Little Dream" b/w "Midnight Voyage"
(Dunhill 4145)
June 1968
Note: Officially released as "Mama Cass with The Mamas & The Papas," and marketed as Cass's debut "solo" single.
(Debuted on the Billboard charts July 6, 1968—peaking at #12 during its 12-week run).

"For the Love of Ivy" b/w "Strange Young Girls"
(Dunhill 4150)
July 1968

"Do You Wanna Dance" b/w "My Girl"
(Dunhill 4171)
October 1968

"Step Out" b/w "Shooting Star"
(Dunhill 44301)
January 1972

SELECTED COMPILATIONS/ANTHOLOGIES

Farewell to the First Golden Era
(Dunhill 50025)
November 1967
Released during the group's lifetime, it included the then-current single, "12:30 (Young Girls Are Coming to the Canyon)."

A Gathering Of Flowers
(Dunhill 50073)
March 1970
An excellent (and now very rare) double album anthology 'box set,' *Gathering* contains all of the group's biggest hits, as well as some excellent album cuts. A superb 12-page booklet with an exceptional essay by Andy Wickham (who wrote the liner notes for the first two albums) and dozens of previously unpublished photos round out this truly deluxe package. In addition to the fine song selection, there is some interesting studio conversation and run-

throughs, such as Cass coaching John on his lead vocal for "I Can't Wait," and a funny alternate take during the vocal session of "Once Was a Time I Thought." Some of this material, along with bits of the between-song interviews (from John and Cass), was later used on the *Creeque Alley* anthology. Even scarcer is the "white label" radio station–only promotional copy, which includes a seven-inch, 33¹/₃ RPM "open-ended" extended interview with Cass and John on alternate sides. Most of this material appears in this book, by permission of Universal Music.

Creeque Alley: The History of The Mamas & The Papas
(MCA/Universal MCAD2-10195)
November 1991
A two-CD anthology, this set not only includes the hits but also a myriad of well-selected album tracks. In addition, disc one opens up with cuts by The Big Three, The Mugwumps, Barry McGuire's "This Precious Time" (with The Mamas & The Papas backing vocals), and disc two closes with solo material from all four members. Sort of an "audio documentary," it is highly recommended.

All the Leaves Are Brown: The Golden Era Collection
(MCA/Universal 088 122 653-2)
September 2001
All four original The Mamas & The Papas albums in their complete form, and omitting the near-disposable *People Like Us*. Several superb, hard to find (and radically different) mono mixes of singles ("I Saw Her Again," Words of Love," and "Creeque Alley") round out the set, which also includes "Glad to Be Unhappy." Liner notes by the author of this book.

UNRELEASED MATERIAL

[*Editor's note: As indicated in other places in this book, there is little or no known unreleased material from the group. However, the few exceptions are noted here. When I interviewed John in 1998, he said that he had "one or two original, unreleased, and complete songs . . . " from The Mamas & The Papas (pre-'reunion album' period, meaning 1968 or earlier), and added that they had been in "rough mix" form. The titles, whereabouts, and in fact their very existence is unknown. They may, in fact, be some of the titles listed here. —M.G.*]

"Here in My Arms," recorded in 1966 for an ABC television special named "Rodgers & Hart Today." Denny sings the song straight as Michelle and Cass "echo" his vocal much like "No Salt on Her Tail." A fabulous studio recording.

"My Funny Valentine" was sung along with entertainer Arthur Godfrey on another television special in 1967. This was not studio-recorded and not available in any form except a bootlegged video.

[*Editor's note: According to studio logs, several Beatles songs other than "I Call Your Name" were attempted during the sessions for the first album. Some of the titles include "Nowhere Man," We Can Work It Out," and "Michelle." According to ASCAP records, a Phillips/Gilliam song entitled "Hide in Plain Sight (cues)" was copyrighted in 1968. It obviously appears to have been written for a film or television show, but remains unreleased and quite possibly unrecorded. A logical theory is that it was written along with "For the Love of Ivy" for inclusion in the film of the same name or the 1968 film "Hide in Plain Sight" starring James Caan. —M.G.*]

People Like Us —The "Reunion" album
(ABC/Dunhill DSX 50106)
October 1971
Produced by John Phillips

NOTES: It was ridiculously cold in the record store the day I pulled this album from the bin. That feeling has never left the aura of the album. This is not a bad album for it has some really good songs etched into its vinyl. The sounds have always made me sad because I know that in its heart it isn't really a Mamas & Papas album. It is an after-thought that does not merit comparison to the real Mamas & Papas albums that start with "Monday, Monday" and end with "Midnight Voyage." Cass's contributions on this album are minimal at best. It is almost a New Journeymen's album by default. It has some astounding moments of Mamas & Papas clarity and more than its share of originality, but it has no heart. The original album came with an 8x11 lyric sheet that is printed in the same brownish sepia tone as the album cover. It looks great matted and framed. [*Editor's note: This album was recorded for the sole reason of avoiding a lawsuit from ABC/Dunhill for "failure to deliver product," as the group owed ABC/Dunhill one more album of original material in accordance with the contract extension of mid-1967. See Denny and Michelle's quotes in Chapter Eight— M.G.*]

SIDE ONE

"People Like Us"
"Pacific Coast Highway"
"Snow Queen of Texas"
"Shooting Star"
"Step Out"
"Lady Genevieve"

"No Dough"
"European Blueboy"
"Pearl"
"I Wanna Be a Star" (Michelle Phillips)
"Grasshopper"
"Blueberries for Breakfast"
All songs written by John Phillips, except where noted.

As an avid follower of these remarkable songs and the talent behind them I cannot express what a true part of my life they have all been. It maybe sounds trite and contrived, but they have all played a great part in me being the person I am today. I loved music as a child before I heard The Mamas & The Papas but it became a profound part of my life because I did hear The Mamas & The Papas. I thank you collectively and individually.

SANDY GRANGER

Acknowledgments

Yes, I indeed had a lot of help here. Although I conducted almost all of the interviews myself, most of the contacts actually came from the participants, the names of whom you're probably already familiar with by now. It was a virtual domino effect, one person leading to three others, and so on and so forth, and I'd like to thank everyone who sang here for the open minds, calendars, and phone books—especially Denny Doherty and Michelle Phillips. They only asked for one thing: an honest book. I sincerely hope and think they got it.

But there were also a lot of other people who, aside from helping set up interviews and contacts, provided insight, sustenance, objective and constructive criticism, feedback, and inspiration throughout the course of this project. To that end, I wish to thank:

Andrea Michelle Holland, Joe Shapiro and L. B. Holland at 4449 for the living cone, camaraderie, and support . . . Thomas 'Jonsie' Jones—a true musical and spiritual soldier who helped me fight hard for all the right reasons . . . Helen Donlon, Bob Merlis, and Bill Bentley at Warner Bros. for a critical eye and help with the contacts . . . Alan "Ruby" Rubens, a true friend and that's a lot . . . Paul Williams, Cindy Lee Berryhill, Ellen Sander, and the entire *Crawdaddy!* family . . . Irv, Mitchell, Marc and Gloria Greenwald, through thick and thin . . . the staff of The Rock and Roll Hall of Fame (Cleveland), Michael Simmons, Chrissie Hynde, Jim Marshall, Sam Andrew, Michael Ochs Archives, David Ponak, Jeffery Spearitt, Michael Laine, The Beverly Hills Hotel bar for coolness and comfort after a hot day in Laurel Canyon, Richie Unterberger, Pete Howard and Bill Wasserzieher at Ice Magazine, Dave Zimmer, L. A. Johnson, Newcastle Brown . . . Craig Rutherford, a true

Mamas & Papas fan who helped immensely with the British angle . . . my great agent Sheree Bykofsky . . . Richard Campbell, a gentleman and great Mamas & The Papas archivist . . . Melissa Levine, Arthur Lee, Esperanza, Van Dyke and Sally Parks, Stuart Rosenberg, Darian Sahanaja, Rick Bell, Chris Carter, Taro Yoshida—*mi compadre* and partner in crime . . . the amazing and wonderful Tess Taylor, Michael Jensen, Bryan Alsop, Judy Collins, Cheryl Smith, Mac Holbert at Nash Editions, Pamela Koslyn, attorney deluxe . . . Alice and Bernie Maltz for their constant enthusiasm . . . Owen Elliott Kugel, Chris Woodstra and all the gang at All Music Guide, Taco El Toro, John Koenig at Discoveries, Buffalo Springfield, Luther Russell, John Densmore, Bill Payne, Dr. Robert Titcher, Ted Alvy for the news bulletins . . . Cathy Tushinsky, Michael Fremer, Paul Surriatt, Gene Clark, John Marcus, Herb Alpert, Ken Belding, Hal Lifson, David Leaf, Skip Heller . . . Steven Peasant at Experience Hendrix . . . Jennifer Ballyentine, Andy McKaie and all the staff at MCA/Universal, Geoffrey Tozier, Hilary Hicks, Emberly and John Doherty for putting up with the unexpected calls . . . Elliott Kendall, Warren and Holly Caswell, Roy Trankin at *Hits! Magazine* . . . Kevin Delaney, Saul Davis and Carla Olsen, Dave Bagley, Phillippe Aubuchon . . . all those at The Monterey Historical Society, Stan Cornyn, Tony Asselta, Jeff Albright, Steve Stanley . . . all the gang at Cooper Square Press—especially Michael Dorr, Michael Messina, Ross Plotkin, Hector DeJean, Ginger Strader, and Barbara Werden who believed in this project from the beginning . . . Michael Ansaldo, Bill Crandall, and the old gang at *BAM* magazine . . . Mr. Dan Epstein, a great friend and fellow journalist who knew what I was going through and helped me hike through the tough hills . . . Arthur Leavy at Arista Records, Harve at the Bravo Network (Canada) for making me look good . . . Kazuhiro Goda, Gilberto Diaz, and Redbeard . . . Claudia and Ron Shapiro, Jac Holzman, Joe Smith, the entire staff at Record Collectors/Japan, Lee Hirshberg, The Whisky A-Go-Go, the staff at The Roxy for a great night remembering John . . . all at the Adler office (Howard, Julie, Woju) for keeping me in touch . . . Spankey McFarlane, Gavan Daws, Dan Bourgoise, Denise Sullivan, Ben Edmonds, the staff at The Hotel

Halifax for the unnecessary but welcome VIP treatment . . . Howard, Bob, and all the staff at Moby Disc Records/Sherman Oaks, Josh Mills, Greg Moscow, Barry Jacobs, Thomas "Doc" Cavalier, Lenny Waronker and Gail Pierson at Dreamworks, Stephen Barncard, Angela Murray and all at the Neptune Theatre in Halifax, Mark Felsot, Sid Griffin, Cindy Kado, Jonathan and Crystalann Lea, George Hamilton the 4th, Janan McCoy . . . Cole Cartwright and Gary Stewart at Rhino Records, Harvey Kubernick, Stuart Lippman—a good friend who put up with a lot and retained a sense of humor—D. Whitney and Elizabeth Quinn, Marv's Deli, Cosmo Topper, Dan Matovina, the staff at G.D.A., Randy Hoffman . . . Barbara and Kevin Higgins for being—and being Texans . . . and Andrew Loog Oldham, who was much more than a voice in this book. . . .

A very, very special thanks go out to Gus Duffy and Sandy Granger, without whom this book would not have existed. And lastly, all those on the *Creeque Alley* mailing list, who provided virtually endless support and enthusiasm, especially Kelly and Willow, my "5th Mamas" for their fabulous web sites that kept the word out from day one. . . .

http://www.angelfire.com/ma2/mamasandpapas/book.html

Other Cooper Square Press Titles of Interest

ANY OLD WAY YOU CHOOSE IT
Rock and Other Pop Music, 1967–1973
Expanded Edition
Robert Christgau
360 pp.
0-8154-1041-7
$16.95

THE ART PEPPER COMPANION
Writings on a Jazz Original
Edited by Todd Selbert
200 pp., 4 color photos, 16 b/w photos
0-8154-1067-0
$30.00 cloth

BACKSTAGE PASSES
Life on the Wild Side with David Bowie
Angela Bowie with Patrick Carr
368 pp., 36 b/w photos
0-8154-1001-8
$17.95

BEHIND BLUE EYES
The Life of Pete Townshend
with new afterword
Geoffrey Giuliano
376 pp., 17 b/w photos
0-8154-1070-0
$17.95

THE BITTER END
Hanging Out at America's Nightclub
Paul Colby and Martin Fitzpatrick
Foreword by Kris Kristofferson
296 pp., 32 b/w photos
0-8154-1206-1
$26.95 cloth

THE BLUES
In Images and Interviews
Robert Neff and Anthony Connor
152 pp., 84 b/w photos
0-8154-1003-4
$17.95

CHER
If You Believe
Mark Bego
Foreword by Mary Wilson
464 pp., 50 b/w photos
0-8154-1153-7
$27.95 cloth

COLONEL TOM PARKER
The Curious Life of Elvis Presley's Eccentric Manager
James L. Dickerson
310 pp., 35 b/w photos
0-8154-1088-3
$28.95 cloth

DEPECHE MODE
A Biography
Steve Malins
280 pp., 24 b/w photos
0-8154-1142-1
$17.95

DESPERADOS
The Roots of Country Rock
John Einarson
304 pp., 16 pp. of b/w photos
0-8154-1065-4
$19.95

DID THEY MENTION THE MUSIC?
The Autobiography of Henry Mancini
Updated Edition
Henry Mancini with Gene Lees
312 pp., 44 b/w photos
0-8154-1175-8
$18.95

DREAMGIRL AND SUPREME FAITH
My Life as a Supreme
Updated Edition
Mary Wilson
732 pp., 150 b/w photos, 15 color photos
0-8154-1000-X
$19.95

Other Cooper Square Press Titles of Interest

FAITHFULL
An Autobiography
Marianne Faithfull with
David Dalton
320 pp., 32 b/w photos
0-8154-1046-8
$16.95

FREAKSHOW
*Misadventures in the
Counterculture, 1959–1971*
Albert Goldman
416 pp.
0-8154-1169-3
$17.95

**GOIN' BACK TO
MEMPHIS**
*A Century of Blues,
Rock 'n' Roll, and
Glorious Soul*
James Dickerson
284 pp., 58 b/w photos
0-8154-1049-2
$16.95

**HARMONICAS, HARPS,
AND HEAVY
BREATHERS**
*The Evolution of the People's
Instrument*
Updated Edition
Kim Field
392 pp., 44 b/w photos
0-8154-1020-4
$18.95

HE'S A REBEL
*Phil Spector—Rock and
Roll's Legendary Producer*
Mark Ribowsky
368 pp., 35 b/w photos
0-8154-1044-1
$18.95

JOHN CAGE: WRITER
Selected Texts
Edited and introduced by
Richard Kostelanetz
304 pp., 15 illustrations,
facsimiles, and
reproductions
0-8154-1034-4
$17.95

JUST FOR A THRILL
*Lil Hardin Armstrong,
First Lady of Jazz*
James L. Dickerson
350 pp., 15 b/w photos
0-8154-1195-2
$28.95 cloth

LENNON IN AMERICA
*1971–1980, Based in Part on
the Lost Lennon Diaries*
Geoffrey Giuliano
320 pp., 68 b/w photos
0-8154-1157-X
$17.95

**LIVING WITH THE
DEAD**
*Twenty Years on the Bus
with Garcia and
The Grateful Dead*
Rock Scully with
David Dalton
408 pp., 31 b/w photos
0-8154-1163-4
$17.95

LOUIS' CHILDREN
American Jazz Singers
Updated Edition
Leslie Gourse
384 pp.
0-8154-1114-6
$18.95

MADONNA
Blonde Ambition
Updated Edition
Mark Bego
368 pp., 57 b/w photos
0-8154-1051-4
$18.95

MICK JAGGER
Primitive Cool
Updated Edition
Chris Sandford
352 pp., 56 b/w photos
0-8154-1002-6
$16.95

OSCAR PETERSON
The Will to Swing
Updated Edition
Gene Lees
328 pp., 15 b/w photos
0-8154-1021-2
$18.95

**REMINISCING WITH
NOBLE SISSLE AND
EUBIE BLAKE**
Robert Kimball and
William Bolcom
256 pp., 244 b/w photos
0-8154-1045-X
$24.95

ROCK 100
*The Greatest Stars of
Rock's Golden Age*
with a new introduction
David Dalton and
Lenny Kaye
288 pp., 195 b/w photos
0-8154-1017-4
$19.95